UNDER A FULL MOON

THE LAST LYNCHING IN KANSAS

ALICE KAY HILL

WILDBLUE
PRESS
WildBluePress.com

UNDER A FULL MOON is the story of real people in authentic locations and is researched and reality based. The names of the primary characters are accurate. Situations, individuals' thoughts, conversations, and some fictional characters were added to complete the telling.

UNDER A FULL MOON published by:
WILDBLUE PRESS
P.O. Box 102440
Denver, Colorado 80250

WILDBLUE PRESS is registered at the U.S. Patent and Trademark Offices.

ISBN 978-1-952225-19-2 Trade Paperback
ISBN 978-1-952225-18-5 eBook

Cover design © 2020 WildBlue Press. All rights reserved.

Book Cover Design by Villa Design

Interior Formatting by Elijah Toten
www.totencreative.com

UNDER A
FULL MOON

For Scott + Jenny,
Your Kindness + Integrity
are Powerful!
Alice Kay Hall
7-13-20

"If no one turned round when we entered, answered when we spoke, or minded what we did, but if every person we met 'cut us dead,' and acted as if we were non-existing things, a kind of rage and impotent despair would ere long well up in us, from which the cruelest bodily tortures would be a relief; for these would make us feel that, however bad might be our plight, we had not sunk to such a depth as to be unworthy of attention at all." (James, 1890/1950, p. 293-294).

FOUNDATION STONES

My mother came home
to the farm of her childhood.
Nothing remained but the
foundation stones.

The stories she told
as I lay in my bed,
of haylofts and wheat fields
and unpainted sheds
tied the earth to my heart
held me rooted like grass.
Now my mother comes home,
a handful of ash.

Layers of time
as layers of soil
deepened by death
watered by tears…
Another generation blown by the years.

My feet step the ground
of grandmothers great;
I scatter my mother
on soil that will wait.

This book is dedicated to
Phyllis Charline Bockhold Kay (1925-
1999) and those who preceded her.

INTRODUCTION

Primal rage: an instinctual response to a heinous breach of moral law; a reactive urge to punish with finality.

In the spring of 1932 a mob of citizens from Thomas, Sheridan and Rawlins counties of Northwest Kansas were driven by primal rage when they forcefully removed fifty-three-year-old Pleasant Richardson Read from the protective custody of the Cheyenne County, Kansas jail. With vindictive fury they then bound and hung him for the brutal rape and murder of eight-year-old Dorothy Eileen Hunter. This is the story of that event, the last lynching in Kansas, and the collective history of the individuals and their families who became entwined by this act.

What led to this writing?

The story begins with childhood summers spent in Atwood, Kansas with our maternal grandmother, Freda Cochran Bockhold and great-grandfather, Edwin Ruthvin Cochran. My siblings and I listened in delight to their pioneer stories. These were told with the authority of people who had lived the settling of Rawlins County. The first baby born in Atwood (1880) was a Cochran, so our family claimed a measure of ownership in the transition from empty prairie to the well-established farms and towns that now exceed a century mark.

One story our bloodthirsty hearts desired to hear repeatedly was about the murder of a little girl and the resulting hanging of the man who'd done it. There was a connection to the story that made it personal: the lynching had taken place on land owned by Edwin Lyman, the husband of our great-grandfather's sister.

Tied into the gruesome tale was a lesson in safety: "never take candy from a stranger" or "never get into a car with anyone you don't know". Exciting hints of brutality in the story of her death intrigued us further. I felt attuned to this vulnerable girl child left hidden in a straw stack and took into my heart a strong awareness of evil.

When I asked why anyone would hurt a little girl, I was told the man was 'retarded' (a commonly used term in the 1960s) and didn't know better. At that time of my life this answer satisfied.

In 1975 I married my high-school sweetheart, a young man from Atwood whose farm family's roots also went deep. In doing so I tied myself to the land just as my forebears had done. We raised our two daughters and moved into middle life doing all we could, just as those before us had, to keep our land and preserve a family farm.

In 2002, with inheritance from my mother's death, we purchased the 1907 Shirley Opera House, a faltering building, with the intention of restoring it to its original use. One of our goals was to see it listed on the Kansas Register of Historic Places. As part of that application process, we were required to document its significance in the community.

While researching archived newspapers, I found mention of the Owl Café as one of the many businesses housed on the main floor. Further reading in other reference materials led to the discovery that this café was named as the place Richard Read took Dorothy just before her violent death. In an overwhelming rush the stories heard in my childhood came back to me as I realized this was the event my grandmother had horrified us with and that I was now walking the very same floor that they had.

The Shirley Opera House is well known by locals to have spirits within its walls. One story is of an Indian woman who was thrown to her death from the second floor during a time when it housed a raucous saloon. Another is of a barroom shooting that killed a man, also occurring upstairs. Thus we were primed for 'events of a spiritual nature'.

As our family worked to create the Aberdeen Steakhouse and our first granddaughter spent her early years alongside us, there were a few occurrences that gave us reason to believe a younger spirit also roamed the interior. The sensitivity of small people to the spirit world is well accepted. She was, unwillingly, 'in tune' to the energies lingering from the past.

A particularly impacting event was when she looked up from her play, her face pinched with anxiety and said "Little girl crying." I asked if she heard someone crying and she answered, "Uh, huh. Little girl wants her mommy." I heard nothing, but certainly felt the power of that momentary connection. Other auditory and visual glimpses into forces trapped within those brick walls occurred regularly.

In 2007, coinciding with its 100th birthday, the building was accepted by both the Kansas and National Registries for its authenticity of the period and its example of a time when public entertainment venues were developed in Kansas communities during the late 1800's and early 1900s. This acceptance led to the honor of two Heritage Trust Fund grants for the preservation and protection of the second floor and south face of the Opera House. Months of planning, labor and oversight were required to bring this to completion.

Concurrently, our family was preparing meals for guests of the Aberdeen Steakhouse and developing a live music venue to recapture the entertainment portion of the building's heritage. This meant hours of time spent within the building. Much of that time I spent alone. I frequently felt I'd stepped into a past era and was repeating the actions of people long dead.

Night dreams and unbidden day images as I worked within the Opera House walls pressed me to research and record Dorothy Hunter's brief life and the forces that placed her in the path of Richard Read. Despite our very hectic life, this urge would not go unmet. I felt compelled to tell the story.

I began to research. I learned Richard Read was a repeat offender. In 1916 he was incarcerated for the rape of a fifteen year old in Kit Carson County, Colorado. This knowledge intrigued me, but I could find no details locally.

In time, I arranged trips to the Denver Library to squint at newspaper accounts on microfilm and to the Colorado State Archives for prison records. Museum visits included Old Town in Burlington, Colorado, the Prairie Museum in Colby, Kansas, the St. Francis Museum, St. Francis, KS and the Sheridan County Museum in Hoxie, KS. I also toured the St. Francis Court House and saw the cell in which Richard Read was held prior to his lynching. The Rawlins County Museum keeps a file on the event along with the murder weapon used to crush Dorothy's skull.

My feelings twisted unexpectedly when a photo copy of Richard Read's mug shot from the Colorado State Archives arrived in the mail and I saw his signature on the Colorado State Penitentiary log book. While my attention had previously been placed on Dorothy, he suddenly became a real person with his own story.

I had fully expected to hate the man, just as everyone had, calling him monster. Instead, I felt heartache as intense as if he'd been a son or brother. Pleasant Richardson Read's eyes implored me to tell his story, too.

Thus began the writing of *Under a Full Moon.*

*****

I apologize wholeheartedly for any and all inaccuracies as they are unintentional. I ask forgiveness from any descendants or families affected by this writing.

With this writing I pray the souls of Dorothy Eileen Hunter and Pleasant Richardson Read are at peace.

CHAPTERS

LIST OF PRIMARY PERSONS

Pleasant Richardson Read: Last man lynched in Kansas

Jacob Hoffman & Mary Ellen (Kell) Read
– Pleasant Richardson's parents

Sarah Lou – Pleasant Richardson's sister

Edward Henry McGinley: Arresting
sheriff in Thomas County, KS

John James & Mary Ann McGinley – Ed's parents

John Rice (J.R.) Ruberson: Arresting
sheriff in Kit Carson County, CO

Addison Alanson (A.A.) Bacon: Sheriff
in Cheyenne County, KS

Pauline Weisshaar: first victim in Kit Carson County,
CO John & Christina Weisshaar - Pauline's parents

Dorothy Hunter: second victim - killed
in Rawlins County, KS

Floyd & Jennie Lucille Hunter – Dorothy's parents

William L. Thomas: member of the lynch mob

CHAPTER 1

Coming to Kansas

I was born in Johnson County, Iowa in the first month of 1879, the first child of Jacob and Mary Ellen "Kell" Cardwell Read during their first year of marriage. Throughout my life I've heard many many times the story of how I nearly killed Mother with my birth.

I was too large for a firstborn. I made her suffer agonies that no young wife should endure.

Father heard her screams; screams that went on and on until even her eyes became red with ruptured vessels and she cried tears of blood. I was finally pulled from her womb, purple and lifeless. The midwife exclaimed in fury "You will not die, you lug of a baby! Not after all this work!" and she threaded her fingers tight against my greasy ankles to raise me high. With a lifting and dropping motion she forced air into my lungs. When I gasped my first breath in a rasping wail, Mother turned her head from me to weep at the sound.

Pleasant is a family name on my mother's side. I was named for her father who was called 'Pleas'. This brought no benefit to me.

Father's people came from Pennsylvania. He is a man of determination and brooks no slack in himself or others. He is a man of firm rules. No affection need be expressed. Commands need not be repeated. I am the oldest; I would abide and obey and carry the weight.

We came to Kansas in early fall of 1881, following Mother's family who had settled in Republic County the year I was born. They were established.

I see my feet when I remember coming to Kansas: my feet walking and walking and walking. Puffs of dust, grey and soft, rise and settle on my bare toes and legs until they fade out of sight and I am afraid they are gone. I look back and see the path behind me, little round marks from my heels pushing against the soft earth. I want to turn around and run fast.

I have always felt torn in two. When Mother says, "I'm just not myself today," I know what she means. Pleasant needs and wants, but it is Richardson who takes.

Richardson hates the wagon with its darkness and clatter and cramped space, so when Father tells me to walk Richardson steps out. Pleasant loves to ride inside, tucked into the quilts that wrap around Mother's china hutch; the quilts that still smell of home, a place of plenty and Granny Read's warm lap, a place of cookies and Christmas sweets.

Pleasant doesn't believe in Kansas. Pleasant wants to hide in the quilts and imagine the horses circling back for home, undoing the steps we have already walked like Granny pulls yarn from her crocheting when she sees a mistake.

Instead, Richardson makes me hurry forward. He wants to beat Indians to death. He wants to eat rattlesnakes. He loves the wide open sky at night; a black bowl that makes me feel like I might drown. After supper he squints at the cooking fire to see flames dance. I long to crawl on Mother's lap, but it is full with Sarah and she pushes me away with her baby arm, cuddling close. I sit near the wagon wheel with Buster, the dog Granny Read gave me last year. He leans his heavy shoulder against my back, warm and solid.

I think we will travel forever.

Father says, "Toughen up, Boy."

Mother tries to give me extra biscuits, but if Father catches her at it, he snatches them for Sarah. If I see Mother looking her sad face at me I turn away. Richardson dry spits on the ground and thinks about how Sarah might get fat like a little shoat from all those biscuits, and then he'll eat her.

I try to shut Richardson out of my head, but he will have his say.

CHAPTER 2

1881: PLEASANT RICHARDSON READ
Republic City, KS

Father's eyes looked wet and sore when we crossed the Nebraska state line into Kansas. Republic City, named for the nearby Republican River, was where mother's people had homesteaded. All that day I'd watched close, thinking we'd drive the wagon over something like a belt dividing a shirt from pants.

Father said, "What's that fool boy doing now? What's he starin' at the ground for?"

Mother's soft voice answered, "You told us we'd be crossing the state line today. Your son listens to you."

That brought a bitter laugh and a shaking of his head.

Mother tried to explain a state line wasn't something to be seen unless you studied a map. "He just hears what you say, Jacob. He can't know the meaning."

Every morning Mother was slower to get up, holding her hand against her belly and pinching her lips into a white crease. Sarah Lou cried at the slightest thing and was whiny between times. Her thin baby hair was bleached white from sun and wind, her cheeks rashy and raw. For days and nights it had been oven hot with harsh winds sucking moisture. My cracked lips, like everyone's, bled if I smiled. There were few smiles.

Father had promised a rest when we reached Mother's family, though he'd warned we couldn't stay too long or winter would catch us. I'd looked behind to see if winter was chasing us, but Father gripped my skull in his strong fingers, turning me around saying, "Look ahead, Boy. This is the beginning of a new life for the Read family and we are going to meet it head on!"

That's when I saw his red rimmed eyes; eyes that had stared ahead for weeks but not yet seen what they were looking for. He looked at me with the same dissatisfaction.

Mother says, "Pleasant, aren't you excited to see Grandmother and Grandfather? You won't know them and neither will Sarah Lou. They left Iowa not long after you were born. They will be surprised at how big you've grown!"

I don't understand what Mother means. I watch her face and her mouth moves up on the edges but it means nothing to me. I am hungry and tired and I need to squat in the grass. I don't know excited.

As our wagon rolls into town Sarah Lou quiets at the sights and sounds. The noise is a sharp change: clanging iron at the blacksmith's, loud yells as our cattle move down the main road, dogs barking at our wheels. Father asks a boy which way to the Cardwell's and we go west toward a line of trees visible past the stores. Sun streaks through dust filled air. I smell grease and outhouses and fresh cut boards. I don't like the noise. It bangs in my head and I need to squat now; my gut is telling me, now!

Mother's hands guide the team into the yard of a small white house with red chickens scratching in the dust. She sets the brake and raises a hand to a lady coming out of the house. I climb down and look at the dust. More dust. Always dust.

Father turns the herd into a corral where a tall man holds the gate open. The man is waving and yelling, "Hello, folks! Hello and welcome to Kansas!"

Father has come to the wagon and taps my head with a knuckle. I go rigid.

He says, "I'll unhitch the team. Take the bucket for water." He points to a pump near the corral. He takes the wash tub off the wagon and holds it at his side. "The horses need to be watered. The poultry, too."

My bowels release. The smell is strong and familiar and I see Father's face darken. I turn away to get the bucket from the wagon. Father says hot words under his breath.

"Agh!" he growls, "Kell, your son has soiled himself. Again! Give Sarah Lou to your ma and get him cleaned up."

I am large; everyone who sees me says so, but they say it funny like it's something wrong. Father is dark with big arms full of power. If folks say I look just like him he gets squinty.

When Mother explains I'm coming three, they shake their heads in amazement, claim I'm the size of a child twice that and wish they had a big son like me to help. Mother smiles, but Father's jaw clenches tight.

Mother says, "Pleasant, come with me now. Let's get you fixed up so you can meet your family. My sisters and brothers will be here too – your aunts and uncles. There will be cousins to get to know and play with."

Her mother, Grandmother Sarah, has taken Sarah Lou inside the white house. I hear a bang as the door shuts. It looks like a dark mouth to me.

Mother uses her sing-y voice; the one she uses when she's going to do something I hate. Like washing. I hate water. It burns my skin. If it goes in my eyes and nose and mouth I won't see or breathe ever again. I see her come slow, slow towards me; she keeps her hands behind her back. She looks at Father and moves her head side to side, telling him to stay away without words. If he comes close I will run. She knows.

A breeze lifts the air and sun sparks on the leaves over us, the leaves of a big cottonwood tree. The leaves dance and glitter. For a while that is all I see, as Mother drops my pants, unpins the soiled diaper and washes me with a cold rag. I don't look at her face. I listen to the wind, watch the glittering leaves and hear the song she sings when she washes me, like a hum inside my head.

When I am wearing dry clothes, Father sets the bucket beside me. I hear his words, like rocks dropping, and it breaks the hum, stops the sun sparks. "The animals are waiting."

Mother does not look up at Father. She grunts when she stands, gathers my soiled things and goes into the house's mouth. I hear girl sounds, squeals, and laughter.

The team and Dancer are tied to a tether line. The wash tub is in front of Dancer. He paws the ground. Flies are rising up in clouds from fresh mounds of horse biscuits and green cow slop. They bite my neck and ankles with hot stings. The bucket is too heavy when full, so I make lots of trips back and forth to the pump like Father has shown me to do. The screech and cry of the pump scare me at first until I hear their music. It is hard work, bringing the water up from the well. When Dancer has his share, I drag the tub over to the team. The animals drink faster than I can fill. They switch their tails and stomp against the flies, shaking their heads impatiently.

Something goes wrong. I don't know what. Suddenly I am in the middle of horse legs and shoving butts. The washtub is hit by a kicking hoof, a loud clanging-clatter. I cover my ears, pressing hard to stop the noise. The tether rope snaps past me, the horses wheel in panic.

I feel a whistle of wind, hear Father's muffled roar. Hooves thud and a hammer slams into my head as the team pounds away. I taste a rolling mouthful of dusty crap. Then everything is black.

Mother is sponging my scraped cheeks, her hot tears plopping on my neck, when I awaken. "Oh, Lord. Oh, dear, dear Lord, my little boy. What will we do with you?" I roll over and throw up on her lap. Blackness returns.

One of the horses had clipped me squarely behind my left ear as they fled. A hoof shaped wound leaks pinkish yellow fluid and blood trickles from my ears and nostrils. Doctor Stone, Republic's physician, doesn't hold out much hope, but he's stitched me together with fine cat-gut. I heave every time I try to open my swollen eyes.

While I lie there, I hear speaking. Most of the time I can't make any sense of what is said and at other times it is a dream voice I hear. That one comes the clearest.

Richardson holds my hand while we walk along a bright stream. The water is golden. I can smell it - biting and sweet - reminding me of the cooling feel when Mother brought down a fever with an alcohol rub; her touch so tender. Richardson holds my hand as we walk together and he speaks in a firm, reassuring way, "I am here with you… always… I will protect you. No one will hurt you again." The golden stream gurgles and glugs like something being poured from a jug.

I hear Mother's voice, words begging in harsh whisper. She says, "He's a little boy, Jacob. He is not to do a man's job anymore until he's grown. You'll have to find another way until then. We could have lost our son!"

Father replies in words spit between clenched teeth, without mercy, "You keep babying him, Kell, and he'll never grow up. He's nearly a dullard already and I've not much to work with. You've got a girl to help you and I need a son. A real son who can hold his own and make something of the Read farm. Not a momma's boy. Not an idiot. If you spoil him, he'll be good for nothing!"

Mother says, sadder and softer, "If you kill him, he'll just be dead!"

Richardson says, "I'll take care of you, Pleasant. I'll take care of you. Together we are Richard."

Doctor Stone comes twice a day, speaking with Mother in soothing but guarded tones as each day passes. "Mrs. Read…that was a mighty bad knock for your son. Only time will tell if he's going to pull through. A hit like that… well, you never know the damage. I've not seen much worse, especially in a child. But he's big for his age. He might surprise us all. I've done all I can for him. A tincture of time, that's what he needs."

Mother's family comes and goes, looking at me and shaking their heads. Some want to touch me, but Mother says no, it's best not to. I hear and know this, but I don't wake.

When I do open my eyes, the edges of things are fuzzy and don't make sense. Then a day comes when I can stay awake without retching. Mother spoons me salty broth. Her hands shake. She uses both to bring the spoon to my mouth. "Pleasant Richardson, you are breaking my heart."

In my ears I hear a song low as hissing snow in deep winter. I follow the sound with my eyes, searching within, and echo its path with breath through my nose. Mother pauses to listen, her grey eyes shadowed and deep as she looks at me. Her soft hum matches mine as she dips the spoon again and again. Richard sips at the broth. His hand holds mine and it is steady. We are Richard.

CHAPTER 3

I've always said the ones who left deserved to fail. They
were spineless quitters. I saw proof in the crumbling dirt
walls of half-built homes, rusting stove pipe and wagon
parts scattered like old bones along our trail. To my
credit, I was able to gather items of usefulness from those
abandoned places.

Kell hasn't spoken much on our final day of travel.
She is worn. I understand. Each time I look back at her,
driving the wagon as she has for so many weeks, I long for
a smile. Her mouth is firm, downturned. I see no softening.
The boy has grieved her some and carrying our third child
is straining her more than I expected. She'll soon rally,
though. She comes from strong stock.

Pride swells my chest when our wagon creaks to a stop
along the Prairie Dog Creek, shushing its jangle and thump.
It is early afternoon and we've not had lunch in order to
arrive as early as possible this last day. I thrill to a sense of
manly power and keenness of hunger for our future.

I draw back on Dancer's reins and watch Kell assess the
land we will call home. She is silent, supporting her womb
with both arms. Sarah Lou holds the edges of the safe-
box where she sits securely alongside Kell and leans her
little chin on her hands. She looks at me and grins. There's
my smile! She's a keeper, I think to myself. Too bad she's
female.

The boy, sitting at the back of the wagon, has his head downcast, staring at his feet. God he makes me hot! Here we are at the start of our new life and he's looking at his toes! For Kell's sake I grit my teeth to hold back words I feel pushing like vomit into my throat.

I step off Dancer and loosen the rig, putting my anger into action. "Our journey is done! Let's unload that wagon! We sleep at home tonight!"

When Dancer is secured with hobbles around her front hocks, I give her a quick rub with sacking. She drops her head to crop grass with a tearing sound. I pull the wagon-tree pin free of the hitch to lead the team aside. Unharnessed and freed from their strapping they roll, their plate sized hooves flailing at the sky, their light colored bellies wider than barrels. Heaving up, they lower their heads between their front legs and shake vigorously, throwing dust and grass in a cloud. Both are carrying colts that will come in early spring and they'll soon be put to breaking sod. I tie them to stakes pounded deep in the soil and take a few minutes to survey the area.

Tall grasses of several varieties grow along the sides of U-shaped hollows between up-sloping hills. Seed heads of different colors, bent and lifted by wind, seem to flow like water. On the flatter ground, where the wagon sits, curly buffalo grass grows, crunching under our feet. East of us the Prairie Dog Creek runs from southwest to northeast. Cottonwoods, willows and low bushes create pockets of green and shade.

Our property is 160 acres for homestead and another 160 as timber claim. It is virgin grass and begs to be broken! We've brought sixteen hens and a rooster, black and white Dominikers that are eager to get out of their wooden crates and scratch for crickets in the grass. Kell's milk cow Forsythia, named for the bright blooms of spring, is due to calve again when winter breaks. Her heifer calf, fully weaned now and part of the beef herd, will be ready to breed next summer. I have ten red cows that were exposed to a purebred bull in Iowa before we left. The calves that have traveled alongside them will need to be separated soon, the heifers kept and the steers sold for meat. The horses and milk cow are tethered close to the wagon, but the beef cows and their calves have already begun to range, grazing steadily, tails swinging side to side.

Buster noses under the wagon and snaps at the big hoppers that jump in the grass. I count on him to keep varmints away from the stock. Shelters and corrals will need built before winter.

Everyone and everything must earn their keep. My eyes scan the area as I imagine the swine we'll bring to the farm once we are settled and can raise corn for their feed. Pigs on a farm are mortgage makers!

For months of evenings, well over a year in fact, long after everyone slept, I've written it all out, my plans for stallions and mares, bulls and cows, boars and sows, wheat, corn, oats and hay, eggs and butter for trade. Now we are here, at our new home and I thrum with anxious energy to start.

I had hoped Kell would recover some during the time in Republic City. Being with her family gave her joy, but I was impatient to go. We'd been delayed so long, and these last days of travel I've pushed hard. The unfortunate event with Richard was a mistake, but how was I to have known he'd get hisself kicked?

I note her slumped shoulders and flat eyes. Her spark is gone. I miss the young woman I married, the one who colored so prettily when our eyes met. Just three years ago. If only she had not been rent by a child who should never have lived! If only that monstrous child had not hurt her so! Sarah Lou came so easily, like spitting a watermelon seed. I pray her spark will return. Surely it will in this grand new land!

CHAPTER 4

1881: RICHARD READ

Part 1: Prairie Dog Creek

Father climbs into the wagon to unload. "Stand clear!" he yells at me. "Move those trunks out of the way!" I drag items aside as fast as I can, grunting at their weight. I squint against the pounding behind my eyes. Dr. Stone had told Mother I might have headaches for months.

I look up at Sarah Lou who is sitting securely on a quilted pad in her safe-box. Mother has nursed her so at least she isn't hungry like the rest of us. She watches us work, but her eyes are droopy from her feeding. Father gave Buster the stay command, so he lies next to her, his head on his paws. His eyebrows twitch up and down as he watches us work. I would like to sit beside Buster with my belly full of sweet milk.

Mother points to where she wants things to go, organizing the unloading, and suggests softly that Father should be cautious with her precious belongings. I heave, push and drag until all the things we'll need for the next days are on the ground in proper piles.

Father lists my chores as we clear a fire ring for cooking and set up the tripod for Mother's kettles. He sends me to search out dry tinder for the fire. I gather an armful, stacking as much as I can carry. Father puts dry grass in a mound below the branches and the fire lights quickly.

He says, "Fetch another load and put it safely away from the heat, but close enough for Mother to reach easily." He checks the wind and scrapes a larger space clear of grass. "Bring what you can carry and break up the longer branches. I'll take my ax to the big stuff when I have time. Until then you are responsible for the firewood."

His voice runs on and on, "Keep the water barrels full, not half full, but always full. Do not let the cows muck up the creek near the home place. Watch where the hens lay their eggs and you damn well better not break any when you gather." The hens have been released from their crate. They chuckle at their freedom, turning their heads this way and that as they peck among the grasses. Mother has a loop of twine around the leg of the rooster to secure him to their crate. This will help keep the flock from wandering far until a hen house is built.

I keep my head down, watching the hens, and stand farther away than Father's hand can reach. My gut bites with hunger and churns at his voice. Every instruction makes me feel sure I will fail.

Father says to Mother, "Tomorrow I will dig a hole in the creek bank for the zinc box. That live water will keep our milk and eggs cool."

Then he turns to me and says, "You're not to play in the water near it and only open it if Mother asks you to."

I look up to meet his eyes.

He barks, "There something you want to say, boy?" But I know he isn't asking.

He thinks I will take food without asking, but he should know how I hate water, how I would never want to play in it. When I take the buckets to the creek, I will find a way not to get wet.

Mother begins preparing our meal. Over the fire she has a pot filled with chunks of salt pork, potatoes and turnips. In her crock bowl she mixes corn meal and flour with a finger of lard and a bit of salt till it is crumbly, then adds eggs and water to form a thick batter for corn cakes. I watch her fingers working and working, mixing and mixing with spidery moves. She greases a flat iron skillet with more lard, heats it till a drip of water spits and sizzles and then places pats of dough on it to brown. The toasting smell makes my knees weak.

Father's voice makes me jump. "Get a move on! Those barrels won't fill themselves."

I get the two buckets and walk to the shady creek. The water runs clear in a steady flow. Where the sun shines on the banks juicy looking grass grows but below the trees the earth is bare. Thick roots loop like ropes tethering the big trees to the bank. Some roots have been washed free of soil and circle back as they reach for solid ground. It is on one of these smooth roots that I crouch to dip the buckets in.

After I haul them back to our campsite I step up on a small tool chest to pour the water into the tall barrels. The bails of the buckets dig into my palms. Worse yet is the splashing drops that hit my face, making me gasp.

When I am done with the last load, Buster joins me by the creek. He noses around some old logs, scrabbles with his paws and pounces when he smells a mouse. I see him catch two and swallow them whole. I wonder if I can swallow a mouse like he does; I am that hungry. He keeps searching.

Out of a woven-grass nest wiggle four pink naked babies. I shove Buster away and scoop them up in my palm. Their squeaks are almost too tiny to hear. They aren't much bigger than raisins. They jerk about and tickle my hand. I pinch one up to look closer. Its skin is wrinkled, like it has room to grow into but so thin I can see into its insides. I sniff it and it smells sweet and earthy with a little musk. These tiny things can't live without their mother, I think. They are weak and soft.

Just as I bring it up to my mouth, Father's voice roars "Quit your woolgathering! The fire needs wood now!"

My hand jerks, dropping the mice, and Buster snuffles them up quick, quick. I push him aside to fetch up more wood. His tongue comes out, licking his smiling lips.

For a time home is in and under the wagon, just like it has been all during the weeks we've been traveling. The only pleasure I feel is knowing we won't be moving on in the morning and the quiet. I like the quiet.

Father and I sleep on the ground, Mother and Sarah Lou in the wagon bed, for several nights while Father worked to open up a space in the south facing bank above the flood plain. He had looked a long time to be sure the creek had never risen that high, that the north winds would go up and over the hill behind the dugout and that there was good grass close in with level places nearby for the sheds that would soon be built. He explained all this to Mother, his arms waving into the air like he was pulling his dreams from the sky.

After he'd dug into the bank about ten feet wide, ten feet back and five feet down he cut another foot of sod all around the top edge one foot down. This made a rim. He pulled the side boards off the wagon, carefully putting the nails in a pouch to be reused, and laid these boards over the top, setting the ends on the rim to support them, creating a flat roof, slatted with spaces between. My job was to carry off the dirt from the dugout, to clear it from the front of our new home. I used it to fill in low places, making the yard more level. Mother worked alongside me and she sang all the songs she knew over and over. I followed her songs without words, humming low when she sang high.

At the far end, closest to the back wall, Father set up our cast iron box stove and ran its smoke pipe through an open space. He cut tall grass with the curved scythe and after supper we twisted them into long bundles using more stems of grass for twine. These we put as an overlay atop the boards, mounding them into a humped shape to shed water.

The wagon's stiff waxed canvas went over the bundled grass and we laid piles of dirt clods and rocks along the edges to hold it in place. All the time we worked Father talked about the real house we'd soon have with glass windows and wooden floors, two chimneys and a cooking stove.

"Kell," he said, "You'll be inviting ladies to tea one day and proud to do it!" Her smile was thin in reply.

Father was careful to keep the grass and canvas away from the stove pipe. He placed flat rocks around it like a chimney, packing sticky mud into the gaps. I was told to bring him mud from the creek and Father had to belt me before I'd put my hands in the black stuff. His words cut as deep as the leather strap.

Even with the front of the 'house' still open to the world Mother made it a home. Her china hutch stood against one wall. It was held in place with wedges of wood so it wouldn't topple over on the uneven floor. Her trunks lined the walls.

Once the roof was finished Mother spread our bedrolls out to sun and air. The first night indoors I suck the clean grass smell from my pillow until Father's roar tells me to "stop that slobbering!"

"Shush, Richard honey, shush," Mother's singing voice reaches out to me in the dark.

"Goddamn, Kell! A man's got to sleep if he's going to work all day!"

One morning after breakfast and chores are done, Mother takes folds of muslin from a round backed trunk, measures it to the ceiling boards and begins tacking it up like a net to catch the dust and grass sifting through the cracks. She stands me on a box to hold the fabric in place while she hits shiny silver tacks with Father's hammer. Her arms, stretched at their full length, just reach the boards. I watch her fine fingers grip the wooden hammer handle and remember them bringing music from Granny's piano. Now, red and chapped at the knuckles, they seem stronger. I feel odd standing on the box above her, seeing the top of her head and I giggle. She looks at me with her fog grey eyes and smiles just a bit. I go quiet, wondering what she wants.

When we finish and I'm standing on the dirt floor again, she reaches out to me. I flinch away. I wish I didn't.

"Richard, I know you've been through a lot and I'm proud of you," she says softly.

I steady, watching dust motes floating in the slanting sun, and let her fingers trace the curved scar behind my ear. The edges are puckered and tender. Scabs that I can't leave alone peel and ooze juice that crusts when I sleep. No hair has grown over it, though the places around the wound have filled in. Her touch sends shivers over my scalp.

The muslin hangs like a cloud above us. My eyes get trapped in the pattern of the weave and I wave my fingers at it, breaking the shapes into more and more patterns. I feel a vibration of sound that settles my chest. Mother's hand drops from head to my shoulder softly, so softly, and then she turns away from me.

She sighs and bends to Sarah Lou who is walking her first steps away from us, fingers spread to catch the sparkling dust. "This baby is going to be harder to watch now that she can manage her own feet. I'm glad she was slow to walk. We'll have to watch her all the time, keep her safe."

Mother sighs again and, plopping Sarah Lou on her hip, drapes the skinny toddler's leg over her swelling belly. "I'll need you even more, son. I'll need you even more." I wonder how I can give her anything when Father takes so much of me.

Mother spends evenings twisting grass mats to cover the earth floor. She binds them with colored yarns from her mending box, bringing a bright pattern to the red/gold grass. Sometimes her cracked knuckles color the grass, too. Our walls are moist with hairy roots showing through and decorated with little white bones and layers of color, pale ash and sparkly black. The room is dark a few feet in and holds the night's cool air till midday. We are still cooking outdoors, but the weather is changing.

I hear Mother say, "Jacob, winter will soon push us inside. I know you are eager to get the corrals built, but the dugout needs finished. I want a wall and door."

Father says, "I'll start cutting sod tomorrow, Kell. The wall will go up fast, once I've got the blocks cut. I've got it all worked out, don't you worry."

CHAPTER 5

1881: JACOB HOFFMAN READ

Part 2: Prairie Dog Creek

During the time the dugout was being built the team grazed and rested, but now I catch up the mares and lay the harness over their backs. They are twitchy with unused energy. "Settle, Pearl. Easy, now. You'll soon work off your vinegar. Whoa there, girl."

I hitch them to a sod cutter. I've never used one, but have been told how they work. Surely, I can manage easily enough. I walk alongside the team using voice cues to move them away from the homestead with the cutter upside down. It slides along the grass with a hissing sound. We walk a distance along the high ground where the buffalo grass is tightly woven. I flip the cutter over and unhitch the mares. We return to the home site to chain several heavy logs together to act as weight for the cutter. The rectangular blade must penetrate the soil for it to work properly.

I call Richard over to help roll the logs together atop the chain. I try to keep my voice low as I tell him what I want him to do. His flat expression and slow speech make me itchy, but he's one more layer of strength that I sorely need for jobs like this.

In two days I have enough sod cut for the dugout to be enclosed. The blocks are six inch thick sections two feet long and one foot wide, furry with grass on top, dense roots binding the base. Richard helps me put them onto a skid for the team to haul homeward. He struggles with their weight, grunting and humming in an annoying way.

"Can't you work without the noise?" I ask.

His face is crunched in what looks like pain. Well, its hard work we have ahead of us. It's no more than he should expect.

I have paced off the distance and figured in a door size. The wall should go up fast. I start out laying the first course lengthwise, grass side down, with the next course spaced to cover the cut ends and so on to tie the wall together. It is lumpy and bumpy, but as straight as can be managed. To reach the top courses I lay a wide board at an angle to slide the cut sod uphill to the highest row. Eventually, the only light coming into the home is through the open doorway.

I frame up the door's opening with as near straight cottonwood poles as I can find. I patch together a slab-wood door, covering it with bark shingles split from a trunk to overlay the cracks. Though I'd brought iron hinges in my tool box, I didn't want to use them on this temporary home so I hung the door with heavy leather strips and fit an inside latch to secure it.

It pleased me greatly when Kell stood outside of her enclosed 'house' and smiled for the first time since our arrival. Her womanly fear of predators and night dangers is diminished by this wall and door. It might be crude compared to what we had in Iowa, but it's a start.

"Providence shines on the Reads!" I declare when we've been on our home site for a full month and enjoyed nothing but good weather. The house is as tight as it will get. We've carved a dug out for the hens and geese, put a lean-to on the south side for Sythi and the horses and built a corral of cottonwood poles to keep the herd gathered at night. The calves are weaned and in their own pen. I know the days are shortening and have been hard pressed to get so much done.

The livestock pens are built along the lower part of the creek, sheltered from the north winds by a high bank. There is good water here with enough flow to keep ice from forming when winter comes. I tie Buster near the pens at night to warn me of anything wanting to taste our beef.

A few feet from the house is our privy, protected from the wind and made private by willows on three sides. Kell has stocked it with cattails which are softer than the grass wipes we'd used before. She has a way of gentling everything she does. I believe we are near ready for our first winter in Kansas.

CHAPTER 6

1881: Richard Read

Part 2: Prairie Dog Creek

I haul water several times a day to fill the home barrels and my path is worn clean of grass. The trees are nearly bare now. I don't want the good weather to end. Father has spent many days scything tall grass and stacking it in a natural hollow near the horses' lean-to. My job has been to tromp it and pack it down with each load. It was fun for the first hour, but soon became just plain itchy work. Father said if we squeeze all the air spaces out of it the grass will keep better. He doesn't know what our first Kansas winter will be like, but he wants plenty of ready grass for the milk cow and horses in case of heavy snows.

After the grass was cut short he turned the sod with a single plow, rolling the earth over in black curls. The roots held the soil in ridges, but Father claimed the winter would help break them into fine tillable earth. Our seed bags hang from the dugout's roof to keep mice from stealing our precious supply and Father talks to them at night as though they are old friends. He has three bushel bags of oats, five of wheat, two of barley and two of corn.

Mother's box of garden seed holds squash and pumpkin, cabbage and kohlrabi, turnips, beets, carrots and seven kinds of beans. Sometimes Mother lets Sarah Lou play with the bean seeds, making her promise not to eat any. Each type has its own cloth bag. Sarah Lou sits on the floor chattering about their colors and names: Soldier, Brown Dutch, Navy Pea, Appaloosa, Bird Egg, and Money. Her favorite is one she thinks was named for her daddy. It is a spotted bean called Jacob's Cattle, but she calls it Faddar's Cows. Sarah had been slow to walk, but quick with talking. Mother teaches her new words every day and Sarah claps happily when she catches on.

The potatoes that had sprouted since leaving Iowa are hanging in a muslin bag in the cool front of the dugout. They will go into the ground next spring. It is hard to leave them for seed, but if we eat them now there won't be any next year. Mother tells me, "For every eye we put in the ground, we should get ten potatoes to eat. Nature is very generous, Richard. All she needs is for us to do our share of planting and tending." Then she shows me what she means by 'eye' and watches my face to be sure I understand.

Mother has asked Father to open her garden patch in rich soil close to the creek and I dug channels with a grubbing hoe to bring water between the rows when the plants start to grow. Father warned it might get flooded in the spring, but Mother insisted she didn't want to haul water if she didn't have to. Father plowed what he called a 'diversion' ditch above the garden site and sent me with a shovel to build a ridge around it. This raised ground should send high water around Mother's garden. The soil here is moist black and smells sweet. On the high fields, where Father cut the sod and broke out the fields for our grains, the soil is grey and dry.

One afternoon when Mother and I are gathering wood up creek, I hear her shout, "A treasure, Richard! Watercress!" The cress is deep green with plump round leaves, growing from under an overhanging ledge of white rock. She gathers a handful and nibbles hungrily. I take a sprig from her, smelling its brisk odor. It burns in my mouth with a sweet pepper bite. I am surprised by how much Mother is eating and the happy sounds she makes, but it has been a long while since we've had anything fresh.

"Richard, can you keep the cows away from this place? They would eat it all and ruin the spot." She speaks seriously. "This cress will give us important fresh greens to keep us well and we should be careful never to overharvest." I am glad to do something just for Mother, something she asks just of me.

After taking the cows to graze the next day I go back to the cress patch and haul dead branches and logs to build a stout fence around it. Looking closer at the shiny plants I see a little spring running fresh water below their shallow roots, keeping it clean. This hollow feels like a secret between Mother and me and I hum a song to match the trickling water sounds.

The herd grazes every day and moving them is one of my chores. Father expects me to be in charge of the cows, the chickens and geese, the water and the firewood all the while keeping an eye on Sarah Lou if Mother needs me to. I am hard pressed to stay one step ahead of Father's next order. I try to see what he'll want before his hard words hit me, but I am never smart enough.

"You numbskull! Why is that hen door flapping in the wind? By God, boy! You know better than to leave a door open and loose. Snakes and possums will be in there waiting when the hens go to roost!" I had only just let the hens out for the morning and had to set the water bucket down to fill their trough. But Father seemed sure I'd left it open on purpose.

Sarah Lou is walking fine now and likes to disappear on me. She is little enough that if she sits in a low spot I can't see her. She never answers my calls, though I try to sound nice and not scary like Father. If it weren't for Buster, I'd lose her for sure. He sniffs her out and then sits thumping his tail while she pulls his ears. I finally put a rope around her waist and tie her to a rock that I can move from place to place as I work. She pats and soothes the rock, singing to it like Mother sings to her.

When she is wet or soiled, she cries and I take her to Mother to be changed. One afternoon Mother is standing over the washing kettle, stirring our clothes with a heavy wooden paddle as the water steams above the fire. I can see she is busy and tired. Her hard belly juts out before her like a heavy stone. Sarah is crying hard, so I take her inside and lay her on the floor to clean her.

Father comes through the door just as I am lifting Sarah Lou's warm, pale bottom with my hand to look at the places she and I are different. My finger had poked a little at her. His backhanded blow throws me into Mother's square trunk and I feel something pop above my eye. Blood flies in an arc. I see red drops dot the bed quilt. Wet runs down my face; tears and blood and snot. My ears whistle and little sparks dance in the air. Father's roar brings Mother running, one hand holding her skirts, one hand under her belly.

"You dirty little monster! You filthy little monster!" He rises as tall and hot as a wildfire over me. "If I ever see you touch your sister again, I'll beat you senseless! God in Heaven, you're already senseless! What kind of son do I have?!"

Mother stands in the doorway, blocking the sun and my escape. Her hand covers her mouth; her eyes are open wide in fear. I look down at the floor, my head swaying, and crawl on hands and knees towards her. I hear little grunts coming from my chest: unh, unh, unh. I see her booted feet turn to the side to let me pass, but she speaks not a word. I watch a tear of blood drip, hanging in the air like it is hung on a string. Then everything turns black.

Winter set in hard not long after this, but I spend as much time outdoors with the animals as I can stand. There isn't enough space in the dugout for me and Father. I hum and sing to the cows as they graze and they grow to know me. When 'Sythi lays down to chew her cud after filling her gut with grass, I rest with my back against her warm and musical belly making up songs and watching the clouds form magic shapes. The days grow short; dusk is my enemy.

The only time I spend inside was at night and on the days Father is away hunting meat to salt and smoke. The nights last forever and I hide inside my head, hearing the tunes made by the wind and the ticking stove, the shudder and shush of snow falling. Sarah Lou's bed is closest to the stove, then Mother and Father's with my place nearest the door. I like to smell the icy air that leaks under the threshold, like to imagine myself living like a coyote in a den somewhere far from everyone. I do not hear the voices of my family. I hear only the voice of Richardson while my arms wrap around my chest and I stroke my cheek with the side of my thumb.

Father had nailed together boards into a high sided box for the new baby. Mother lined it with her softest, warmest blankets. In early February, on one long night during a bitter cold spell, Mother has her next child.

The odor of blood, urine, shit and something salty filled the air. I try not to listen when Mother screams and whimpers like an animal. The baby's cry of life brings a groan from Father. Another girl: Attie Mae.

CHAPTER 7

1882: Richard Read

Part 1: Prairie Dog Creek, Rexford, KS

It is a hungry time, late winter. Sythi is dry, resting before her next calf, so there is no milk or butter. With nothing green and little grain the hens have stopped giving eggs. They are resting too. The cornmeal and flour barrels show their bottom boards. Now that baby Attie Mae is a month old Father has made plans to go for supplies. I hear him talk to Mother about taking me or leaving me with her.

"I can't watch stock and babies both, Jacob. If you are delayed I would be without help. Please leave Richard with me. He's good with the hens and cattle." Her soft voice convinces Father to travel without me.

On the first day of March, long before dawn, Father prods me out of my pallet with his boot toe to help harness the team. He had watched the weather patterns and waited for a red sunset as signal of a dry day to follow. The days are still winter short. His anxiety about leaving us shows in exaggerated impatience and gruffness with the horses. When he climbs onto the wagon seat, the old boards creak with his weight. His hunched back does not muffle his commanding voice.

"You better watch out hard for trouble and don't let any find you while I'm gone. Your mother's still puny and should she tell me you gave her any problems your hide will get a good brushing. Keep the stove warm and don't mess with the babies. I'll be home by dark or soon after and will want help unloading." He clucked the horses to move out in a southwestern direction.

I stand until I no longer hear the clinking harness and clopping hooves. I draw in a full breath, the morning air so cold it stiffens the hairs in my nose and makes me cough. There is yet no color in the east, but I can feel dawn's edge. Stars burn and spark in my watering eyes. A heavy weight lifts as Father leaves the farm. His day away passes too quickly, but Mother is thrilled to see him return just before nightfall.

Mother begins to talk about neighbors. A few wagons, loaded with shy children and worn out women roll past our farm, following the Prairie Dog Creek. Mother greets them with a welcome smile and encouragement, but they move on, searching for their own homes. Father puts me to watching the stock more closely, worried that someone might take advantage of a stray animal to feed their hungry brood.

In April Forsythia comes fresh with a heifer calf. This calf is pure-bred Jersey, small as a fawn and gentle as a kitten. She will grow to be a milk cow in a couple of years and though Father takes credit for our luck Forsythia was a gift from Mother's family. Mother smiles with joy. "She will be called Windy because she came on a blustery day."

Father laughs, "In Kansas almost every day is a windy one!"

In a few days, when we can start using the milk, Sarah Lou drinks until her belly bulges. Mother drinks her fill, too. During the winter her cheeks had hollowed out scary. She says Attie Mae is a little milk pig, hungry all the time and maybe her own milk has been too thin to satisfy. She laughs when Sarah Lou smacks her lips and holds her cup out for more. She says, "Looks like I have two little milk pigs." Mother insists I have a glass full at every meal.

We have good luck during calving. Each of the cows gives a live birth. The mommas like to calve off from the herd, so we keep close watch. Father blusters at me after each new calf is located, threatening harm if I don't get a good count when putting them in the evening corral. Coyotes and wolves smell the birthing blood and are drawn to weak newborns. Being corralled at night helps the cows protect their babies. Buster stays between me and the cows when we round them up.

Father ropes the new calves when they are still weak and uses his sharp knife to cut open their bull sacks if they are males. He knows it is easier on the animal with less blood spilled than later when weaning time comes. When they are small he can do this alone without asking for help. He also cuts triangle notches in their ears to mark them as his: one high notch on the right and two low notches on the left. The momma cows carry the same markings.

When the last cow calves and Father thinks he can be gone for a couple of days, he makes plans to drive all but one of the yearlings into Oberlin where there is a rail head. The remaining steer will fatten on grass all summer for fall butchering. He is put into the pen with Windy until he adjusts. This steer is huge next to Windy and wild, but he'll soon settle and she seems to like the company. Father and Dancer have been moving the steers from graze to graze apart from the cows since the grass first greened up and they've learned to stay grouped.

He hopes the steers will bring enough cash to buy a bull. Our mother cows, the ones that had traveled pregnant from Iowa, are ready to rebreed. Father has kept three heifers to join the herd and they are ready for breeding, too, but we have no bull.

Mother has written a list of items she needs. This is the first cash crop from the Read Farm and Father is tense and short tempered. Not knowing what the market for beef is makes him nervous. He writes long columns of numbers and talks to Mother about the highs and lows they represent. She is busy cooking and tending the two girls and does not answer often. When she does, Father says "Well, what would you know about it?"

The beeves go to Oberlin to be sold, combined with others, and put into a boxcar for Chicago. Father is gone for a few days. While he is away Mother has more time for fun. She sings silly songs to the girls and plays peek-a-boo with her apron. Sarah Lou is too small to carry Attie, but Mother puts the baby in Sarah's lap for her to rock. Sarah Lou croons and sings to her little sister. I watch from the doorway and hum.

Father comes home with more seed, supplies and cash hidden in his boots. He brings sugar, coffee, flour, cornmeal, and muslin cloth. His return crowds the dugout.

CHAPTER 8

While in Oberlin delivering the steers I learned of a man with breeding bulls for sale in Sheridan County. Mr. Hausafus was reported to have a good herd of young Herefords ready for service.

"Kell, I've enough to purchase a bull and now seems a good time for me to make this trip. I will be gone at least three days, maybe more. Is there anything you need done before I leave?"

My wife looks around the dugout and shakes her head. "No, Jacob. I think we will be fine while you are away. Perhaps you could chop some of the bigger wood pieces for the stove. I don't want Richard using the ax."

My instinct is to say something harsh about that idea, but I don't want to leave with Kell angry, so I stay quiet. "I will bring up a good supply for you. Never know when spring might decide to backtrack to winter around these parts."

I leave early while it is still dark, feeling a freedom in my heart. Dancer takes me twenty miles south and east, crossing the North Fork of the Solomon, South Bow Creek and a long draw towards Sand Creek the first day. The owner of the Oberlin Mercantile had told me the route and said I'd find the Hausafus' farm on the south side of Sand Creek. In between the creek valleys the high divide gave me views of empty, empty prairie. I spot a group of wild horses and vow to make use of this free source of stock.

Dancer pushes hard to draw close to the herd. I see some good horseflesh in the bunch.

It is late when I arrive at the Hausafus Farm. I'm pleased to learn the family members are big eaters and Mr. Hausafus brews a German beer that he is rightfully proud of, though Kansas is a dry state. By the end of the meal I have laughed more at their table than I can recall. "If you don't mind me saying so, you are a prosperous man, Hermann! You've done very well and I admire your work."

Hermann Hausafus had told me his people had also come from Iowa, he as a young boy, and were part of the original homesteaders arriving in the late 1860's. He knows well what it takes to make it in western Kansas: luck, good planning, never ending work, and luck. I believe he sees in me a man of determination and, with providence on my side, one who might succeed. I feel emotion filling my chest as he thumps my back and sends me to my bed.

The next day, after choosing a prime bull, I tour the Hausafus' farm, staying over a second night. Their warm hospitality and conversation is balm. I see all they have done, the solid buildings, growing crops and healthy livestock as proof that my place can be just as fine and well established. After admiring Mr. Hausafus' Poland China swine pens and enjoying smoked bacon two mornings in a row, I make a promise to Mr. Hausafus that I will return in the fall for a bred sow. The thought of smoked pork served at our table is almost overpowering.

The return trip takes me two long days as I match my pace to that of the young bull. Now and then the animal balks, trying to turn for home. I am ready with a heavy quirt that I bring down on the animal's nose, pivoting on Dancer until the bull faces the right direction. It isn't long before a pattern of obedience is set and I can relax.

This trip has given me renewed belief in my dream and I see a much clearer vision of my family's future. I watch the well fleshed bull striding westward and share in his virility.

While I'm setting up camp under the brilliant stars I hear coyotes yip-yip-yowl on the edge of the earth. I feel assured that Dancer and the bull are safe from such clowns of the prairie. I give a few yips and howls just for the joy of it!

My only sourness comes with thoughts of Richard. What a man needs most is a son he can be proud of; a thinking son, a companion to discuss plans and strategies. Just the thought of that lumbering, oafish boy, his dark eyes sliding earthward or looking vacantly into the distance, his slow speech and stutter, makes me clench my teeth in frustration. Our two daughters are fine, but the boy seems hopeless. Maybe luck will be better on the next child. As I drift into sleep, wrapped tightly in my coat and blanket, I think of Kell's plushness against my hard belly.

CHAPTER 9

Father's distant yell of "halloo the house" late on the fourth day sets Buster to barking, alerting us. Mother wraps Attie Mae in a shawl and lifts Sarah Lou to her hip. "Come, Richard. Father will need our help."

The yard is hazed golden in the setting sun. When the bull catches the cows' scent, his bellow ululates as though he's in pain. I meet Father at the corral, ready to open the gate. Mother and the girls catch up to where I stand.

Father yells, "Open that gate now, for crying out loud!" The gate is made from peeled bark poles, heavy and dragging. Mother helps me swing it wide enough so the bull can see a way in.

Buster spins in circles to keep the cows from pushing forward and the bull charges into the herd. Heads up, their ears flap in agitation. Father dismounts and shuts the gate easily, securing it in three places.

"Do you see this, Kell? Do you see this fine beast? Won't he do us proud next spring and for years to come!" His arm wraps around her shoulders and he hugs her close. I see a fire in his eyes and am drawn to them, but his glance sends me off to stand with Buster.

Mother soon turns back to the house, uncomfortable with the powerful drive of the animals. I slip around the other side of the pen to the bole of a thick cottonwood and stand in open mouthed astonishment at what I see. From the bull's belly a glistening red rod pokes forward as he shoves his bulk among the milling cows. He is heavy in the shoulders, red as oak leaves, and wears curling white hair on his flat forehead. Polished horns curve towards his dark marble eyes. His moans and calls stir the cows further until one separates herself to stand with her rump in his face. The bull's hips are smeared with green manure by his thrashing tail. A cloud of early flies hovers about him. He curls his upper lip at her tail head and paws with his right front hoof, sending clods of soil into the air. Then, with a grunt, he heaves himself onto the cow's back, shoving her forward and down with his weight. She braces, widens her back legs and holds steady. With thrusts and dancing steps, the bull connects with the cow, spearing with his rod. There he remains, half his weight upon her back, servicing her with heaving energy.

Father whoops and says with pride, "Our first Kansas calf just got its start!' I tingle with gooseflesh even though it is warm. Excited and overcome with what I've just seen, I wonder at the strength of the bull and the willingness of the cow to endure him. I have a moment's thought about Father and Mother, but push the image away before it fully forms.

I smell the rankness of the bull as he dismounts, trailing milky fluid from his diminishing organ. The cows continue to circle around and against him. His head rises to scent the air and he paws the earth again, first one hoof and then the other, throwing clumps of earth onto his back.

Father waves me over to him. "Take my bags to the house. I'll leave these beasts to their fun and settle Dancer for the night." He hefts his bedroll and valise over to me. I carry them into the dugout, breathing in the steamy supper smells, and set them down alongside the doorway.

When Father has Dancer rubbed down and fed, he walks into the dugout with a strange look on his face. He calls Sarah Lou over to him and lifts her to his lap.

"Mrs. Hausafus sent you a little something, Sari girl."

I stand by the door watching as he reaches into his coat pocket and pulls out a grey puff of fur. A tiny kitten mews, its pink tongue showing in the lamplight. Sarah Lou squeals with delight, though she'd never seen a kitten and didn't know a thing about cats. From long ago, I remembered stroking Granny's calico as she licked milk from a flowery china dish. Wanting to help, I rush in to pour milk from the pitcher, but trip over Father's bedroll. I crash into Sarah as she holds the kitten close, knocking her into the table. Her bottom lip splits open. The kitten flies from her hands into Attie's bed and, in terror, little claws rake across the baby's tender face.

I run ahead of Father, ducking and weaving to escape his rage. Buster barks and gets between us, but Father kicks him out of the way, coming after me. "You clumsy, worthless horse turd! You better keep running!"

I hear Mother's yells, "Jacob! Jacob, it was an accident! Jacob, stop!"

I slide down the creek bank and into the darker places under the trees. Buster and I have a hide-out we'd found, a hollow place under a plum thicket that is barely big enough for a rabbit. I scoot inside, ignoring the scratch of plum bush spurs and hold my sobs of terror and shame inside. Buster stays by me until full dark. I hear Father's command for Buster to 'watch the stock!' and he looks at me sadly before slipping away. He knows his job well.

I sleep in the hole that night, wrapped in my own arms, my legs tucked tight against my belly, wishing I could die and be done with it all. Richardson's voice whispers, "He's a mean, mean man; he's a mean, mean man…" over and over until it becomes a humming song.

Hunger draws me back in early morning. I start my chores on an empty belly and suck a couple of stolen eggs when I come over dizzy. Knowing this is wrong I crush the shells into fine white dust and scuff that into the dry dirt of the hen house. Mother might suspect she was short the usual number, but I hoped she wouldn't mention it.

When Sarah Lou comes out of the house with her kitten held gently in her arms, I can't bear to look at her face. She says, "Rich-ud, 'wanna see my kitty? Her is a girl, like me. Her called Wittle Biskit."

I walk away like I don't hear and go to milk Sythi. Windy is bawling for her share and I work fast to get the milking done before Father is bothered by the noise and comes for me again. I drink as much as I can, warm from Sythi, putting my mouth on the bucket's edge, tasting the sour scrim where milk collects between the wooden staves. I am careful not to let any stain my shirt, dirty though it is from my dirt cave, careful not to drip any on my chin or I'd be found out. I save a little milk for Sarah Lou's kitten, putting it in an old lid, and leave it where she plays near Mother's clothesline.

CHAPTER 10

1882: SARAH LOU READ (1880-1968)
Prairie Dog Creek

"Poor Brudder. Poor old Brudder", I whisper soft. "He's always sad. He's always shadowing like a rainy-cloud." I see him coming out of the hen's home and he's got his frowning mouth on. He's dirty and he's got a bloody mess face.

I call over, "Rich-ud, you wanna see my kitty? Her is a girl like me. Her called Lil Biskit." He won't even look at me. I think he wished he could disappear.

I am sorry about the roarin' Father made and the screechin' cries of Baby Sis. I think a thunnerstorm hit our home last night. Mama shush, shushes us all an tried to make everything better, but Father yells and yells and shakes his big head like a cow with flies, back-and -forth, throwing slobber.

I'm going to give Rich-ud a surprise today. I'm going to fix him a special dessert for dinner. I'm going to put lots of sugar on his bread. He's going to like all that sweet and maybe he'll smile!

I cuddle my kitty and I sing her a love-a-by. I sit on the dry dirt by Mama's clothes line. I like to hear the whup-whup of our washing in the wind. I like the smell the hot sun drying the cloth.

In just awhile Rich-ud puts a bit of milk down for Lil Biskit. He's humming sounds like kitty purrs, but his hummings not happy like kitty purrs; it drags my chest like a cough.

"Thank you, Brudder. Thank you for my kitty milk." I try to see into his dark eyes. They are the color of Mama's purple pansies when the nighttime pulls away the bright. They are deep eyes, not soft like Mama's or shiny like Baby Sis. They give me a shuddery feel, like the shuddery breath that comes after I've been crying hard.

I smile at him, thinking about the sugar bread dessert. The wind lifts his brown hair up like feathers and I think he smiles back.

CHAPTER 11

1883: RICHARD READ

Prairie Dog Creek

We have lived in Kansas for two years. I have a routine to follow each day: caring for our animals, planting crops, weeding and watering and harvesting. I eat my fill of foods I've tended from seed to plate. Work is expected of me, but it is work I know. Each season eases into the next without disruption.

Mother's gardens are large enough to fill our root cellar for winter's needs. This is a cool and moist place with shelves and bins for holding potatoes, onions, turnips, beets and carrots, winter squashes and pumpkins. Crocks, bought in Rexford, hold fermenting pickles and kraut while heads of storage cabbages are wrapped in paper so they will keep. When I open the wooden door to carry something in or bring out what Mother needs, I breathe the smells of all these foods like sucking soup.

Father brought home a Poland China boar and five bred sows from Mr. Hausafus last fall. Piglets came in batches of ten to twelve. Father and I have built several pens and movable shelters for the swine. When the herd grazes and roots their paddocks into a barren space we move them to a new area, then harrow and seed the old ground with oats or barley. In time there will be a series of these rotating paddocks. The creek runs alongside this field, giving the pigs shade, water and wallow. When I am not busy, I sit with my back to a tree watching the piglets race and wrestle. I share the joy of their outdoor lives.

I am milking two cows now. Mother separates the cream, skimming it with a shallow ladle, and she churns it into butter. The skimmed milk is poured into a tub of grain to soak overnight for the pigs. In the morning I scoop the thick mash into troughs for them to slurp. The mix grows piglets up fast and fat. Mother's hens race to the troughs for their share then scratch and peck at the pig waste.

The hen flock has expanded with fluffy chicks that grow to layers in a season. The roosters become dinner meat. There are enough hens for Father to take eggs to Rexford regularly now. He takes butter, too, and is finding buyers for beef and pork. His trips to town excite him and he returns with mouthfuls of news.

"The town is growing by leaps and bounds, Kell! You should see the stream of folks coming in. The hammering and commotion that's going on, well you would hardly believe it. Folks say there'll be upwards of two thousand in the county by next year if the pace continues. These people are hungry for good farm products, Kell. We'll have a ready market for everything we can grow. I see a very bright future. I do indeed."

My choring time takes longer every month but I don't mind being with the animals. Their morning sounds, their wanting out, wanting food, wanting water are like a greeting without words. At the end of the day when everyone is safe for the night, I feel my efforts are good.

Father has broken new fields of sod for alfalfa and expanded the corn, wheat and oat fields. Nothing seems to stand in his way. He sows and he reaps. Rains have come in good times and in amounts to make the crops.

Nearly one year to the day we had first pulled onto the Read Farm, Father stepped out the site for a real house. That winter he promised Mother that her next child would be not be born in the side of a hill like a rabbit.

True to his word the new soddy, while still made of grass and soil blocks, has bright white plaster walls, a wooden floor and wavy glass in the window frames. It is a square home with a tin roof pitched towards a center chimney from its four sides. A cast iron range in the kitchen heats the main room and holds a reservoir for hot water.

There is one room for the girls and one for Father and Mother with a cradle alongside their bed. I sleep on a pallet by the stove to keep it loaded during the night. In the summer I'll have the attic space.

The front door and windows look south towards the creek and the north windows look out onto the prairie. Plans for a roofed porch to wrap around the east, south and west sides are drawn on brown wrapping paper. It all feels bright and clean after living in the earth home so long. There is space for the girls to play, for Mother to sew and mend, for Father to work his figures on a table in the evening with a lantern for light.

Mother delivers her second son the first day of November, 1883. It is a fast birth. In the security of this home with clean oak floors I watch Father hold this new boy close to his heart and gaze at the baby with a look I'll never receive: complete pride. This is Little Jake.

CHAPTER 12

Everything sparkles. It is near Christmas and Mother has baked for days to fill the house with sweet smells. Sarah Lou is the official cookie decorator and she gives it her full attention. She slips the 'oopses' into her apron pocket and shares them with Attie Mae and Little Jake. Cookie crumbs dust their lips and chins.

Life in Kansas has gotten easier. Father says, "The first years were tough, Kell. I'll give you that. But we're getting on towards starting our fifth year and look at all we've done!"

"It has been a full few years. I am pleased, Jacob. This will be a fine Christmas and our little ones will only remember the good times." Mother's gentle smile warms us all.

My trips to the creek for water are over. Last summer a crew arrived, dug a well and put up a windmill. The clanking circle of blades, flashing as they turn high in the air, fills a cistern of water protected by an earthen well-house. When the cistern is full the mill is kept from turning by a brake. To draw the wooden handle downwards I must hang my full weight upon it. It is then secured with a U-shaped iron ring that pivots into place.

From the cistern the water flows into a limestone creamery where a trough holds milk cans and butter crocks. The air is cool and damp in the creamery, even during hot summer days making a perfect place for wrapped cheeses to ripen on shelves. Mother has become quite skilled at her cheese wheels. Thick rock walls and a double door prevent the water from freezing in winter.

As the water leaves the creamery it is piped to tanks and troughs for the horses and cows. In really cold weather I am careful to shut the valves so that the tanks don't freeze up. The livestock drink what they need each morning and afternoon, sucking greedily when I open the flow. When most have finished I close the system and let the herd drain the tanks.

Getting the well was timely. The Prairie Dog has begun to dry up following two droughty years and the springs have slowed, only running after a heavy rain. The seep where the watercress grows hasn't dried up yet, but Mother is worried it will. Last summer I put up a strong fence to protect it from thirsty animals. With such a dry spell behind us, Mother prays for a wet spring at every meal. Without real moisture soon all our work might be lost.

The well water is pure and sweet as it comes from deep in the earth. Unlike the creek water, there aren't any bugs, leaves or dirt to strain out. Next year Father plans to pipe water to the house. For now I still carry buckets and fill barrels beside the kitchen door, but the walk is short and I've grown strong enough to carry two full ones. We are all very grateful to have the windmill and well, but I am the most grateful.

In late fall Father had gone on a wild horse round-up. Dancer was fast and loved to run so the cowboys welcomed Father into their business. They searched out a band, whooped and hollered them into a narrow canyon with no outlet and roped them one by one. Whoever got a rope on one claimed it. It was dangerous and exhilarating work for men just as tough as the horses they caught.

Father had practiced every night with steers and pigs and even chickens until he could put a loop over anything, every time. He thought it was great fun to catch me around the middle and toss me earthward. When I stopped running away it took the fun out of it for him, so he quit.

He said, "If you were a horse you'd be pretty safe. They'd turn you back rather than take you home."

The new horses added considerable to Father's herd. Some of the horses had good lines with classic heads. Others had plow horse mixed in and Father planned for those mares to be mated with a Percheron stallion he had his heart set on. According to the Rexford newspaper there was a stallion for sale located west of us, clear into Colorado. Father would drive him back, pulling a newer wagon that he'd arranged for in Burlington. If the price could be managed, he'd bring home a papered mare, too. His dream of being seen as a 'man who knows a good horse' was coming true.

After Christmas the weather stayed mild and dry with milky blue skies and light winds. The sun, though low in the sky, had strength. We spent the short days outside working on jobs put off during the busy summer.

Father had just about decided to make his trip west, when something in his gut told him to stay home. All morning he'd been irritable and jumpy. Midday, after his usual short rest following lunch, he saddled Dancer and rode out onto the high ground. It was warm enough for Sarah Lou and Attie Mae to play on the south side of Mother's lilacs, serving tea to their dollies from tiny china cups. In a short while Father came at a hard gallop into the yard, scattering the hens and throwing dust into the air. "Kell, come out here now! Girls, get indoors!"

Mother hurried out of the house, pushing loose hair back into her bun. "What is it, Jacob? Fire? Is it a wildfire?"

Father was unsaddling Dancer as fast as he could and leading her towards the shed. "Bad weather is coming and it's moving fast!" He looked over at me, waving his arms wildly. "Put the poultry inside now. Mother, check on the milk cows, make sure they're tied up secure. By God, boy, what are you waiting for? Do as I say, then get down to the herd and double tie the corral gates!"

Buster hunkered low and ran in circles to gather the scattered hens. They squawked and flapped their wings in hysterical panic unused to being put indoors during the day. I smelled a bitter tang in the air and hurried toward the corrals. The windmill head turned first one direction and then the other, the blades screeching as they shifted. I needed to pull the brake before the wind climbed too high.

The day was changing. It felt like the air was sinking, like the high dome of sky was dropping upon us. Blue-grey clouds tore across the sun in ragged wisps and streams, becoming a boiling grey-black wall in seconds. North winds gusted over the ridge behind me making the bare cottonwoods moan and creak. I pulled the gates tight with wire latches. One cow after another gave anxious voice and they circled with their heads down. The horses were held in a pen up the creek a ways and I saw the wild ones raise their heads, nostrils flaring into the wind. A few bucked and kicked the sky. Even the steady team, wintering with the herd, shifted nervously, turning their tails to meet the cold gusts. I checked their gate, too.

Along the north bank, outside the corral, the prairie grass Father had cut each summer was piled and packed for winter feed. Every year winter had ended without this grass hay being used, but yearly we added more to the stack. I had to wonder if this storm wasn't the one Father had been preparing for.

Mother was feeding baby Jake and the girls were settled near the stove when I came inside. Everything was as safe as we could make it. Father had brought a shovel and several lengths of rope into the house and stacked more wood alongside the wall. The wood bin was full, our water barrels full, the stores of food secure, our animals as protected as we could manage.

I slipped into the girls' room to sit with my back against the west wall. I wrapped a patched quilt around my shoulders and head. Tucked low between the beds where no one could hear me, I began to hum, matching my tone to the sound of the rising, wailing wind.

With each gust the wind grew stronger. It rattled against the house like thrown stones. I felt the house shudder. The temperature dropped and my ears throbbed. I thought about facing the strength of this storm without protection and I thought about how Father might have been caught out there on the prairie, on Dancer. My hum ranged low and high, growing as the wind grew.

From the main room I heard Father say, "This could be the drought breaker, Kell. Your prayers may have been answered, but rain would have been nice."

CHAPTER 13

1886: RICHARD READ

Prairie Dog Creek

Spring came with torrents of melting snow filling the creeks and making early planting impossible. Father talks of a new type of wheat, one planted in the fall, resistant to smut and giving better yields. It is a hard-red wheat, good for baking and in demand back east. He's learned that the Russian settlement near Burlington grows it and he plans to bring home seed when he makes his long postponed trip to Colorado.

The high ground was worked as soon as it was dry enough to put in the oats and the corn fields are ready for planting. The lower, wetter fields were held back for the new wheat, called Turkey Red.

Mother is not well. I suspect she is carrying another baby, but this is something not discussed. Little Jake is 2 ½, Attie 4, Sarah Lou just turned 6 and I am 7. Father says he will take her to Republic City for a rest. Grandmother and Grandfather Cardwell have been encouraging a visit and want to meet the little ones.

On the seventh of April, in the greying of a chilly morning, Father lifts the younger children into the back of the wagon. It is packed with bedding and food for the journey. Each child is protected from falling by boxes of supplies and gifts for the Cardwell family. Father's new gelding, a son of Dancer, is on a lead rope tied to the back. His return trip will be much faster on his own without the team and wagon which he will leave at the Cardwells.

At the last he helps Mother climb onto the seat beside him. Her face is waxy and pale as winter butter. She is wrapped in a heavy woolen coat and a scarf covers her head. She has suffered through the bitter months that followed the New Year's blizzard.

Father says to me, "You know how to run the place and I hold you to do just so until I return." Then he climbs up next to Mother.

Mother calls me over to her and even though she sits high on the springboard seat, I am tall enough for her to place a hand on my head. She leans down towards me and says, "Son, we are counting on you. Father will be back just as soon as he's got me settled. The McAfoos family will help you if anything goes wrong. You can go over anytime you want, you know. Mr. McAfoos might stop in now and then to check on things, so you don't have to feel lonely."

My eyes burn and I nod, keeping my head down. I sense Father's impatience, so I step back away from the wagon, letting them go. I raise my eyes as they begin their eastward journey. Sarah Lou's face is stained with tears and Attie Mae waves her dolly's arm my way, but Little Jake is too young to care. He is in Father's lap and holds the team's reins just below Father's hands.

My days alone are fine. I don't need the neighbors and hope no one stops by. I stretch my voice into the empty spaces above and sing to Buster. The grass is lush from winter snowmelt so the cattle graze in a bunch, making it easy for me to hold them in place. I ride Jigs, one of the smaller mustangs that Father brought into our herd and broke to saddle. Buster keeps the stragglers in place with little nips and barks. My days are full and I fall asleep easily at the end of them. I feel this is what I was born to do; tend living things and keep them safe.

The only upset is the bull. He is separate from the cows so they don't breed back too soon. Father takes pride in having all his calves born over a two month stretch and not in the dead of winter like some ranchers whose bulls stay with the herd year round. The spring air has the bull slobbering and pawing his pen. When I give him his feed he charges forward, shaking his horns and throwing strings of spit. His urine is strong, vinegary, and biting to my nostrils. He pees on the earth and paws at the sour mud, throwing it over his humped back.

A week after the family had gone, I am giving the bull his late feed. I watch the moon's edge rising above the eastern hills. It will be full tonight, bright as a lantern. In the stillness I hear a horse blow behind me and Buster begins a low growl. I turn to the sound, surprised, and meet the piercing gaze of a mounted man watching me work. It is not one of our neighbors.

"Well, boy. You got a fine bull there. He looks ready and able. Where's you kin?"

I feel my belly squeeze and my bowels loosen. Buster drops low at my feet, his growl a steady warning to me. There is something wrong with this man. His look is hungry and mean. He wears whiskers that should have hid his mouth, but don't. His lips are thick and red, moist and puckered in a way that turns my stomach. His teeth, when he leans to spit brown baccy juice and grimaces at me, are black.

I cough to clear phlegm before I answer him. I have trouble getting my words. Father says you can milk a cow faster than I speak. Talking aloud pains me. "Mister… there ain't… nothing here… for you."

"What's a matter wit' you? You a bit slow? I bin watchin' you, boy. I don't think you got any kin 'round. I think you're on your own, keepin' this real nice place all by you self."

"Mister… town's… just… a few… miles… south. You… can find… grub there."

"Ain't grub I'm needin', son."

He steps off his horse real slow and loops the reins over the corral post. "You a big boy, now ain't ya. I think you do just fine."

I back up to the feed stack and can't go any further. He and his horse have blocked me in a tight space with only one way out, through the bull's pen. The bull is stamping and blowing, not interested in his feed. His round eyes reflect the moon's light as it rises behind the man, milky white.

I watch as the man loosens his belt. A belt means a beating, but it didn't make sense from a stranger. Maybe Father had sent this man to check on me and told him to give me a whalloping 'cause he was sure I deserved one.

Darting forward, he kicks out with his cracked boot and snags me behind my knee, bringing me down to the ground in a lifting sweep of his leg. It happens so fast! He spins me over so that my back is facing him. I can smell his sour rankness, like the vinegar must of the bull mixed with rotten breath, blowing over my shoulder. I struggle to get away from his warm, moist huffing against my cheek. His belt snaps around my throat and he pulls it tight.

With the other hand, he yanks my pants free and they tangle about my ankles. I thrash and claw at the belt, choking and crying. Buster comes out of the dark, snapping and snarling at the stranger. Slick and quick the man slips a knife out of his boot, the blade glowing silver, and casually flips it into Buster's side, sinking it with precision between his ribs. Buster's cries of pain make me scream in high pitched rage, but the man's grip never loosens on the belt.

I wheeze in breaths and cough them out. With Buster no longer aggravating him, he reaches around my waist and hoists me until my buttocks are in his lap. I scream again in my own pain as he spreads my legs with his feet, spits a glob of thick spit onto his free hand to smear on me, takes hold of my dick and thrusts his hot and hard into my rear. Unendurable pain ruptures through my center and I squeal in misery, choking on spit and vomit, strangled by the belt. His thrusts continue until he shudders and groans, releasing me to fall on my knees. Breathlessly, he says, "Son, I ain't had that much fun in a coon's age."

Warm, sticky wetness runs between my legs. I gasp and retch for air. The belt has loosened from my neck. I collapse onto my side against the feed stack. My out flung hand lands on something solid; cold metal. The pitchfork that I had used to feed the bull is resting, tines up, on the ground. In one smooth motion, I grip the pitchfork handle with both hands, twist around and sink it into his hairy belly where it rises above me. I feel the tines slide into him with such ease that I think I've somehow missed, but there he stands, his glistening mouth and eyes wide open, his face going from pleasure to shock to agony in quick succession. The full measure of the tines are buried from just above his limp member to above his hairy navel, the wooden handle horizontal to the ground. It wobbles up and down slightly.

His scream is piercing, girlish. He falls to his knees, screams and screams for me to "pull it out, pull it out!" Then he begins to mewl, a hurt pup sound, and slides sideways onto the ground. The three of us lay close as bedmates.

The bull is snorting wild with the noise and the blood smell. I worry he'll come through the corral to join the fight. I take a shallow, shuddery breath and began to hum, then to sing softly. The stranger quiets; I hope he's dead. With the stillness the bull begins to calm.

I hug my knees to my chest, the pain in my backsides a burning fire, bringing bile into my mouth. I work my way closer to where Buster lays and pull the blade from his side. It clatters on the earth between us. My friend is gone. I put my face against his warm side, smelling his fur, feeling it tickle softly as the night breeze lifts and drops his white neck ruff. It shines bright in the moonlight, sparkling with my tears. I sing to him until I pass out of awareness. Sweet puffs of plum blossom scent drop, mixing with the odor of feces and blood and sour sweat as the air cools and sinks.

Sometime in the night, the moon shining through the new spring leaves straight above me, I wake. I shiver so hard my teeth clack. Buster is hard and cold under my hand. The man's eyes are lit by the moon, too. Curled around his belly, the pitchfork handle quivering with each breath, he has not moved. He hasn't died.

I get to my knees and stand up slowly, whimpering. I feel dried blood and the sticky remnants of violation pulling against my legs. I drag at my pants and grip them, unable to manage the fasteners. The man's gaze follows my movements and he tries to reach out a hand. His voice comes in a breathy high pitch, squeezed through his nose, "Son, I need hep real bad. Ride to town for me, won't ya? Bring a doc here fast. I'm certainteed dyin." His words come in gasps and his breath is foul, like air from the privy.

I ease past him and hobble up to the house. The stove holds some coals and I lay a few thin wood slivers to get a flame going, heat water and wash myself with a rag. I soak my pants in the wash bucket when I am done, throwing some salt in the water like I'd seen Mother do to take out blood stains. I swallow a bit of bread to soak up the acid that has risen in my belly, drink water and lay down in bed, putting a pad of rags between my legs to soak the fresh blood. Wrapping a quilt over my bruised self, humming brings me solace. It is a grieving song and a song of rage.

Dawn wakes me. Normally I would have been well into chores by now, but I fight to roll out of bed and pull on my spare pants, those that are short in the legs and tight in the waist. I cannot stand the pressure, so I wrap a small blanket around my waist and secure it with a length of rope. I feel ill-used. My raw throat is gritty as sand. It is hard to swallow, but I sip water and begin the morning's routine.

I let the poultry out into the yard, milk the cows, strain the milk and put it in the creamery to cool, feed the pigs, fill water troughs, turn the cows out for grazing and load the wood box. Tears run past my nose and mix with snot. Bubbles of mucus form at my humming lips. I shuffle from job to job, trying not to strain when I lift. As I move toward the corral to feed the horses I remember where the pitchfork is.

The man is still alive. His face is the color of wet ashes and he wears purple bruising around his ears and lips. His breaths are shallow with a gurgle on the exhales. Yellow brown ooze stains his flesh where the tines penetrate. I walk alongside him and pull the pitchfork free. His scream sends birds flying from trees and the bull into short hopping bucks.

I untie his horse, a flea bitten grey gelding that has not grazed well in weeks, and lead him, slowly, to the barn. His saddle has a high horn and might be useful someday, but after pulling it free from his back, I bury it as best as I can under the far end of the straw pile. The man did not carry much with him, just a water jug made from a gourd, a sack of wormy cornmeal and a sour smelling striped wool blanket for a bedroll. I drop it all in a corner to burn later.

The horse is rawboned with badly worn feet. I don't know what to do with him. Turn him loose and someone might recognize him. Keep him and the same might happen. I am too tired and hurt to care much. For now, I give him a small scoop of oats, put grass hay in the bunk, fill a water bucket for him and leave him in the stall.

I go back to the corral to finish feeding but I don't look at the man. I can't lift Buster, so I ease him onto a burlap feedbag that I can pull. With slow steps I take him to our place under the plum thicket, singing past the pain in my heart and body, and lay him to rest in the cool overhang. It takes me a long time to find enough stones to set a wall around him and I cry out each time I lift one, but I don't want coyotes to pick at his body. He's always been with me and I will miss him.

The cows graze and I move them, real slow, on foot until mid-afternoon. I smell rain in the air and lightning flickers through a western cloud bank. Everything is locked up safe with the evening chores done early when the first drops fall. It rains heavy and I grieve for Buster lying cold and still, hoping the overhang of rock is keeping him dry.

I wake with hunger gnawing at me. I had hard boiled some eggs the day the stranger came so I peel one and mash it onto bread for a sandwich, washing it down with cold coffee from two nights ago. In a whoosh it all comes back up. Pain clenches my lower belly in spasms, chasing away hunger.

My washed pants have dried so I won't have to wear a blanket today. There is a dark stain in the crotch that I hope Mother won't notice.

Morning chores eventually lead me back to the man. His skin has gone all speckly purple-grey, his clothes are sodden, but his chest still rises and falls in a jagged pattern. A stinking green-brown drool oozes from the holes in his swelled up belly. I bend down slow to look at him and his eyes try to turn towards me, but he isn't seeing. "Go... ahead... and die... Mister. I... can't... bury you... till then." I walk away and finish choring.

As the morning warms my pain eases some. While following the cows I keep an eye out for a good place to put the stranger's body and towards noon find just what I need. An old badger's den has caved in during the spring melt. It is off the usual path of the grazing herd and nowhere near a worked field. I decide, dead or not, that I'll drag the man there before nightfall.

The herd is quiet, most of them resting on their bellies chewing cud, so I walk back to the farm and halter Jigs. I know I can't rise into a saddle, but I put his gear on and take a rope off the barn wall. I lead him down to the bull corral and have to sing soft and easy to work Jigs over close to the man's foul body. I consider putting the rope's loop around the man's neck, but something keeps me from it.

He is still curled as though protecting a precious package so I snug the rope around his ankles and take a wrap around the saddle horn. When Jigs moves out to my clucks, a sigh puffs from the man's lips and liquid runs from his belly. I only care that he doesn't hang up on our way to the hole. His belt falls from his grip and I pick it up to bury with him.

It takes a bit to work him up the creek bank, his body bouncing and snagging on yucca and rocks until we are over the top, but soon he is sliding along at a fair pace. Jigs dances some when a moan escapes the man, but I keep him paying attention with clucks till he steadies. My jaws ache from clenching against my pain.

When we reach the badger hole, I slip the rope from the horn and untie the stranger's feet. I ground tie Jigs so he'll stay near. He crow hops a few feet away to graze. The man is nearly full dead, breaths barely coming with long stretches between. I want to roll him into the gaping earth to get him out of my sight, but again, something keeps me from it.

I sit down gently, putting my weight on one haunch, and wait for his chest to quit rising. He holds on what seems a long time. I look at his worthless carcass, measuring his badness, and consider taking his boots. They look to be a size that might fit my feet, and I'd never had much by way of shoes, but I knew I didn't want a thing on me that had touched him. Keeping his horse and saddle were enough of a burden.

Finally he lets his spirit go. It escapes him in a final wheeze of air and he seems to shrink before me. I wait to the count of 60 before I'm sure, then wait awhile longer. Leveraging my back against a hump in the prairie, I shove him into the hole with my feet, screaming at the effort and feeling fresh blood leak into my breeches.

Covering him will have to wait for tomorrow. I am played out and still have evening chores to do. It has been two days since I'd last held any food. I see sparks of black and hear a whine inside my ears, feeling cold and hot both by the time the day's work is done. I spend a wretched time clearing my bowels in the privy, wiping bright blood when done. I am clammy and shivering, but I feel better for it.

Father is away for nearly a whole moon cycle. It is moving towards full again on the evening he rides into the yard and halloo's the house. I come out of the barn. I'd moved my bed into the stall where the saddle is buried under the straw. The grey gelding is grazing with the other horses and I have a story of how he'd just wandered in to join them. He doesn't wear a brand and already looks like a different horse, having fattened up with good grass and oats. I'd brushed the dry coat off him, pulled the burrs from his mane and tail and cleaned up his hooves. He'd gotten real friendly with me, pricking up his ears whenever I come within sight. I'd named him Speck.

Over supper of biscuits and gravy Father reported on the family. Mother and the children were settled in and enjoying the relatives. Father had worked while in Republic City, making money in the brick yard. He was real pleased to have brought back a great wrapped bundle of apple tree transplants. These would go on the timber claim. He'd brought Russian apricots and pie cherries, too. We were to have an orchard.

Father was full of plans and talked on and on of what he'd seen possible in Republic City. Folks in Rexford would soon come to the Reads for the finest horses, cows and pigs. He planned to go west for that Percheron pair as soon as we had the orchard planted.

It was a one man conversation, but it was the most he'd ever spoken in my presence. I knew he had no interest in me except as a way to get these jobs done. I missed the solitude of the past weeks and was not sad to hear he'd soon be leaving again.

"Where's the dog?" Father asks as he walks about the farm the next morning, looking to find something I'd neglected.

"Sn...ake," I answer, swallowing hard and not looking up.

"Hmph. I'd a thought he was too smart for a snake. We'll miss him with the stock." Father had taken my answer. I was ready to never speak of Buster or that time again.

After the corn and fruit trees were planted Father rode west into Colorado. Three weeks later he drove back with a new grain wagon pulled by a powerful black team. He'd sold the gelding, getting acquainted with the horse traders in that area with a thought to the future.

The Percheron stallion was immense with hairy fetlocks and a thick curly tail. He was quiet in nature and would work or breed, depending on what was asked of him. Father was going to use him to cover the mares gathered on his wild horse hunts and also offer him for stud. The black mare, smaller and feminine, was already in foal by another stallion. Her offspring would carry a different bloodline. It wouldn't matter if she gave us a filly or a horse colt, either would work for his breeding plans. Father was puffed full of a future with great horses.

He had bought new duds for himself while passing through Goodland, a market town east of the Colorado state line, and he gave me his old ones. "You grow like nothing I've ever seen. It ain't normal, the size you've gotten to. It just ain't normal."

I was nearly as tall as Father, my arms and legs pushing out of my clothes. I'd had to split the fronts of my shirts to fit them over my shoulders which seemed to hump up around my neck. Father's clothes were faded and patched, but they covered me without binding. I had burned the stained pants along with the stranger's things and was glad for these castoffs.

Our crops came in well, though it stayed dry, and we broke more ground. Father was gone much of the time. He was content to give me jobs and leave me to them. I was content to stay busy. The fruit trees needed to be watered which meant buckets and buckets. To keep weeds and grass from choking the saplings I had to hoe around them, too. Otherwise I spent most of the days alone with the stock.

With all the barns in place and the house finished, Father had more time for town. He went often to Rexford, the trail clearly marked and almost a road now, taking the extra eggs and milk. Since the rest of the family was away, we had much more than could be used. Without Mother here to churn I was freed from separating the cream, lessening the twice daily milking chore. Sometimes he stayed away all night, 'getting the feel of the community', he said. Summer and early fall passed.

He was beginning to make the name for himself that he'd always wanted. Many of the new-comers had gone, pulling out after the blizzard losses. Others left by fall when acres of crops were ruined by a tremendous hail storm just before corn harvest. That opened up more opportunity for the ones who stayed.

We had a quiet winter. Father brought home a new dog, a buff colored pup with a dark face and feet, but he kept it with him and it learned not to wander my way. I went inside the house only to keep the wood box full and to haul ashes from the stoves. We took turns fixing the meals, though when it was my turn, Father found reasons to work outside. I had gotten into such a habit of humming to myself that I was startled when Father suddenly yelled, "Quit that God-forsaken yowling!"

During dry days as winter came to an end, Father joined a group of men to trap badgers. It was known that horses and cattle could break legs when they stepped into their deeply dug holes. Litters of up to five were common and the men were determined to get ahead of those numbers. I ran cold sweat when Father told me what he was doing. My mind flashed back to the stranger's dull thump when he hit the bottom of that washed out den. I knew he was well hidden. The grass had mostly grown over the bare place, leaving just a swale that looked no different from other low places on that part of our range, but I carried a horror of seeing some part of the stranger revealed. His ghost rode my back.

Mother didn't return until the following spring, bringing home a new boy. Tim Johnson Read was six months old before I met him. Father had been away for a month to fetch them and I had spent the last days getting the house free of dust and clutter. Sarah Lou was shy and sweet, but the others hardly knew who I was, believing I was hired help, and seemed afraid of me.

By sleeping in the barn I gave Mother more room in the house for the little ones. She looked herself again, with color in her cheeks and shine in her hair. The wagon held many nice things for her house: fabric for curtains, rugs for the floors, ornate mirrors and pictures for the walls. She'd also brought something special for me: a music box.

Mother says, "Let me show you how it works, Richard. I hope you'll like it. It has a goodly sound."

I touched it with a finger. It was smooth polished wood, red-gold and silky-warm. A key, secured behind a drop down door on one side, wound the mechanism. Under the hinged lid a cylinder with tiny bumps spun slowly, plucking true notes from brass teeth that lifted and dropped as it turned. I heard four tunes, their names written in fancy script under the lid. When she watched me listening to the beautiful sounds, Mother's eyes made me think of sunshine caught in morning frost. I had no words for her. She didn't need any.

I felt too large for the room. I had to back myself close to the door to remain inside. Sarah Lou and Attie danced about with their hands in the air, tiptoeing to the tinkling sounds. I saw their pale legs and bare feet lifting under their skirts. Little Jake chuckled and Tim hooted with glee. Mother took a few dance steps herself and smiled at Father in happiness. I heard myself humming, a worrying sound, and a voice, the one that spoke between my ears, say "We don't belong. We are not a part of this."

"Richard? Are you all right?" Mother starts towards me with her arms outstretched, palms up in a beseeching way. I feel the air leave my lungs in a whoosh, just as it had when the stranger clamped my ribs in his grip. The room dims and my ears whistle. I find the door knob and flee to the barn.

I hear Father's voice or maybe the voice still inside my head say, "He's not right, Mother. He'll never be right."

Mother came out to my stall later that night. I catch her woman smell, so different from the barn, so different from my own. She cradles the music box in her arms, wrapped in a piece of quilting to keep it free from dust.

"Richard. This is for you. It will always be yours. You listen to it when and where you want." She sets it on a shelf above my bed, pushing it safe against the wall. I see her wipe a tear and I think of the saddle still hidden behind me and the man in the hole and the pain. Her tender heart is too good.

CHAPTER 14

The steam powered train stops jerkily with screeching hisses and clunks. It has arrived, literally, at the end of the rails at Oakley, KS. Tracks will be laid westward in the upcoming years, but this is the furthest the McGinley family can ride. They stand ready, gripping the rough boards of the doors and brace themselves against the braking movements.

Spring winds gust and blow cinders into their eyes as John James McGinley, Edward and young John slide open the boxcar's doors. Odors of manure and coal smoke are strong.

Opening these doors ends an exhausting journey which began with the loading of the family's mules and wagon, farming tools and poultry into an emigrant boxcar in Springfield, Illinois. Stacked along the walls are trunks and crated household items. Canvas bags of quilts and linens hang from iron hooks.

Edward Henry is twelve-years-old, the second oldest child. His father, John James, had come from Ireland to New York as an eighteen-year-old stowaway. Dreams of success firmly in mind, John worked his way westward to join his older sister Ann and her husband Patrick Daily who lived in Illinois.

His older sister's children had also emigrated to America between 1878-1880 carrying the last name Brogan. They settled in Nebraska. Their letters of encouragement were important in the McGinley family's decision to go west.

With his foundation of poverty in a starving country, John's vision is of a future owing to no one. It has steered him to this place. At age thirty-five John has brought his family of seven children and very pregnant twenty-nine-year-old wife, Mary Ann, to claim their share of free Kansas land.

In Kansas City their boxcar was transferred to the Kansas Pacific Railroad Line. Young Edward is thrilled by the knowledge that this route follows the western journey of Marshal (Wild Bill) Hickok, his hero in all ways, twenty years earlier: Fort Riley, where Mr. Hickok was appointed Deputy U.S. Marshal and became friends with Lt. Col. George Armstrong Custer; Abilene, 'Queen of the Cowtowns', whose farm families he'd protected from lawless Texas herdsmen; and Hays City, where he became known as 'guardian of the city'. Edward's boyish mind polishes these jewels of knowledge faithfully.

Each time the train stops for fuel and water the family clears their car of human and animal waste, stretches their legs and replenishes their own supplies. Edward's searching eyes absorb the terrain of the towns where James Butler Hickok brought terror to evildoers. His imagination places the tall lawman, stern of face, defender of children and women, at every station along the way. Edward's copy of DeWitt's Ten Cent Romances is his most treasured possession. Its cover features a pencil drawing of Mr. Hickok, drooping mustache and flowing shoulder-length hair enhancing his masculine strength.

Edward believes, had they met, he would have been recognized as a kindred spirit by this great man. Edward's internal longing to right injustices, to stand taller than others, to be known for swift, decisive action on the side of moral right echo the daring stories about his hero. His intense blue Irish eyes might well have caught the attention of his idol, whose English ancestry results in similar features. They even share Illinois as their birth state.

The boy sadly knows this can never happen. He mourned the death of Mr. Hickok after discovering that tragic event had come one year after his own birth. Reading the tales of this grand man as a child and now finding himself, as a growing boy, following the Sheriff's path, Edward feels especially aligned with the charismatic character. He imagines himself leaving a mark as lasting as that of Sheriff Hickok in the raw lands of western Kansas.

John and Mary Ann are relieved to be free of the stink and confinement of sharing a train car with bored children and nervous animals. John steps onto the wooden loading platform and takes his wife's arm to steady her. Mary Ann feels as though the platform is moving under her feet and sways, chuckling at the sensation. The children crowd alongside their parents. They blink at the glaring brightness, so contrasting to the dim boxcar they've lived in. They listen to horse whinnies, mule brays, bawling cows and the clatter of wagons along with shouts from teamsters and others crowding the streets. The town of Oakley is bustling.

Clots of blackened snow melt into mud channels on the north side of buildings. Brilliant white clouds race with the wind, revealing a sky bluer than the family has ever seen. Three boys wearing overalls and clomping boots run forward and offer to help lead the skittish mules down the boxcar ramp and to roll the wagon into place behind them, hoping they can earn a few coins. John turns the boys away with a curt, "We can manage!" Most of the family's money is sewn into Mary Ann's skirts, safe from pilfering hands and less tempting to spend.

John directs Edward to help him lead the four dark mules to a nearby hitching post. Their nostrils flare and blow at these new surroundings. Edward pays close attention to the nervous beasts, soothing them with shushing sounds and firm handling and is relieved when they are secure. Without being told Edward rubs the lead mule Pete with a burlap cloth to smooth his coat and prepare him for the harness.

Edward moves with assuredness, having helped his father daily on his grandmother's Illinois farm. He finishes Pete and does the same for Pat, Dobbin and Dick.

The harnesses which have hung, jingling pleasantly, on harness hooks during the journey are laid upon the mules one by one. Though their alert ears twitch forward and back and their eyes are shiny with nervousness, the four animals stand quietly as John secures the collars and hames around their necks, snugs the leather belly straps and adjusts the breaching. Each mule has its own set of harness, fit to prevent wear on their pressure points. John moves surely and efficiently, settling the mules further with his words and the routine of harnessing. Then he removes the harness hooks from the boxcar walls and bolts them onto the sides of the wagon where they will stay until a place for them is built at the new farm.

Everyone except Mary Ann and the little boys help roll the empty wagon from the boxcar to level ground. John controls the tongue to direct and slow its descent. Suzella, (14) and Edward stand on either side at the front wheels while John (10) and Hugh (6) manage the rear wheels, alternately pushing forward and holding back based on Da's commands. Mam bites her lip until the job is done, calling out to Hugh to "keep your hands free of the spokes, stay to the side and don't get in front of the wheel!" She supports Thomas (2) on her hip and holds Charles Robert's (4) hand tight.

Time is short to get their belongings off the train; the rail bosses holler at them and the other emigrants to "move it fast or pay the delay!" Da has told the family that the railroad can charge an extra fee if they don't unload fast enough to prevent a delay in the train's schedule. Da stands in the wagon, organizing the family's belongings to his particular plan as the items are brought to the end gate. His Irish temper and intolerance is evident to everyone and they struggle to please him.

Edward knows he has to hurry, but he restrains his excitement and curiosity. His eyes jump to see everything possible between trips to and from the boxcar. He notices a monstrous mound of grey-white bones piled near the rails and he taps a passing man who looks like he knows his way around. "What are those?" he points to the mountain.

"Last of the buffalo, boy. Last of the buffalo. Haulin' 'em East and grindin' 'em up fer fert'lizer. Hmmph! Took 'em no time to kill off them herds. Bin here forever; rivers of 'em. Black rivers of the beasts. Thund'rous shaggy rivers. All thar's left is bones, boy. Only bones and now them's leaven', too." He spits a long stream of thin dark juice from the tobacco chaw wedged in his lower lip. Edward hears a wet splat. Dribbles stain the old man's yellowed chin whiskers; bristling ash colored eyebrows shade a long-distance gaze. He swipes his wrist across the drool, ragged cuff stiff with filth, and shakes his head in sorrow at the changes he's witnessed.

Edward nods like he understands. He is overwhelmed. Tears prick unbidden, as a loss for something he'll never see clenches his chest: a river of thundering beasts flowing across the plains as they'd done for centuries. Before becoming a lawman Mr. Hickok had shot buffalo to feed troops; his eyes and ears full of their immensity.

Edward turns his face downward, blinks back the sting, and loads a third crate of hens onto the wagon. The black and white birds have dropped feathers, revealing bumpy red flesh paling near their pinched vents; their feet caked with sticky, ammonia smelling droppings. "I am here too late," he thinks. "I should have been with Wild Bill. I could have been his pard. And here I am haulin' chickens!" An angry eyed rooster glares sideways at him between the crate's dowels. "Don't frown at me, Master R. You've got a few more days in that cage and I can't do a thing for ya!"

"Son!" Da yells. "Stop your gallivanting!"

Edward and Suzella work together to bring the last of the trunks to the wagon just as the train whistle toots a warning. Da has sorted the wagon so that the heavy items are to the front and well balanced for the mules. It is a full load with an empty space left for supplies and Edward admires his father's skill. He takes a final look through the boxcar and slides the train's door closed to show they are done.

John makes arrangements for Mary Ann, Suzella, Hugh, Charles Robert and Thomas to take the mail coach north-west to Colby. The Thurford Post Office stop allows for a change of horses and will give the passengers a chance to stretch and attend to personal needs, but the coach runs hard between towns. It won't be an easy trip for them.

Edward and young John remain with Da to drive the team and wagon. They will meet up in two-and-a-half days and then travel to the homestead site another three miles west and four miles south of town.

The family clusters around Mam, not willing to be separated, but the trunks holding Mam's and the children's clothes are loaded and the stage driver looks irritable. Da puts an arm around Mam, leans into her and whispers too low for the children to hear his words except, "Acushia – pulse of my heart."

She smiles warmly and gathers her skirts below her swollen abdomen, covered discretely by folds and drapes of cloth. Da helps her into the coach and then hands the small ones up to her. Suzella climbs in, squeezes between Mam and Hugh and places Tom on her lap. Charles Robert sits on the floor between Suzella's feet. Da puts a finger to his lips in a last farewell, closes the door and taps on it to let the driver know they are cleared to start away.

The carriage is an abused Concord. It has lost all its original shine and reeks of humanity. Cracked leather curtains block the wind and the enclosed space soon becomes too strong for Mam. She requests permission from the other passengers to roll up the one beside her. Fine dust filters in, lifted by the spinning wheels and dancing hooves of the team, creating a dry fog, but the odors subside a bit.

Mary Ann is queasy. The stage's rocking motion, very different from the train's movement, has brought hot bile into her throat. She has not taken a whole meal in weeks. Heartburn and nausea have plagued her throughout this pregnancy. She yearns for something green and crisp or for fruit, clean and sweet and full of juice. She swallows down sourness, imagines sucking on an Illinois peach and focuses on the land passing beside her. She sees low treeless hills covered with tawny short grass, clumps of silver-grey sagebrush and grey-green yucca. There is nothing of height to break the horizon, not even fences to create boundaries. Mary Ann's eyes ache with the dry distances. Suzella sits upright with her eyes closed and the children doze like pups in a basket.

Part II

In Oakley the harnessed mules are secured to the wagon, the chain tugs set for a hard pull. John had pre-greased the axles while the wagon was still on the train and it was thoroughly reinforced before they left Illinois. A waxed canvas tarp can be laid over the load to protect it from rain, but this is rolled tightly and tied to the seat back for now.

Da leaves the boys in the wagon while he purchases some items to replenish what they had used or couldn't carry on the journey. He's been told prices are higher further west. Little John and Edward watch the bustle of the Oakley station and point out sights to each other. The boys jump and the mules jolt forward when the long whistle blows for the outgoing train. Edward has been holding tight to the leather reins and draws them in. He's glad the handbrake was set, too. He and John giggle at the excitement and to release their tension. They are very glad not to be trapped in the enclosed space of the departed stage coach.

Large sacks of oats, potatoes, flour, cornmeal and dry beans are placed in the wagon by workers, adding to the homesteader's basic supply. Da has bought a tin can of lard, a crock jug of molasses and small sacks of baking soda, baking powder, salt and a tin of tea. He has also spent a few extra pennies to buy each of his children a striped peppermint stick, but these are hidden until the family is together on their own land. He climbs onto the wagon seat, takes the reins from Edward, releases the brake and clucks to the mules. The four beasts lean into the harness to break inertia.

John James directs the mules to draw up to the community cistern which is close to the tracks. He partially fills their water barrels, two on each side of the wagon, from a canvas spout. They will be topped off in Colby. This is water will be used to get them that far. He lets the mules drink at the brimming tank. Others are doing the same and folks chat while waiting their turn. Weather, prices and local news are discussed, but no personal details are shared. Several accents are noticeable. Some speak with foreign languages.

Guiding the team in a wide circle, John turns them north-westward. They follow the trail used by the stage. He talks to his sons, "Boys, we are going to make our home, an honest grand home, here in Kansas. It won't be easy, but we've got our kip and the wherewithal. We have it in us to stick to the land. You boys will work for your family and yourselves, not some laird and master. You will be the owners! God willin'." Edward's heart swells with the power of this big land and his father's promise.

The McGinleys are not alone on the trail. Families move slowly along the ruts in various styles of transportation, some facing west as this family does and some facing east, returning to tamer lands. Hands are raised in greeting, yet an inherent isolation is attached to each family.

The shadows behind them lengthen and it is soon evident their first night on Kansas soil will be spent not far from

Oakley. This suits the mules, stiff from their train journey and hungry for fresh grazing. Da gives the 'haw' command and the mules point their ears left, southward. He drives them far off the trail to a place where last year's dry grass and some few green blades of spring grass can feed them through the night. A limestone bluff, creviced and scoured white as bone, runs southwest and blocks the strengthening north wind; a good place to camp. Da sets the wagon's brake and unhitches the mules, tying them to picket stakes he's pounded into the hard earth, enough distance between each animal to prevent tangled ropes. He slides off their harness and puts the equipment on the wagon hooks matching the positions the mules hold when pulling.

Edward rubs the animals smooth and checks their feet for stones. He brings them each a bucket of water, standing at their heads while they suck and swallow. He speaks to the animals, calling them by name and praising their hard work. Edward understands these mules are vital to the family's wellbeing and success. He is very fond of them and thinks of them as friends. A measure of rolled oats is poured onto the grass in a pale cone for each animal and the mules lip and tongue it up eagerly. As Edward straightens up he's relieved to see the sunset is clear. Gold-red streaks light up the opposite bluff.

Little John has scraped clear an old campfire site ringed with limestone chunks and filled it with dry manure and grass clumps. There is no wood in sight. Da measures the rising wind, shakes his head and announces they will do without a warming blaze. He has heard tales of wildfires that can't be stopped. This country is very different from Illinois and must be learned. He would prefer not to learn the hard way.

After feeding and watering the poultry the men share a cold supper of heavy bread spread with lard and molasses, a chunk of dry beef and a salt crunch pickle. A hot meal was wanting, but this assortment satisfies their need for fat, sweet, protein and salt. Colby's well water, which carries a tang they are unaccustomed to, quenches. Da wishes for a cuppa strong tea, but does not complain.

Stepping away from the wagon site the boys relieve themselves, hearing the sound of their streams in the crystal stillness. The sky dome above is pearl blue, shading to bruise purple. Coyote chorus close and far breaks the silence and the boys race back toward Da, whooping to cover their fear. His chuckle reassures them. "Coyotes are little fellows. They won't be botherin' you." He does not mention the wolves that can.

The brothers wrap themselves in blankets and lay back to back in the wagon bed, heads tucked under the seat with barrels and boxes between them and the wagon sides. Edward marvels at the feeling of a great sky wheeling above them and the turn of the earth below. Da lights a lantern, checks the mules and then climbs up beside them, putting little John in the middle. It takes no time for the McGinley men to fall into dreamless sleep.

Part III

The stage arrives in Colby later that night. The horses blow and shudder under their harness, eager for release from the day's work. The children try not to whimper as their legs uncramp. Mary Ann is near collapse. The stage driver, longing for strong drink to wash the dust from his throat, takes special care of her. Asking the men passengers to unload the bags and trunks and taking only the mail bag slung over one shoulder he leads her, Suzella and the small ones to the Windsor Hotel, into the care of Madge Miller who owns the establishment with her husband Herb. His relief at handing over this worn family to the matron is evident.

"Damn landgrabbers!" he mutters under his breath as he returns to the coach. "No place for wimenfolk. No place for little ones or young girls, neither!" He has seen uncounted graves during his years as a freighter; so many abandoned dugouts with nothing to show for the wasted lives except scrap-board crosses to mark the buried. "Blast and damn the men who do this to their families!"

The McGinleys are led upstairs by Ma Miller into a room occupied by a couple of elderly women sharing one of four iron beds, two each set against opposing walls. Faded but colorful quilts cover the muslin sheets. There is just space enough to walk between the beds, the wooden floor shiny with use. At the far end is a 'comfort' station with a wash stand and chair commode hidden behind a fabric screen. One window, closed and draped heavily, is opposite the door. The room is clean and smells as fresh as the unwashed bodies crowding it allow. Mary Ann is too tired to eat and gratefully releases her family to the hotel matron's care.

She removes her garments down to her shift and relieves herself in the commode. Her urine is strong, concentrated. She's restricted her water intake to reduce the difficulties of finding places for toileting during the trip. It is difficult to pull off her shoes, to bend around her thickness and she grunts and gasps louder than she wishes. She rolls her cotton stockings, greasy and soiled, into balls and massages her swollen, spongy feet gently. She rinses her hands and face in the enamel basin then pulls pins from her heavy dark hair. With eyes already closing, Mary Ann crawls into one of the beds, pulling the quilt over her shoulders. Curling onto her side, her arms wrapped to support her gravidness, Mary Ann gives in to exhaustion.

Ma Miller plops Tom onto her wide hip, his short legs spraddled front and back of her round frame, grabs Hugh's hand and leads Suzella with Charles in tow down the stairs to the hotel's warm kitchen. Seating the children around her work table she fusses and bustles about, ladling thick barley stew into earthenware bowls, arranges slices of buttered bread on a plate and pours scalded milk into cups with a sprinkling of cinnamon sugar for sweetening. "Now, young folks, tell me everything!" Ma Miller feeds on people's stories. She views it as fair exchange.

"Da's got us a farm!" Hugh turns on his best smile for this kind lady. His rosy cheeks, bright eyes and dimpled chin reflect his sunny nature. "We're from Ill'nois but now we're Kansans!"

He speaks like a future mayor of Colby, Ma Miller thinks, laughing at his enthusiasm.

"You've come a long way, son. But you sure aren't wore out yet! Well, this area needs young men like you and we're glad you've come. Welcome, welcome!"

Charles Robert sits on his knees to reach the table and pulls the bowl to just below his chin. His full attention is on eating. Let Hugh do the talking, that's fine with him. He is a silent boy, much different than outgoing Hugh. His darker coloring, slim build and quietness help him to stay unnoticed. He is independent, almost secretive by nature. Ma Miller observes him while she smiles and chats with Hugh, watches as he shovels his stew, slips a second piece of bread onto his lap and gulps his milk without pausing for breath and her heart aches for the tyke.

Suzella spoons cooled soup into Tom's open mouth. She is gentle natured like her mother and loves her brothers deeply. When Da got land fever, she considered staying in Illinois with her grandmother, Ann Higgins, but Granny promised she would join them after they settled. The older woman has been a vital part of Suzella's life and she grieves at their separation. Meeting Ma Miller helps her feel less lonely and the pleasant featured, red-headed Suzella is drawn to her.

Mam was fifteen when Suzella was born in 1873. Grandpa Higgins died the same year. John McGinley, five years after arriving in America, had been working on the Higgins' forty acre farm as live-in hired help. With a second pregnancy in an advanced state John and Mary Ann were married in a civil ceremony. The following day the union was blessed by a Catholic priest. Three months later, Suzella, then four, was given a brother to love, Edward Henry – named after Mary Ann's deceased brother.

Ma Miller would never hear these stories, of course. It was obvious to Suzella that her parents lived for each other. Children were the result. She had only recently realized she is near the age Mam was when she found herself 'in the family way'. The shock of that discovery ran deep and made her feel very protective of Mam and, for a short time, awkward around Da.

Suzella explains, without going into detail, the path that has led them to Thomas County, KS. She shares the names of her parents and siblings and the information of where they will be locating their farm.

"Oh!" Ma Miller nods knowingly. "That'll be Four Mile Corner." She chuckles with delight. "Some call it Little Ireland, because so many Irish families are settling in that neighborhood. I must say, they are a hard working bunch!"

Suzella does not detect any insincerity in Ma Miller. She seems genuinely happy to see more families come to the area. Da had warned the children there might be some who didn't care for Irish Catholics, but also said that this is a grand big country and surely there was room for all.

Jaw-cracking yawns make their rounds, so Suzella thanks Ma Miller for the fine meal and prompts the children to do the same. Jumping up from his seat, Hugh races around the table to wrap his arms around Ma's thighs and gives her a tight hug, his nose inhaling the fragrance of clean fabric and cooking. Ma Miller dabs her eyes with her apron corner. She has no little ones of her own and has taken a particular liking to this family.

She says diplomatically to Suzella, "I've got a tub full of wash water and there's no sense for it going to waste. You bring down those travel clothes when you can, young miss, and I'll get them clean for you before your Da arrives. It will be awhile before you folks are set up to do washing on your new place."

Quiet as possible, Suzella takes the children upstairs, shows them the lidded commode, helps them to undress and runs a washcloth over their worst places. No one's had a proper bath since leaving Granny's farm. Suzella notes her own odor and knows it is unpleasant. She appreciates very much Ma Miller's kindnesses as she gathers the family's outerwear into a bundle, holding back an over-cloak to cover herself as she takes them downstairs. Tomorrow they will exchange their soiled underthings for fresh items out of the travel trunk.

Mam doesn't rouse as the children climb into bed. Tom and Charles share Suzella's bed; Hugh curls up next to Mam. That leaves one empty bed which is filled sometime after midnight by another emigrant mother and two small daughters, who don't bother to undress at all.

Morning streams through the hotel window, chases sleep from the room. A clatter and thump of feet outside their door announces guests moving toward the dining room for breakfast. The other roommates have already vacated. Mam stretches carefully and steps behind the privacy screen to use the commode, noting its fullness and wondering if she should ask where to empty it.

She is much improved by the night's rest and believes a real breakfast will do her that much better. She knows John won't arrive until tomorrow and misses him terribly but is glad for the time to recover.

They have rarely been apart since she first fell into his lake blue eyes. Though he is six years older than she this did not seem unusual to Mary Ann, whose father was eleven years senior to her mother. She is educated and has been teaching her children to read, write and keep accounts as they become old enough. Though John has learned much from her during their 15 years together, he relies on her and she leans on him.

Suzella is next up and shares with Mam the events of the evening. Together they sort out fresh clothing from the trunk and dress the children for breakfast. Bundling their soiled clothing in a tidy pile the family joins the other diners.

Breakfast is hearty and generous. Ma Miller competes well with the other Colby hotels and has built a good reputation that she works hard to maintain. She is a woman of great energy and compassion for others. Suzella watches her greet guests by name and is cheered by how her eyes light up when she sees the McGinleys.

Mam carries herself with dignity. Others move aside for her and two gentlemen stand to offer her and Suzella their places at the long communal table. The little ones stand alongside until open spots on the bench become available. Bowls of steaming cereal, plates of corn cake, sausages and eggs, biscuits and jugs of gravy are passed from hand to hand. The young girls who help Ma Miller make a steady circuit from kitchen to table, placing full serving dishes and removing the empties.

Ma greets Mrs. McGinley politely. "I must say, your fine family is sure welcome! We hope we'll see you often in town. Don't get so busy building up your farm to forget about your town friends. This community is just bursting with plans for betterment! Do you play an instrument, by any chance? There is to be a 4th of July celebration featuring all our local musicians. We'd sure welcome you to join us!"

Mary Ann's fine features are warmed by this friendly speech. "I do not play, but I do love to listen. Perhaps we will be settled in by then and can make a day of it. Thank you ever so for the care you gave my children last night. I cannot express what it means to me and I have no doubt my husband John will feel just as obliged."

"Think nothing of it!" Ma Miller says reassuringly. "Your little ones and that beautiful daughter gave me the pleasure of their company, in spite how tired out they was. I so love fresh conversation. Yes, it was my pleasure! Now, do you need anything while you are waiting on your husband and sons?"

"Perhaps we can discuss a few things in a more private setting, Mrs. Miller." Mam is not going to ask about personal needs in this public space.

"Why of course! I'll be through with this rush soon. Anytime at all, Mrs. McGinley. And please call me Ma. Everybody does!" She gathers and stacks plates, layering them onto her broad forearm as she speaks, eyes sweeping the long table to judge the need for more food while moving towards the kitchen chatting and smiling at the guests.

Mam gets a few more bites of oatmeal into Tom. He has been so busy watching the table activity that he's forgotten to eat. She gathers the children, looking to Suzella for help, and finds Ma Miller coming from the kitchen with another enamel coffeepot full and hot, holding the handle with her wrapped apron. "Be right with you, Mrs. Just let me set this down for the table."

"I wonder," Mam asks Mrs. Miller quietly, her back to the busy dining-room, "is there a method for the children and myself to wash fully? And the night soil…how is it disposed?"

"Oh, Dearie, we take care of all that, of course," says Ma as she leads the family to a lean-to built at the back of the hotel. "Already freshened, your room is. My girls know their jobs, all right! Now, this is what you'll be wanting. It will do quite nicely for you, I'm sure." She opens a door with an ornate brass sign identifying the room as PRIVATE – GUESTS ONLY.

"You see, Mrs., here's a nice copper tub, towels and soap. The water comes right from the kitchen range which is hot day and night, so we never run out – you see, right through that wall there? The cold is piped in from a cistern. Now, sometimes that will freeze up, but we're past those rough weeks for this year. Just turn those knobs to fill and when you're all done, lift this handle and the water drains out to my garden. We grow lots of vegetables, I must say! Grow them and serve them, we do. Now, just tell me when you want to reserve the bath and I'll make sure no one disturbs you folks."

Mam is thrilled to imagine herself and all her chicks clean once again. "How much extra for this, Mrs. Miller?" She can't bring herself to call this delightful woman Ma, though her motherly nature suits the nickname.

"We don't charge a nickel extra, dear. I think being able to wash is the least I can offer my women guests. Travel is hard enough. Uprooting yourself and your children and leaving home and family – well, if you can at least feel clean that is one less endurance." Her large brown eyes fill with tears. She is so tenderhearted that she feels everyone's misery and does what she can to relieve it so that her own burden is lightened. "I told Pa Miller when we built the Windsor that the women's needs come first. Them and the children, poor little tykes! I've not been sorry, either. Business is good and we are grateful for folks like you who are moving in. Good for the community, I say!"

"I can't thank you enough, Mrs. Miller. You will wear a crown in heaven, I'm sure." Mam's soft voice quavers a bit; seeing this strong survivor of the prairie and feeling the outpouring of her generous spirit. "We will get our personal things and return promptly."

"Sure thing. Have one of your children tell me when you are done so I can have the girls ready it for the next guest. We scrub it between, you know. I like things as clean as we can make it – blowing dust and all!"

The morning was spent with soaking and scrubbing and combing. Mary Ann had never known such relief before. Going without truly made her appreciate having!

Mam bathed the boys – all three fit in the tub together and they had a grand time pouring water over themselves and each other. Suzella scrubbed the soiled undergarments in a basin, proud not to have this job done by Ma Miller. The soap was good quality and left their hair and clothes with a fresh scent. Ma Miller told her later that she added wild sage to her soap mix and used the roots of yucca plants, also known as soapweeds.

"It's hard digging them and harder still to mash them up, but a good axe will do it. Makes the nicest suds for washing 'bout anything." She chuckled at the thought. "Another thing about those soapweeds you should know… the blossoms are edible, but you have to be fast because the cows and horses like them, too. Fresh tasting they are, just as fresh as how they wash things."

Later, after enjoying a light lunch and nap, the family strolls through the streets of Colby. It is a mild day, the first of April. In the center of town a windmill turns steadily, pumping clear, cold water into a livestock tank. The dirt streets are hard rutted and dry except around the well. Only a few flies have hatched this early in the year. Later they will be a misery.

On one corner stands Donelan's General Store. Hugh notices a flurry of activity on the wooden sidewalk in front of the store. He races ahead of his sister who is in charge of him, while Mam holds the younger boys' hands, walking slow to match baby Tom's steps.

Hugh watches from behind a hitching post as person after person stoops down to pick up a fallen coin. He soon realizes it has been stuck with a bit of solder onto the boardwalk and the prankster is standing just inside the store enjoying his joke. In a flash Hugh pulls out his penknife and, just as Suzella catches up to him, pries the coin free and pops it and the knife into his pocket.

The jokester is so surprised by this little man's act that he laughs loud and long as he steps outside. "Well, son. Guess the joke's on me! You earned that fair and square. Just don't spend it all in one place, ha ha!" He tips his hat to Suzella, noting her flaming cheeks and golden-red hair.

Mam hurriedly joins them, believing she might have to intervene.

Thinking he wants to learn more about this family, the young man smiles again at Hugh and hands him another couple of quarters. "Happy April Fool on me, son. Give these to your little brothers with my compliments."

"Thank you, sir!" cries Hugh, gazing at the shining coins. "Mam, Mam! We're rich!" The gentleman laughs again and is proud to give so much pleasure to the lad.

Hugh steps forward and puts out his hand to shake. His natural ease with people is evident. "Pleased to meet you, sir. I am Hugh McGinley and I am a Kansan!"

"The pleasure is mine, Master Hugh. Arthur Kleinhan at your service, blacksmith apprentice at Sam Yousse's livery stable across the way." Art tips his hat once more, this time to Mrs. McGinley as he has sensed her concern and wishes to reassure her. "Welcome to Colby, Ma'am, the oasis of the plains."

Mary Ann nods briefly at him, but gathers the children and places herself between Suzella and this bold young man. His neatly trimmed dark hair, wide smile and clean shaven face do not lead her to fear him, but her natural protectiveness is evident.

"Come children. We shall return to the Windsor for an early supper. Your Da and brothers are on their way now."

The slight mistruth is not lost on Suzella. Da and the boys won't be arriving until midmorning tomorrow, if all has gone well for them. She recognizes how Mam has deftly set up a barrier preventing unwanted attentions. Mary Ann leads the children on a direct path back to the hotel and the afternoon is spent in the parlor, enjoying the chatter of the guests and busy activity of the town.

"Charles Robert!" Mam looks about her frantically. She had dozed for a moment and awoken to find the boy gone. "Suzella, did you see where he went?" The 4-year old is a master of escape and can disappear in a blink. Slipping away is a game he has nearly perfected. In Illinois he was frequently placed in a shoulder harness that Da designed which could be secured to the clothes- line. This had frustrated him mightily.

"No, Mam." Suzella had been reading the Thomas Cat, a newspaper listing all the doings of the community and had become very absorbed with the news. Tom was curled up under a bench and snoring gently. Hugh had been drawing pictures on some scrap paper.

"Oh my land!" Mary Ann is horrified. "I'll stay here with Tom and Hugh and ask everyone if they've seen him. You go back to Donelan's. Check the well, too!"

Suzella runs out of the hotel's door towards the town's well. She hopes to find him there. Charles Robert is drawn towards gears, pipes and mechanics – everything that a windmill offers. The splash of water into the tank, coming as it does in gushes and pauses from the turning blades as they raise and lower the pump shaft, would be an added delight for the small boy.

Her eyes search among the wagons and horses and she notices a team of hairy oxen, their long horns topped by brass nobs to prevent accidental goring. Their cream colored hides are speckled and spotted red brown. The freight wagon they are hitched to is well built and stocked high with supplies. The oxens' muzzles dip in the tank and they drink heavily. There stands Charles Robert behind a great iron capped wooden wheel at the wagon's rear, small enough that the driver will never see him when he backs up the team. Charles Robert's attention has been caught by a spinning-wheel, tied in place onto the baggage, which is turning slowly, glints of light flashing on its highly polished spokes.

"Nooo…" Suzella cries as the wagon driver lifts the reins and gives the 'heads up' command, readying the team for backing. She is too far to reach her brother.

Suddenly a strong hand grips the boy by the nape of his neck and he is heaved out of the way. The lead ox catches the movement behind him and comes to a full stop, the driver caught off balance by this abrupt action. "What in the…!" he hollers, but the well trained team stands steady.

"Got him!" It is the jokester who had given the boys coins earlier. He is holding Charles Robert carefully now, Suzella's squirming brother unaware of how close he had been to mighty injury.

"Oh my land! Oh my goodness! Thank you so, so much!" Suzella reaches out to take Charles Robert from Mr. Kleinhan's embrace, dropping into a crouch to get eye level with her brother. "You scoundrel! You hooligan!" She shakes the child's shoulders in her grip. "You bad, bad boy!"

The team's driver pales when he realizes the near miss. His own little son comes to mind and he thanks the Lord God that this boy has come to no harm through his actions. "Lady, you'd best keep a closer eye on that child!"

Tears the size of dimes are squeezed from his eyes as Charles Robert tries to understand what has gone so wrong. He drops his face and rubs his toes into the dirt road. "Me just want to touch the spinny thing," he sobs.

"Well not today and not without someone with you! You scared us so!" Suzella stands and thanks the boy's protector once again. "I think we might have lost him if you hadn't acted so quickly. Da will surely want to meet and thank you himself." She reaches a small hand out to shake the blacksmith's and is surprised by the gentleness in his touch. "I must get back now to tell Mam this rascal is found and safe."

"Allow me to escort you, Miss. Please, it is no bother. I'd like to be sure you are both safe at the Hotel."

"Well," she pauses and considers, "I thank you again for your kindness." Suzella meets Mr. Kleinhan's eyes briefly and feels heat rise in her neck, between her breasts and across her cheeks. His smile is reassuring, not threatening, and she feels a sense of protectiveness about him as he steps between her and the busy street. He is careful not to touch her.

"Miss McGinley, I would be pleased to meet your father when he arrives and to introduce the services of our livery and blacksmith shop. We do wagon and field implement repair, which your father might require in the future. I could direct him to the business folks in Colby who can be trusted. It helps to know who you are dealing with, especially when you are new to a community. We like to be sure our area farmers get a good start."

Suzella had never spoken with a grown man privately and was discomfited on how to respond. "Yes," she murmured. "Thank you, I'm sure."

Charles Robert skips at her side, having forgotten his disgrace. "Can me see the shop? Me wants to see a…" He pauses and frowns, trying to remember the word he'd heard Da use. "Farge? No, that's not right. What it called?"

"The forge. You want to see the forge? I'd be happy to show you, sir. Perhaps you could join your father when he arrives." Art is hopeful.

At the Windsor Mary Ann rushes out to place her hands on Charles Robert's cheeks, looking for damage. "Where was he?" she asks Suzella and then sees Mr. Kleinhan standing at a little distance.

"Mam, Mr. Kleinhan has saved our Charles Robert. He was almost crushed by a wagon!"

Mary Ann sways with emotion. She pulls herself up and reaches out a hand to the young man. "Thank you! I will forever be in your debt!"

Art raises his hat briefly and shakes his head humbly. "No Ma'am. It was nothing. I'm just happy I was in the right place at the right time."

He steps away from the family, saying "Good day to you all." His strides are long and sure as he walks towards the livery. It has been a good first day of April for young Art.

The remainder of the evening, following supper and the retrieval of their clean clothes from Ma Miller, is spent reorganizing the travel trunk in preparation for Da, young John and Edward's arrival tomorrow. Mam is feeling much rested and gathers her children close to read aloud from McGuffey's Reader. Hers is a soft, soothing voice with clear enunciation and variability of tone. The children love to hear her read and lie very still. Soon, they have all drifted to sleep. Mary Ann sends a silent prayer into the night for her husband and sons, hopeful and happy to think they will be together the next day.

Part IV

John and the boys traveled hard on their second day, getting an early start and stopping at Thurford just long enough for a hot lunch and to rest the mules. They have seen many other travelers heading west, wagons top heavy and trailing herds of cows behind. John is anxious to get to his claim, worried that the best land will be taken, concerned over the safety of his wife and children. He frets that they must spend another night apart, but is pleased to think they will arrive mid-morning of April 2nd.

The rising sun glows red below low clouds that have moved in overnight. A damp east wind gusts at their backs as the wagon once again starts its journey toward Colby. Farmsteads appear more frequently from the flat ground as they approach the town. Most are square wood or rectangular sod homes with lean-to sheds. A few look more established, with corrals and broken ground showing greening oats. It is too early for corn planting, but the fields are more numerous and larger than those on the outlying farms. It all looks very poor compared to the barns and cultivated ground of Illinois. Surely their farm will be better.

John has rushed the boys this morning. They are cold and stiff, ready for a full meal and to have this long trip over but are anxious to see their gentle mother and are happy to hurry as best they can. Da is short tempered even so. They do not understand their father's mood. While the wagon wheels move round and round they ask Da questions about the new farm until he gets irritated with them. John is ashamed to admit he doesn't know the answers any more than they do, but he has been watching the passing farms carefully to see what others are doing. He is feeling discouraged.

As the town of Colby comes into sight, John brushes the dust and wrinkles from his clothes. He hopes not to feel out of place. His internal image is much grander than his small stature allows and fear is eating away at his decision to leave Illinois behind. His family trusts him completely and he won't let them see his insecurity. It comes out in gruffness.

"Ed, you shorted the mules on brushing this morning! They should be looking their best today."

Edward knows better than to mention his father had told him to skip the brushing in the rush to start. "Yes, Da. I'll do a better job next time."

"Yes and you be sure of that! Young John, when did you last wash your face? You look like one of Granny's shoats after a rainstorm. Take this rag and try to spruce up a bit!"

"Yes, Da." Young John is aware that he'd best be quiet during this last part of the trip. The tension in Da is almost visible. When Da gets like this, the boys refer to him as "Himself" and tread carefully.

It is with relief that the wagon rolls into town and John finds a place near the livery to tie up. Art is hammering a shoe onto a work-worn Belgian mare, but he notices the arrival and believes it to be the remaining McGinleys. He finishes his task and lowers the hoof to the ground gently, pats the mare on her hip and wipes his damp face and hands with a red cloth.

"Mr. McGinley? Welcome to Colby. My name is Arthur Kleinhan. I have met your family through some odd circumstances and have been watching for your wagon."

John's eyes narrow in surprise and distrust as he climbs down. How could this man know his family? "What business have you with my wife and children?" His tone is icy.

"Oh, they are well, Mr. McGinley. They are well and waiting for you at the Windsor. I would be happy to show you the way after we settle your mules and I finish this mare. That was her last shoe. I just need to do a bit of rasping to smooth the nails. Won't take but a moment." Art puts out his hand to shake John's and after a bit, John accepts the offer. Their grasp is nearly equal in power, though the younger man allows John to have the advantage.

"My mules are fresh enough for the remainder of our journey. They won't be needing livery today. If I might just let them remain here while I secure my family I'd be much obliged."

Edward and young John have not moved from their seat, watching the bristling response of their father with this friendly young man. They would like to jump down and explore the town, but know their place. Da glances up at them and nods for them to join him. They clamber down and stand quietly behind their father.

"Well, in that case, Mr. McGinley, I will let Sam know I am away from my post for a few minutes and take you to your family."

"Thank you."

John and the boys brush off their pants and sleeves further and wait for Art to return. Da's wool hat wears a coating of grey dust, but he is unaware and Edward won't say. Wind gusts and blows down the street, raising grit that stings the boys' cheeks. There is a smell of rain in the air, though the clouds have thinned, racing northward in layers.

Art leads them toward the Hotel, pointing out the many shops and businesses that might interest John: Morrison's Grocery, the Colby House restaurant, the general store where Art had become acquainted with the young woman he cannot stop thinking about. He does not mention that event to the stern and silent man beside him.

Edward notices the Thomas County Cat newspaper office and the E.J. Bebb Photograph Studio directly across from it. His heart races to see this busy town his family will call home. After the days on the open prairie the slew of folks feels crowded and a little confining.

The boys try not to gawk, not wanting to look as if they have no culture. After all, they come from a well to do farm in Illinois. Edward imagines himself walking next to Wild Bill, watching the lawman tip his hat to ladies and smile at children, giving a warning eye to rowdy cowboys spurring their horses. It helps him to stand straighter and to calm his breathing. He assumes a stride that he feels would match his hero's.

The reunion of Mary Ann and John is almost painful to see. They are constrained by propriety, but cannot keep from touching and stroking each other and their eyes glow in each other's gaze.

Art clears his throat, bows slightly and begins his return to the blacksmith work. He risks a quick glance at the young woman who has so caught him, but she is fussing with her brothers.

Mary Ann halts him with the words, "A moment, please, Mr. Kleinhan."

He turns back towards the family gathered round their parents. Mary Ann speaks clearly, with a lively lilt. "It is more than fortunate how you have helped us and I wish to thank you once again in the presence of my husband. Please feel free to call upon us at any time."

Art sees again the ice in Mr. McGinley's eyes and recognizes a fire he does not want to fan. "Thank you, Mrs. McGinley. No debt incurred."

Suzella feels a wash of pride that Mr. Kleinhan has not bragged to Da. She stands quietly behind her father, her hand on Charles Robert's head and the young folks exchange smiles. She feels heat rising again, unbidden. Da has not seen the looks pass between his daughter and this stranger. Mam does, but keeps her composure.

Edward watches his father and looks for reassurance from his mother. The tension from his father is unsettling. She smiles at him and at young John.

"Well, boys. Let's get the trunk and be on our way to our new home. I, for one, am very eager to get started."

"Mam, we've not had any breakfast." Young John tries not to sound whiney, but he's been listening to his stomach grumble for hours.

Da laughs to cover the hurt he sees in his wife's face. "Oh, we all wanted to see you so bad we just harnessed up and left. Forgot all about eating; now that would be the truth of it!"

"We won't leave till you've had a hot meal. You boys have earned it, I know!" She gives Da a look and he holds his tongue, though it goes against his nature to spend any more than they've already incurred at the Windsor. "Ma Miller lays a fine lunch table and you'll all be glad we ate well before starting out."

"Let's get a move on, then." Da hurries them through the door and into the dining room. Introductions are made and compliments paid back and forth, then the family seats itself at the long table and does justice to Ma Miller's cooking.

It is a happy lunch, but Da is fidgety which dampens the mood somewhat. "I have the mules just tied up, Mary Ann. I didn't know we'd be delayed. So let's get this passel of children home."

Everyone whoops at the sound of that!

John settles the bill, not knowing the discounted pricing Ma Miller has given him. He feels the pressure of this unexpected delay and anxiety cramps his stomach. It is with relief that he hefts their clothing trunk onto his shoulder and leads his family back to the wagon.

Art has taken the liberty to water the mules. His muscles are tight with anticipation of the McGinley family's return. He has looked over the stacked wagon and notes the neat arrangement. Mr. McGinley is detailed and methodical, he thinks. And a lucky man to have such a fine family. They should make it if anyone can. Art has seen many failures and knows the odds are against anyone who thinks they can make a living on the high plains.

The railroad and town developers have made promises to the settlers so far from reality that Art is amazed they haven't been lynched. But willingness for hard work and solid determination go a long way. Art believes the McGinleys have what it takes.

He is gathering horse biscuits left by the mare into a tidy pile when Charles Robert calls loudly, "Mista, Mista! Can me see the farge? Oh, dang it, forge?" The little boy breaks away from his sister and races towards Art. "Hidy Pete, hidy Pat! How ya doing?" The mules turn their ears towards the child and rattle their nostrils.

Art chuckles at this little man so full of life. Suzella is surprised by this speech from a brother who is normally the last to speak up and raises her eyebrows to Mam. "I think Charles Robert has found a friend, Mam."

Mary Ann notes the blooms in Suzella's cheeks, hoping John misses the signs. "Yes, I believe he has," she answers.

On the way to the livery barn Mary Ann has told John about the events of yesterday. She does not reveal the coin story, though eventually she knows she will need to do so as the boys are sure to tell him about it. John's gruff silence gives her warning not to elaborate. She feels his guilt for having to leave her alone with the children in a strange community and his obsessive protectiveness for her. She reads through his seeming anger to the truth, just as she always does with him.

Art looks for permission to show all the boys the forge and blacksmith tools. John gives a curt nod, but says, "Make it fast, sons. We need to be on the road. The evening will soon be upon us."

He helps Mary Ann and Suzella into the wagon and then loads the trunk into an empty corner, wedging it securely. The boys, led by Art, return quickly, chattering about the heat and bellows and asking to visit again.

"I'd be pleased to give you boys the full show, when it suits your father. Stop by anytime you're in town."

"What do I owe for the mule keep?" John asks. "I'll be sure to use your business when we need smithing work done. Bound to need some."

Art smiles and looks straight into John's eyes. His spine stiffens just a bit tighter. "No charge for water and a place to stand, sir. We will look forward to your business."

John's posture relaxes. He gives the young man the respect earned and leans down from the wagon seat to shake Art's hand properly. "Thank you for watching over my family in my absence, son. I do thank you."

With that he backs the mules, turns them westward and begins the final hours which will take them to their new Kansas home.

CHAPTER 15

In the fall of 1887, when the main crop season is over, I am told to attend school with Sarah Lou and Attie Mae. Now that a teacher is near enough Mother insists. It is a subscription school, Mother explains, with Father paying fifty cents for each of us every month we attend. Little Jake and Tim are too young.

Father allows two days a week are enough for me while the girls will go every day. His words are firm, "The boy is meant for labor and labor only. He's strong as an ox and dumb as one too. Schooling for him would be a pure waste. The farm needs him." Every day, Father finds another job that 'must be done before the boy goes'. I do not want to go, so I put my efforts into the added chores. Mother does not miss this.

Two weeks after the girls start I have my first day. Since I couldn't leave until the chores were done, I wasn't able to go on the wagon with my sisters and must go alone, arriving late. I ride Speck onto the packed earth schoolyard during the mid-morning recess. Sarah Lou had told me about the school day, so I knew why everyone was outdoors.

School is a dugout not much bigger than our first home. I've not been around children except my own family and I feel their eyes upon me. They are divided into huddles of similar sizes, girls and boys in separate groups.

When I slide off Speck's bare back, I hear a rumble of laughter, "Look, it's a monkey riding a circus horse!"

"Ho there, an ape is coming to school."

"That there's a gorilla, boys, a bon-a-fide gorilla!"

I didn't know what any of those things were but I could tell they weren't something I wanted to be.

My lunch pail turns back and forth in my hand, the wire bail digging at my damp fingers, the tin catching sun glints. I try to shut out the wicked sounds of laughter. After a quick glance Sarah Lou and Attie Mae turn their backs. I hum to block the noise.

Mr. Phelps, the teacher, steps out through the school's doorway when he hears the chanting voices: "Ape man! Monkey arms! Ooo-oooo-aahh-aahh!" Hired the year before, Mr. Phelps isn't more than a barely grown boy himself.

I look down at my feet and Speck's dusty hooves. The tops of my ears burn and I feel ants crawling over my scalp.

As slowly as I can I let Speck take a long drink at a mossy trough and then tie him to the end of the hitching pole, away from the other horses who stand with eyes closed against flies feeding on their tears. While I do this, I glance sideways, to see Teacher look me over, gauge the strength of the crowd and make a decision. I sense I will be the only one standing on my side of an invisible line.

Mr. Phelps calls the students to class with a firm "Inside! Now!" The children scramble, pushing each other good-naturedly, through the front door.

I come last into the school, keeping my head low, and Mr. Phelps speaks gruffly from the front of the room. "Master Read, you are delaying this class. Class, Master Read is delaying everyone who has come to learn. Do you believe this to be fair of Master Read?"

"No, Mr. Phelps." The children speak in a unified chorus. Some keep their faces straight ahead; some turn to stare as I stand blinking in the entry, trying to figure what they want of me.

"No indeed!" Mr. Phelps sticks out his arm, holding a rod like a weapon and points. "Master Read, you shall take a seat with the boys in row five – that is the domain for young men aged 12 to 15." Mr. Phelps turns his back and begins to stack slates and chalk onto his desk. I don't dare tell him I am 8.

The small room is crowded and smells of old smoke, earth and sweaty bodies. Most families have at least three children attending, some five or more. The benches are rough boards and children sit by age, girls on the left and boys on the right. The younger ones are in front near the stove and closest to the teacher's desk. I see the braided heads of Sarah Lou and Attie Mae on the first row. They have not looked my way. The boys wear faded bib overalls or loose breeches and muslin shirts; the girls have flour sack dresses. Many are barefoot like me.

I slide onto the bench where the larger boys sit. I put my lunch pail between my feet and try not to knock it over with my shaking legs. I am hungry for air, but too afraid to sit up straight for fear of attracting Mr. Phelp's attention, so I hunch over, my forearms resting on my thighs and try to stop the vibrations I feel overtaking me.

Students who've attended school and know the routines begin a sing-song recitation that I do not know the words to nor the meaning of. I move my lips, but make no sound and hide my face as best I can.

The morning grinds on and on. Students stand and read aloud from primers or work numbers in chalk on a slate. Sweat runs between my shoulders and down my sides. I smell my own onion stench. The boy sitting next to me scooches as far from me as he can and makes retching sounds under his breath. That brings another drenching sweat upon my skin.

After a period of time I feel the children getting restless. They are aware it is close to lunch. Stomachs are growling audibly. Like me, these boys and girls are used to spending most days active and outdoors. They long for release.

Mr. Phelps calls my name and requests that I stand. His high pitched voice brings to mind a yellow jacket's buzz. Terror sinks deep into my bowels. "Master Read, as this is your first day within these halls of learning, please inform the students about yourself."

I stand, feeling the room close around me. My head habitually hangs low on my chest and I feel my neck rasp against my shirt collar, choking me further. I take a gasping breath, but cannot think of nor form any words.

"Master Read? Are you being impudent or perhaps you do not ken the question? Do as I say. Enlighten our class with your history. Where were you born? How long have you lived in this county? What hope do you hold for your future?"

I can bring forth nothing but a hum. It begins softly, low and deep, just air escaping from my burdened lungs through my nose in a steady tone. In the pressure to do as he asks, this grows louder, a quavering melody that rises and falls. The familiar feel of sound heard between my ears and coming safely from within myself, begins to soothe me a bit.

I see Mr. Phelps raise his chin and cock his head as if to hear me more clearly. His thin nose sniffs at the air. With a sharp CRACK he slaps his desk top with the long pointing rod and screeches, "Not only impudent, but impertinent! How dare you make such sounds! Speak up or leave this school!"

My head jerks upright at his words and I feel powerfully tall, but my escape is clumsy with desperation. I heave towards the brightly lit open door, striking my head on the low header board. I hear a crack and feel dirt sift down from the sod onto my neck as I fall outside. The students hoot and bark, "Run monkey boy, run!"

Shaking my head to clear the sudden stars and whine in my ears, I get to my feet and lean into a run. My fists pump to propel me faster. I fear I am to be chased and I am terrified of arms reaching around my ribs.

Snatching Speck's rope from the hitching pole I leap upon his back. He is startled and shies sideways a bit, but moves swiftly in the way I ask of him. We pound up the hill onto the flat plains. I feel the sky spinning over me and my head throbs in a way it hasn't for years. In my ears I hear 'monkey boy, ape boy, stupid ox'.

I never return to school and Mother doesn't mention it again. Father drives Sarah Lou and Attie Mae in the wagon the first three weeks and I go for them in the afternoons to see them safely home, meeting them after they've parted with the neighbor girls. Then Father says, "They know their way and I won't waste good working hours for that anymore."

Sarah Lou tries to share what she learns with me, but I turn from her as she turned from me. I see hurt in her eyes, but hum past it. Mother has given me some primers that have words next to pictures and I've begun to figure it out for myself. I hide these in the straw near the saddle and only look at them when Father is done for the day.

Father starts hiring me out to the neighbors and I ride Speck to their farms after morning chores. I am invited to join them in breaking out new sod, hauling hay, cutting timber, corn harvest or any other job that needs brute force.

I am hungry all the time. The farmers' wives who have food to spare give me a good dinner at noon. I sit away from the other men to eat, my hat pulled low so I don't have to see folks watching me. Father keeps the pay or takes the fee in trade. Sometimes he gets paid with a steer or horse if I've worked long enough at one place. One farmer gave us a sheep for mutton; that is a meat I find good with its heavy oily taste. Father tanned the sheep's skin and made himself some fancy chaps.

I don't mind the jobs that want the same actions over and over: plowing and planting or scything and pitching or sawing and chopping on and on and on. I listen to the rip of the plow, the ticking wheels of the planter, the snick of a grass blade and the slither of slick hay settling onto piles, the burring teeth of a saw chewing through logs and the thunk, crack, plunk of wood chopped into stove lengths. I match these sounds of labor with my own vibrations that come as regular and un-thought of as breathing. Humming is my companion and my solace.

When all the crops have been gathered, when the last of the new farmland is broken from the prairie for the year and fall planting is finally completed, our neighbors gather at the schoolyard to celebrate their efforts and to prepare socially for the upcoming winter. To that I was not invited.

CHAPTER 16

1888: John Rice (J.R.) Ruberson (1888-1960)

Atwood, KS

It may have been the railroad that brought the Ruberson family to Northwest Kansas from Indiana in time for their third child, John Rice (J.R.) to be born. If so, they arrived shortly after a bitter county seat battle had been fought and mostly settled in Atwood's favor. (Supporters for the defeated town of Blakeman, pursued, but failed to win, a mandamus action to reverse the decision by the Kansas Supreme Court in 1890.) The town claiming status as a county seat was bound to thrive while others diminished. Money was to be made!

The Burlington & Missouri River Railroad (B&MR RR) had built a branch line southwest out of Orleans, NE following the Beaver Valley from Herndon through Ludell and on westward. The line lay one mile north of Atwood with the Beaver Creek between the rails and the fast growing town. This was a planned inconvenience for a community the railroad wished to punish. A dray service ran between the town and the depot for freight and passengers.

The track then continued on towards St. Francis in Cheyenne County. Depots were built every ten to fifteen miles in accordance with the distance a wagon could travel from the farthest points to the line and still allow time to return before evening chores. This only held true during the long days of summer.

The Pacific Land Grant enacted by the Federal government to promote a transcontinental railroad gave private investors 17% of Kansas' total acreage. Every other square mile section of land on either side of the track became the property of the railroad. These acres could then be sold to settlers and business hopefuls who believed the hyperbole promoting the lands west of the 100th meridian; promotions generated by the railroads themselves.

This created a pattern of legal thievery and domination which was clearly being exercised in Rawlins County, KS. Representatives of the Lincoln Land Company (also known as the Burlington Townsite Company), whose stock-holders were railroad cronies, chose town locations ahead of the rails. These opportunists then platted the streets into lots and sold them at a rapid rate, fueled by grand promises of wealth for the buyers.

Herndon, whose first settlers arrived in 1879, welcomed the railroad in 1887 to solidify their community. The industrious European immigrants who had seen potential along the Beaver Creek bottomland were given hope by its arrival. Now there would be a method to transport vital goods in and out. New families and new money would be drawn to the area and hope for prosperity lit their hearts like a full moon over the prairie.

Herndon boasts eleven businesses when James Benton Ruberson, his wife Anna and their two children Walter Harris (4) and Alice (3) leave the train for a meal at the Hotel de Herndon. Civil War survivor Captain S.P. Pettys and Maggie Pettys, owners of this homey place of comfort, claim pride in being able to serve seventy-five or more tired and hungry guests when the train pulls into their town for coal and water.

The hotel's nine-year-old dishwasher, Rose Berger, is hard pressed to keep up with the soiled cookware, cups, plates and silverware. A stout girl, heavy and ruddy faced, she is built for hard work and doesn't mind being elbow deep in hot soapy water all day. She is thrilled to have cash money for her family; a dollar and a half a week and one day off. Since her family's homestead lies three miles north of town she boards at the hotel six nights a week. Mrs. Pettys lets her eat her fill at all the meals; something she would not have at home.

Anna Ruberson, nearing the last weeks of her third pregnancy, walks slowly along the board walkways fronting The State Bank of Herndon, the newspaper office and a general store featuring Fancy Herndon and Crowning Glory Flour sacks in pretty printed fabric. This is flour ground from local wheat in Fred Drath's water powered mill. Her smile, obscured by a heavy woolen shawl wrapped against the dry winter wind, is bright. She has hope that her growing family will find a place to settle soon, a place where she can sink roots for future generations. She hears the 'All Aboard' cry and turns to re-board for the final ride to their destination: Atwood.

If fairness and justness are defining character traits of John Rice (J.R.) Ruberson they were perhaps instilled during his first years. The hot subject of 'just folks' pitted against strong-arming railroad men blazed around him. Those who schemed for gain through the misuse of power would rankle J.R. his entire life. An internal balance scale, lodged deep in his chest and unpolluted by personal faults, simplified complex issues for J.R. This early exposure creates a belief that recourse through the law should be successful. It allows him to stand in defense of the working class. He will be found in his adult years providing proof of injury by those in high positions against the common man. His testimony will carry weight in Colorado court rooms.

In May of 1881, seven years before J.R.'s birth, Atwood's founding fathers had received approval from the Governor John P. St. John for their town to hold the temporary county seat for Rawlins County. Six years later the Lincoln Land Company (L.L.C.) in the person of R.O. Phillips informed the community of plans to move the county seat five miles west to 'their' town of Blakeman, justifying this move by announcing a division point at that location and the resulting need to house many men there. Clearly this was self-serving as the L.L.C. could not expect to profit by selling lots in a town already as established as Atwood. They proposed 'generously' to give away one free lot for every lot purchased in Blakeman. The citizens of Atwood declined their offer and the battle began.

J.R. was to hear the story many times of how 'Atwood fought the railroad and won!' He heard how the L.L.C.'s attempts to bribe struggling families with sacks of flour backfired when the petition signers took the flour offered and then signed a strike-off petition to nullify their vote in favor of the move. In retaliation G.W. Holdrege, the railroad's general manager, spoke confidently of a railroad's power to break a town if they chose to. Threats and fear hung like a suffocating fog over the Beaver Valley. The farmers and businesses of Atwood needed the railroad desperately, but not at the price of their town.

J.R.'s first example of men who stood for rightness came from stories about the Kansas State Board of Railroad Commission. Representatives from Atwood, seeking redress from the intolerable behavior of the B&MR RR, brought the issue to the attention of those officials entrusted with oversight. J.R. was hearing the account again:

"We wuz bloody but unbowed! No, siree! That Linkon Land and them railroad men thought they culd whup us, but they wuz wrong!" The talk was hot, hot, months after the Kansas Supreme Court's decision. "No, siree! Them boys in Topeka, by gum! Why they sez 'Ya gotta build them folks a depot for their use, right there where they live!' And those railroad men, they thought they didn't hafta listen and culd do what they a'wanted. But that don't make the Commissioners happy a'tall. They sez, 'Ya better build them folks a depot or we a'gonna come afta ya!"

J.R. watches as the farmer's saliva, thick and creamy white, gather in the corners of his mouth and stretches into strings between his lips as he retells the big fight. The boy is sitting in a newsprint lined coal scuttle by the stove, cold now during the heat of a summer day and a pleasant place for a three year old to park himself, his back against the curved side and his legs dangling over the end. His father has found part time work clerking at James D. Greason's newspaper office and J.R. comes to help mornings; helping mostly by staying out of the way. He listens to the farmers and town people when they come in to buy a paper or swap stories or place an ad. Their pride of place sinks into his soul; their inborn right to defend their homes and hard labors.

"Them Commissioners spoke right up for us, they surely did. I gotta say, never thought we'd get hep all the way from To-peka. They did us fair, awright. They got their teeth into it an bit those railroad boys hard!" He pauses to swallow and run a hand over his mouth, the calloused skin making a rasping sound in the quiet store. He continues reflectively, "Still, lots of buildings had went over tha hill west, hauled on wagins an drug on sleds an had to cum back an that wuz a waste o'time. Lots a folks got hard feelins over it all. Those Ludell folks still mad at Atwood folks, fer that matter. They lost their fight with us, too. Ever'one wants ta have a county seat, but ya can ony have one."

James Benton rubs a hand over his own mouth in sympathy for the dryness this farmer is fighting, both in his body and on his land. It has been a rain scarce spring and summer following a snowless winter. Everywhere there is grit: in the food, in the sheets, in the newest baby's eyes that crust over when she sleeps. He is not sure why the town didn't give in. What could it matter? There's drought and worry everywhere.

Life in Atwood has not gone well. Their family has grown and he's had no breaks. If you aren't connected to someone who's connected to someone, well, the opportunities are few. James Benton is thinking of moving on.

The next Ruberson child will be born in Goodland, KS, further west and nowhere near a pleasant creek.

CHAPTER 17

1889: Addison Alanson (A.A.) Bacon (1889-1969)

McDonald, KS

The Bacon family is weary of traveling, weary of leaving traces of themselves as they search Wisconsin and Nebraska for a home. In 1885 they arrive in northwest Kansas, to a county just south of the Nebraska state line. Mr. Bacon is a believer in fresh starts. Mrs. Bacon has had enough fresh starts for a lifetime.

Alanson and Mary settle for a short time near the town of Celia. Their two wagons are home and they have perfected a very efficient system for managing. Their children are Franklin Fletcher and George Willis, nearly men at ages fifteen and fourteen and able to handle one wagon, Chloe Etta, Ezra Martin, Maybelle Mae, John Lindley (buried at age one in NE), Maude Ellen and Ethel Grace. Mr. Bacon supports his family as a blacksmith and is welcomed into each new community for the vital service he can provide. He wins quick acceptance from their new neighbors by his willingness to throw muscle, his and those of his sons, into whatever jobs need done.

Celia is platted into forty-one building lots on land owned by H.B. and Prulina Franklin and named after their daughter. When the Bacons arrive, it is an almost fully functioning town. From concept to existence, towns on the prairie rose as fast as sod blocks could be cut and laid together. There's no need for more than a dirt floor and waxed paper windows covered by canvas curtains to provide functional shelter. Lumber will arrive with the railroad and the community's optimism is based on that mighty promise. Anticipating this arrival the most northern east/west road is given the name Rail Road Street, though it will be three years before the tracks are laid anywhere close.

The Woods' Boarding House serves those without homes, mostly unmarried men, and features thirty-foot long berths sectioned off into man lengths. An upper and lower level, bunk-bed style, doubles the occupancy potential. Meals can be purchased, church services are held and a school gives the children a place to gather and learn. For serious illness, snakebite or major injury someone rides for Dr. W.C. McIrvin in Burntwood, a hard ride north but closer than the county seat of Atwood.

Fred Eno, publisher of the Celia Enterprise Times, entertains readers with current news, markets, legal notices, weather reports and small town gossip designed to pull a chuckle. Sheets of 'patent papers', preprinted with world and national news and ads for nostrums, are brought in by stage. These are designed with blank back pages to allow each town with access to a typesetter and press to add regional news, local ads and legals while staying informed. Their primary purpose is the posting of letters of patent, notifying the area of land claims.

The Post Office is managed by Carrie Eno, Fred's sister. These siblings take their positions as the 'village voice' very seriously, believing all news belong to them first. Their combined office has established itself as the hub of information for newcomers and locals alike. When Alanson stops his wagons on Main Street, he is directed to this office. Fred and Carrie take his measure and rejoice that another hard working family will be calling Celia home.

The town's well is centrally located, drawing cold ancient water from deep below the surface. Wells are hand dug. This is an extremely dangerous job involving many days of digging and removing heavy soil. It is also faith based work. Daily prayers are made that there will be water at the end. It is a prayer which could be and often is unanswered. No springs or creeks are found in this portion of Rawlins County and some wells are greater than 200 feet deep. When a calf fell into the Celia well and drowned, fouling the water, the loss was cruel.

When the rail line did come, it was laid a half mile north of the town site, a burden for the businesses. Still, workers for the railroad were vital for the town of Celia, filling it with hungry and thirsty men who needed lodging. For a period of time the town swelled with noise and construction. Unfortunately, the Burlington Railroad company had its own agenda and as the tracks moved westward the officials would soon make big changes.

The first child born in Kansas to the Bacon family is Roy Leander. Not long after Roy's birth, the town of Celia is dissolved and absorbed by a newly created community called McDonald, three miles west. The Bacons move again and not for the last time. Alanson points out to Mary that they'd been smart not to build while at Celia. Mary's response is swallowed in silence.

The Lincoln Land Company, in cooperation with a major landholder and rancher of the area, Rice McDonald, felt there were benefits for the relocation; primarily for them. They convinced the citizens that McDonald could better meet the needs of a growing community and being built right along the tracks would make business success assured. Of course, the L.L.C. representatives were happy to sell these new building lots. Rice McDonald 'gave' a portion of his land to the L.L.C., helping to 'grease' the wheels of progress.

The Vandell Lutz restaurant served the first meal in McDonald. The Celia Hotel was dismantled, christened the Grapevine Hotel and rebuilt in a convenient location. E.L. Dobbs of Bird City, the next town further west, purchased the Mercantile Store from Celia, hauled it west and restructured it to hold hardware and general merchandise on one side, groceries on the other. A drug store quickly found its place. The newspaper became the McDonald Times. And Alanson Bacon set up his blacksmithing shop once again.

Jobs abound during the flush years of a newly formed town. Alanson and his oldest boys feel this was a 'sticking' kind of place and they find themselves working from "can't see to can't see" most days. Mary insists on a house with a floor, windows and no wheels attached. Hammers ring, hand saws chir through rough boards and buildings rise daily.

Their next son, Alonzo Penuel, comes into this noisy world in July 1887. It had been a hot and tiresome pregnancy. Daughters Chloe, Mae, and Maude had taken over much of the household chores. Even Ethel at age four was expected to do her share and entertaining little Roy was foremost.

A blacksmith in a community frequently takes on a persona of calmness and intelligence in the face of heat as he is asked to repair, rebuild or create hardware essential for a farmer's daily needs. He soon finds himself in the position of being 'in the know' as his location gathers groups of men waiting for horses to be shod, wheels to be re-rimmed or tools to be hammered out of hot iron. His ability to convert raw material into useful objects by controlling fire, air and water gives him mystique.

Alanson Bacon acknowledged that power. He is soon entrenched in the community, giving voice to decisions needed by the city and feels as settled as he's ever felt. Mary and the girls are thriving while his sons are seen as valuable day laborers and treated with respect. It is a good period of life for the Bacon family. Mary plants fruit trees and flowers in her small fenced yard. Permanence is finally in her grasp.

Their son Addison Alanson (A.A.) is born on a spring day in 1889. Children are one crop that can be counted on. Drought, grasshoppers, late freezes and early frosts might take out fields and gardens, but the babies are persistent in their regular arrival. Mary is thirty-eight years old.

In rural homes a girl is trained for motherhood and learns the basics of house management through helping to raise younger siblings. Typically, not long after puberty, she will be married and delivering or nursing babies without let up for most of her life. Often her first daughters have children before she herself is done.

Mary gazes into her squalling newborn's face and knows that his life can be taken in a moment. Though she would never know the numbers, she was clearly aware of childhood mortality. In 1870, two years after her marriage to Alanson and while they were living in Nebraska, 114 deaths occurred in their county. Nearly 100 of those were children, most less than five years of age.

Cholera infantum had taken their little boy, John. Mary would never forget his extreme distress as vomiting and diarrhea drained his life so quickly, his feverish lips cracking like parchment, his skin becoming translucent until she could trace his veins and see his heart thumping below his heaving chest.

Not long after John was buried a near neighbor lost her not quite one-year-old when he choked on a piece of seed corn. The frantic mother carried his lifeless body from home to home while screaming for someone to save her purple faced child. Anything and everything could happen to these defenseless babies. As she puts Addison Alanson to her breast, Mary shivers, teeth chattering from childbirth strain and fatigue without hope or expectation of relief.

CHAPTER 18

1890: EDWARD McGINLEY

Thomas County, Kansas

I stand as rigid as my hoe handle and do my best to stare down the range rider whose herd has just trampled the half-acre of potatoes that I've been hilling for a week. Their rough hooves have scattered plants every which way, gouging deep into the rows I'd worked hard to draw up so the praties don't green up and turn to poison. The cowboy looms over me with not a trace of remorse.

"You damn sodbusters! You're taking good grass to grow poor food! I ain't sorry my herd come through this patch. Maybe you all will give it up like the others and leave the grass to the beeves like God meant it!"

I glare with indignation. "Do not think for a moment you will not be punished, sir. Do not think for one moment your life won't be worsened by this treatment of a family trying to feed itself. You will suffer in your dreams. You will lay on your deathbed wishing to beg our forgiveness. You will hear my little brothers and sisters with hungry bellies calling your name! You are beholden to the McGinley family and you'll always regret your ungenerous ways!"

The man tips his hat back from his weathered face, speechless at my outburst. For a moment there is no sound but the whistle of wind around my hot ears and then he breaks into a loud, raucous laugh and spurs his pony after the herd. They have moved on towards the open Union Pacific Railroad land east of us. He waves a casual back hand to me.

I look over the field, assessing the damage and realize I have it all to do over. There will be some loss and more if I don't get the roots covered fast.

I think about how vital our gardens are and not just to feed our growing family. My work at planting, hoeing and watering will turn into cash money. Beginning last year the Windsor Hotel has contracted with us to grow produce for their restaurant.

This potato field is expected to make fifty or so bushels. If it does well they might want us to expand. To help us get started we were given five bushels of seed potatoes which I cut, cured and planted in early March. We're half-way to harvest time and, until today, the plants were thriving. The sod crop, the first one after turning grass, is always good. Next year this field will be sown to oats and then back to potatoes. Da knows a thing or two about growing praties. Cabbage is another of the crops Mrs. Miller needs along with carrots, onions, turnips, rutabagas and pumpkins. These are all foods she can store in their cellar for the winter months. I scan the field, curse the cowboys with their open range and get to work repairing the harm. What we need is a way to fence these men and animals out!

The family, all eleven of us, live in the dugout that we built soon after arriving at the homestead. It extends fourteen feet into the hillside with a flat, sloping roof. Cottonwood posts support it and sod blocks close off the front. The mules and hens live next door. A dirt wall is all that separates us from them. Da thought it was the fastest way to get everyone indoors, but he didn't expect us to still be living like this.

Two months after we arrived, Mary Teresa was born. Mam got through the birthing time with some help from Mrs. Mary Elizabeth Towslee, our neighbor to the west. The baby was named for her midwife in thanks for the kindly help.

Da has bargained for some cows of our own. These aren't the scrawny limbed, big horned ones that came up from Texas, but a fleshier type that we boys help herd. Hugh is the best at this job. He brags he can out run a rabbit and frequently brings home a long eared jack to prove it. Ma is happy for the fresh meat, but with so many of us it doesn't go far. She usually stews it with vegetables and dumplings to 'fill our gaps' as she says.

When Suzi turned fifteen, she proudly waved her teacher's certificate before Mam and Da and declared she'd be helping the family in a new way. Mam knows her early efforts of teaching her children have paid off.

Our school is only one and a half miles north of the homestead. It is built of sod and has a single outhouse. School runs for three months of the year and we don't go if Da needs us. Mam made sure we all knew our letters early and how to sound out words. Taking time to practice writing every evening is important to her. She quizzes us on times tables and expects the older ones to help prepare the littler ones. Further exposure to knowledge outside of the farm comes in social events called 'literaries'. Mam is mighty proud of what her family can offer at these gatherings.

In the spring of 1890 Mam has another son, Louis Elmer. To stop her gushing tears after the baby came, Da promised her a better home. It is done by the fall, built of 'prairie marble', the local name for sod.

First we cleared the future floor, giving an idea of the new home's size. Measurements were done in two foot increments and Ma helped sketch out the size and shape with a plan for how the rooms would look and what they would be used for. Grandmother Higgins had written to say she was coming to live with us so she would need a room. Da was hopeful she'd see the goodness of the Kansas land and consolidate her wealth with his.

An acre of grass is needed for a sixteen by twenty foot home. Each block weighs about fifty pounds. This makes walls two feet thick with wooden frames for the doors and windows. The roof is made of cottonwood and willow brush cut from the Prairie Dog Creek and covered by more strips of sod. The new home is more spacious and airy than our dugout yet still cool in the summer heat.

If Mam felt this home was still far from the lovely conditions she'd had growing up, she never spoke of it. In contrast to the dugout she feels great relief. Da had gotten a well put in when the windmill crew came to this area, even though it cost a dear price.

John and I played a bad trick on Da. We'd heard about a neighbor who had fallen to his death from a windmill when greasing the hub. He had told his son, who was only a young boy, to release the brake so it would make a turn or two. When a gust of wind caught the blades, the boy wasn't strong enough to draw down the brake. The mill threw the farmer to the ground. This sad story had been told at supper several nights in a row, with Da crossing himself every time and looking wall-eyed at the thought.

One afternoon, Da went to Colby to deliver eggs and turnips to the hotel. We knew he would pass that tower on his way back after dark. Knowing of his fear of the 'Banshee' we climbed it and tied one of Mam's sheets to the tail. Then we hid nearby.

The night was perfect for our game: a gusty wind that rose and fell, a deep black sky with the full moon edging over the east horizon. Just as Da drove the wagon past the tower, the wind gusted causing the mill to creek and moan, the sheet to billow in a ghostly shape. We heard Da shriek and saw him lean over the team with whip in hand, snapping it wildly. They surged forward and galloped like mad for home.

John hooted and slapped his legs, thrilled at giving 'Himself' such a scare. But I felt wrong, like I'd harmed an innocent. It was disrespectful and I regretted the trick deeply. I made John promise never to tell. He was good to his word and never did.

When we got home, the team was still hitched and standing at the barn, blowing. Da had run straight into the soddy without caring for them. I sent John on in, having him carry an armful of stove wood to explain his absence. I unharnessed and brushed down the mules, feeling doubly bad to think the good animals had been abused for our pleasure.

Da never spoke of it but made sure he never traveled after dark again. I carried the heavy load of regret my whole life.

CHAPTER 19

1894: RICHARD READ

Carnival, Rexford, Kansas

I am fifteen this year. I carry my own weight and that is saying something. Despite the crowds I am going to Rexford for the community 4th of July celebration. Father, Mother and the others went ahead in the wagon. Mother has grown flowers to enter in the fair. The display had to be in the tent early for judging so they left before chores were done, knowing I would manage.

Sarah Lou loves the flower garden and should take the credit for the bouquet. She has done the weeding and watering. Mother tried to put Sarah Lou's name on the arrangement of colorful grasses setting off purple larkspur and baby's breath, but she does not want the attention drawn to her. She prefers solitude, much like me. That is hard to find in the house, so she gardens. Our family now has eight children at home. Edmee Emma is five months old. Joe Glenn not quite three. The once spacious house is full and I think Sarah Lou would like to have a quiet place like I do in the barn.

I am riding a new horse, Riser. He is one-quarter Percheron and three-quarters Saddlebred. His size helps me look less large. I don't ride Speck any longer. He's gotten arthritic and stumbles on long rides. Riser is smooth and shiny black. He picks his feet up well in a swinging motion. I try not to let Father see him much. I might lose him to a sale. Father has become known as a horse trader and an expert on illnesses. He does vet work for folks. His colts sell well. Riser was wire cut as a foal, leaving a jagged streak across his back hip that healed slowly and grew white hairs. But he never favors the side and rides long and strong wherever I need him to go.

As I ride over the last ridge into town, I see carnival tents being set up on the edge of the fair grounds. I hear shouts of men and the clang and ring of hammers. I ride closer to watch the swinging heavy sledges as the workmen pound stakes deep into to the earth. Thick ropes draw tight the canvas walls. I notice a slack area, canvas flapping in the rising wind, where another stake should go. I step off Riser, drop his reins to ground tie him and pick up a spare hammer to help.

These are carnival men, rough and harsh and a tribe of their own. They see a willing worker with arms like bull thighs. They let me work with only minimal direction. When the tents are complete, the snap of tethered canvas in the south wind popping like fire-snappers, the lead man halloos me over to join them.

"That's some mighty fine work you did there, boy. Looks like you wuz borned to it. Your momma holler some when ya cum'd outen her? Hammer in your hand an all?" The friends guffaw and bang into each other with their humor. "Shucks, we's just kiddin with ya. Bet ya momma is mighty pretty to have such a brute for a son. Ya daddy big like ya, too?"

"No... bigger... than you... sir." My voice is quiet and I keep my head downturned, taking the July heat on my neck. For some reason I add, "He... thinks... mighty fine... of hisself... though."

"Well, he do, do he?" The man hawks out a laugh. "And ain't no sirs around here. Only sirs is the man'gers and they ain't goin' be found wit no hammer in they hand!"

A greasy haired, pale skinned man with purple spidery veins across his cheeks and chin reaches around to his back pocket and pulls out a metal canteen wrapped in stained canvas. "I think this boy deserves to quench his thirst. What do you say, men? Shall we thank him for his help?" His watery blue, red rimmed eyes peer at me with malice and his thin lips pull up over snaggled teeth.

"Sure, sure. Give this boy a swaller! He's surely earned one, anywho." The lead man takes the container, pulls a swig, throws his head back and does a little dance in the dust. His heavy black shoes scuffle back and forth like a pig with its throat cut. "Whoowee! That'll cut the phlegm!" He hands it over to me.

I take the canteen in my hand; feel the liquid slosh in the half-full tin. I turn my head to the side so that the men don't see me full on. The first swallow spews onto the ground at the men's feet and I cough and retch. It's taken the breath right out of me. The men howl and so do I. Before anyone can retrieve the canteen I upend it, pouring the liquid into my gullet, throat open and glugging. It is a river of biting gold and reminds me somehow of childhood comfort. The part of me that is Richardson welcomes the burn; relishes the sour-sweet taste on my lips.

"Hey there, hold on now! You cain't drink the whole thing! Giver back, son. Giver back." The men are astounded that a first-timer can swallow the rot gut. They are angered by my greed.

I feel liquid heat in my belly, moving through my veins, and a shimmer starts in my tear filled eyes, making the ground crawl like it is a living thing. I raise my head slowly and meet the eyes of the men for the first time. They back away; these men who fear very little.

The crew boss sees in this young bull's eyes a madness that chills him. He also sees an underage boy and realizes there might be in more trouble with the law than usual.

"Go on home, kid" he hollers. "Go on and git!"

My ears are on fire as though the sun has dropped onto my head. A rattlesnake buzz deadens the sounds of the carnival. My lips are numb, my hands ice cold. I feel my head swinging from side to side and the earth heaves beneath my feet. I want to leave, but somehow lurch towards the group of men. Someone shoves me and I stagger into a canvas wall, bounce off and smack headfirst into a support pole. The sky wheels and then blackness comes.

The men hear a thud when Richard hits the earth. He is staring at the sun blindly and his arms and legs twitch spastically. Blood and froth gurgle into his mouth; bubbling, choking sounds sicken the men.

The boss swears under his breath. "Roll him over, quick! I think he's havin' a fit! Stuff a kerchief in his mouth. I hear they kin choke on their own tongues!" The men scramble around Richard, kicking at the boy and stirring a cloud of dirt into the air. It looks like a fight from a distance.

With a bellow of rage, I roar upwards, knocking down the men around me. The filthy red rag crammed in my mouth makes me gag over and over. My hands scrabble at my mouth, smearing and mixing dirt with the vomit and blood. With a hooked finger I pull the rag free.

"Git out of here, you ape," yells the purple faced man and he shoves me between the shoulders. "Git on home and don't come near our tents!"

I try to run, though my legs feel like blocks of wood. I have to spread my steps wide apart to stay upright. I follow a zig-zag path. Tears run, dripping past my nose and fall from my chin. Blurred grass and yucca pass beneath me. Somewhere ahead of me is Riser. I need to find him, but I have no sense of direction. My right foot hits something and I fly forward, landing hard below a shallow out-cropping of limestone. I sense a small space of shade beneath the rock ledge. I long for relief from the monstrous, glaring sun and creep into the shadow. I drop face down in near madness, chomping my teeth, clawing the earth. I bite back the demon racing through my throbbing, screaming head.

I don't know how much time passes before my breathing finally eases. The horrid confusion is ending. I am aware of a hard throb and a heavy heat in my crotch. The earth beneath me presses against this throb and my hips bear down upon it. In my mind I hear "Pound it, pound it!" Spasms take over. My buttocks are tight and I am thrusting downward over and over. I bite my wrist and taste blood. "Pound! Pound!" I hear a keening moan. It comes from behind my gasping breaths and it builds and builds until I'm jerked from inside; jerked and jerked and white lightening surges. I vomit foul liquid until only dry heaves remain.

Milky stars blur and clarify above me when I wake. I smell damp night air and the prairie odor of cooling earth. I smell myself. I am sick with shame; my clothes caked with dirt and waste. My eyes won't stay in focus and a sledge beats my skull. Slowly, afraid movement will bring on more heaving, I climb from under the ledge. I go up the ridge on hands and knees. Standing is misery, but now I can see below me the tiny lights and the dark shapes of buildings that mark Rexford. This gives me direction. I turn away north towards home, knowing I'll find my way eventually. I hope Riser has been found and returned. I see my feet as they were when I was a child coming to Kansas. I see the paths I've left and they are nothing.

The voice is there: "You are nothing. You are nothing! Pound it! Pound it hard!" The hammer behind my eyes is relentless, cruel.

When the farmyard finally appears, the house is dark and silent. I climb into the icy water of the stock tank fully dressed. Feeling the slick sides, green with slime, I submerge myself. I welcome the fire of the chill water on my skin. The iron tang water clears the sour stench from my mouth and the cold dulls my skull ache. A dim memory of sensation passes through my groin. For once I am no longer afraid of water. The icy liquid numbs, erases. If I could sink forever, I would choose to. In the black night I strip free from my clothes, turning everything inside out to wash. I scrub my hulking body with my nails. I am nothing;

I am nothing. Naked and dripping I find my place in the barn. A tuneless hum takes me away.

CHAPTER 20

Da has gone to Colorado. The drought has nearly broken us just as mercilessly as it has others in the past. Da won't speak of giving up. He has helped build a Catholic Church in Colby and says God will provide. In the meantime Da joined with a group of men to find cash paying work. He leaves me in charge of the farm and the family. It has been this way for two years with Da gone for months and then returning just long enough to stir up the house.

Mam had another baby this past year. Ethel was born in April, a month that should have been showing signs of spring greening, but instead followed March's dirty winds with more of the same. The little ones all have coughs that don't seem to clear, even with dosings of horehound syrup. Da brought home slippery elm bark that Grandmother Higgins swore by, but there won't be relief until the air is washed free.

Da has been working on the Cogg Road. He's a teamster, using teams of ox to pull a scrape that levels the road after the dynamiters do their work. He brags this is will be a brick road from Colorado Springs to Denver. I find it hard to imagine a brick road of a length that great.

He also went to work for E. H. Bunford's 12,000 acre operation. Da said this land is owned by a Boston syndicate and Mr. Bunford is in charge. Sixty head of mules, five farm wagons and supplies were bought in one day. Twenty-five men were hired to break the ground. Da tells us there is a rail line for shipping and an irrigation ditch to bring water out of the mountains. He thinks these Boston men are 'in cahoots' with the railroad folks and are squeezing out the local farmers, but he's happy to have cash money for his work. The workers get fed nothing but cornmeal and beans cooked in salty water so he's mighty glad to come to table when he's home.

Not that much is growing here and fresh goods are scarce for everyone. The well is holding, but the soil is so dry that when I run a bucket of water onto the garden the water beads up and runs off into deep cracks, leaving the plants thirsting. Seems the longer things stay dry the less it wants to rain.

While Da was away, Suzi took a teaching job in Levant. She boards through the week and takes the train back to Colby late on Friday, catching a ride home with a neighbor. At least that's what we thought.

One Sunday following church she takes me aside, "Ed, may we speak in private?" She has always been a pretty girl, but today she looks lit from within. I see a grown woman before me, ready for a full life.

"Yes, Sis? What about?"

"Do you recall our first time in Colby? Do you recall the blacksmith shop?" She pauses and watches my face. "Do you recall Mam telling Da how Robert disappeared and was nearly run over by a wagon?"

I did, dimly. "Wasn't there someone from the blacksmith shop that saved him?"

Her smile ran from her heart to her face. "That was Arthur Kleinhan. He never forgot me or I him. He's been meeting the train when I get in from Levant and bringing me home these past months. We've gotten to know each other well and he's asked me to marry him."

"Well now! Isn't that grand! I'm so pleased for you, Suzi, and I can see you are very happy. Have you told Mam?"

"Not yet, Ed. I need your help. I am afraid of Da, what he will say and Mam is so timid of him."

"Where is the problem? You're of age and if I recall, Arthur seemed like a hardworking man."

"He's not Catholic. He's Protestant."

"Ohh…"

"Ed. I need your help. I need you beside me when I tell Mam and Da. I need you to speak up for me!"

"I'll be there for you Suzi. You know I will. I will always be there for you!"

CHAPTER 21

1900: ADDISON ALANSON (A.A.) BACON

Kanona, Kansas

Once again the family members, those who remain of it, have gathered their belongings and blacksmithing equipment into two wagons to travel eastward into the next county: Decatur. Alanson is answering the call for a blacksmith needed in Kanona.

Though another child was born while they lived in McDonald, this baby, Rollo, did not survive. Coming so soon after all the others, Mary believed she'd just run out of anything more to give to an infant. Addison (now being called A.A.) holds his place as the youngest. Mary is nearing fifty and determines not to carry another child. This puts a strain on her marriage, but she believes very soon her woman's final change will come, ending the risk of pregnancy. Regardless, she doubts she will ever again welcome Alanson to her bed.

Maybelle Mae married David Copper. Mary feels it is a good match for her second daughter. She sees contentment in Mae's eyes. Mae taught at the McDonald school for a short time before finding herself betrothed to David. His mother had died when he was young and Mary believes he sees in Mae a grand replacement for mothering as well as a lovely bride. He could do much worse. Mae cares deeply for anyone she turns her heart to. She is loyal, affectionate and a natural mother.

Mary knows the family's sadness tainted Mae's special day, but she found it impossible to feel joy and her sorrow was reflected by the others. That troubles her deeply, but there was no help for it.

Grief over recent events has drained any reservoirs which should contain delight at seeing her children doing well. Chloe Etta, her prize, her joy, her most beautiful daughter, has fled to Colorado, refusing to live in the same household as her father. Harm compounded by harm has taken Mary's dearest companion from her. She does not believe they will ever meet again. It is nearly more than Mary can bear.

Chloe Etta, a skilled seamstress working at the McDonald Mercantile met, was wooed and fell in love with a railroad man who had come in looking for a new set of boots. He took her heart and her virtue. It wasn't until his death in a freak railroad accident revealed an existing marriage with two children and a grieving wife that Chloe Etta became aware of his duplicity.

Edwin had taken her to Lincoln on the train, showing her a glimpse of city glamor and treating her like a queen. While there he'd given her a beautiful ring which folks thought meant she was a married woman when he returned her to McDonald. She had shared a small home with her lover as he came and went on railroad business, believing his whispered promises of marriage "the next time I'm in town long enough to do it properly!" Even Momma and Papa did not know the truth. She had not said outright, but she let them believe what they wanted.

Within days of the tragic event the community knew more than she did. She learned of his double dealing through half-heard conversations and side-long looks. Eventually an article in the paper was published, giving the lurid details of his death, listing his widow and children's names, his home town as Omaha.

Suddenly she was out a job and forced to leave the house Edwin had rented for her. And her darling son Rollo (named for the baby brother she'd helped birth and then held tenderly as he died when she was eighteen) became 'that Bacon bastard' in whispered conversations. With a crushed heart, broken trust and overwhelming shame, she and the five year old boy moved back in with her parents.

Momma wrapped her arms around Chloe Etta, gave Rollo a salted turnip to suck and cried with her daughter. Papa's blacksmith hammer rang on the anvil like a tolling death bell. A. A. and the other children did not know what the tears and anger were about, only that their sister was hurting and Momma too.

For a week the family did not speak more than needed. Rollo couldn't understand why his 'Poppa' no longer wanted him to be near, but soon quit asking, content to play in the house near his Mama and 'Moppa'. He'd sensed quickly not to talk about Daddy, though he longed for the strong arms and scrachety hugs he remembered.

One evening during a silent supper Alanson mentioned he'd been looking into "that job in Kanona" and, considering things, thought they might go. Mary was too broken to respond, the grief for her daughter sucking her strength. It was soon to be worse.

Alanson told the family he had a short job lined up in Benkelman, Nebraska to get them start-up money for the move to Kanona. He then surprised everyone by saying he would take the boy with him. They would leave pre-dawn the next morning.

Chloe Etta was hopeful maybe her stern father was beginning to soften. She gathered together a basket with boiled eggs, cornbread, cold potatoes, peaches and cheese for the trip. Wrapping Rollo's quilt around the curly headed boy, she placed him on the wagon seat and kissed her son goodbye. Rollo's brown eyes were bright with tears and he sucked his bottom lip to keep it from quivering, but he was excited to be spending time with Poppa again. He hoped Poppa would let him drive the team as the wagon turned northward towards the state line of Nebraska. They would be gone several nights as it was a long wagon ride to Benkelman and the job would require some time to complete.

When Alanson finally returned, late enough for the early stars to glimmer, Chloe Etta raced to meet his wagon. Seeing only her father slumped over the reins she ran to the wagon bed to look inside for her sleeping son. Other than the portable forge, anvil and tools, the wagon was empty.

"Papa? Where's Rollo?"

"There's more mouths to feed in this household than I can manage already! Don't you go whinin' about that child. He's got him a good home with folks who'll put him to use. They ain't gonna give him back and they's a long ways gone already. They ain't local neither, so no one is gonna be able to tell you who they is or where they went. Listen here... you don't need no fatherless child to hold you back, Chloe Etta. You cain't support yourself, much less that young 'un. That's the last I'm gonna say and the last I wanna hear bout it!"

Chloe Etta collapsed in the dirt and her father went to the barn to put the tired horses away, leaving her lay there until someone noticed her. He'd been telling himself over and over that someday she would understand he'd done it for her. Now she'd be free to find a husband right and proper. He'd given her a chance and she'd best understand that.

At age twenty-seven, Chloe Etta boarded the westbound train in McCook, NE to find work in Colorado. She would not see her first-born child again until, as a mother of eight daughters, they were reunited by the efforts of her generous hearted husband. Tragically, not long after this joyful reconnection, Rollo was killed in a lime pit accident at a cement factory.

At age eleven, A.A. attended a new school in the town of Kanona, KS. The loss of his favorite sister, his grief over Rollo and the visible tension between his parents brought A.A.'s life to a miserable state. A sense ever present doom settled onto his thin shoulders. This weight would remain throughout his life.

CHAPTER 22

1900: EDWARD McGINLEY
Nebraska Sandhills

There are seven white columns supporting a curved wrap around porch on the McGinley homestead. . Windows gleam, the floors shine with wax and the rooms are spacious. A pump in the kitchen brings easy water. The only lack is the joy Mam should feel over this fine new home. The recent years have broken her and I do not think she'll find her way back.

Suzi and Art had run off to Nebraska, back to his home town, to be wed. Da's fury at a daughter of his marrying outside the faith was terrible. He literally tore up the ground upon hearing the news.

I kept my promise to Suzi and stood up for her. "Da, with respect, Suzella is twenty-one, earning a living, making choices using the level head you gave her. She loves Arthur the way you love Mam! For the sake of the family, Da, don't turn her away!"

Da's fist was on my jaw in a blinding slam. I hit the ground hard, grunting as much in surprise as in pain. His heavy boot connected with my lower back as he tried to kick the seat of my pants.

"Think you know how to be a father? Think you have a say in this affair? Think you can speak to your Da like this? Think again, son!"

The 480 acres were clear of debt but Da had skimped us hard during the tough years to reach this proud accomplishment. Building the house had shaken his sense of security even though, with the death of Grandmother Higgins, Mam had received her inheritance and much of that went towards the house. Mam grieved the loss of her mother more than we could know and losing the companionship of Suzi the same year was unbearable.

When Da started denying the family meat from our own cows, I left for Nebraska to escape the tension and ease Mam's burden. Mam had her 11th child, William, while I was cow-boying with my Brogan cousins on their ranch in the Sandhills north of the Platte River. Suzi delivered a son the same year, Benjamin Arthur.

I liked the Nebraska life. It seemed cleaner than Kansas, with less dust, though the Sandhills were fragile and could get blow-outs if overgrazed. Crops did poorly so less native prairie had been broken out. We hayed the bottoms for winter feed, stacking high mountains of it with good teams, buck rakes and a great contraption called a beaverslide. This was cattle heaven!

I saw in the rounded hills a feminine shape with soft curves and dips. The swales held shallow lakes of ground water that percolated to the surface and reflected the crystal blue sky. Water fowl passed back and forth and made for tasty camp meat. I might have stayed and found a place of my own if not for a tragedy that took me home.

Suzi had a second son in 1896 named Henry, my middle name, which made me proud to be thought of so fondly. She and Art were doing well in their home in Colby. Mam could visit on occasion but Da wouldn't let them come to the farm. Not until Suzella became seriously ill in the spring of '98.

Dr. Eddy did all he could for her, but a cough that had settled in her lungs during the dank days of February turned to pneumonia. My dearest sister, the one who had stood like a warm flame for my entire life, was only twenty-five when she gasped her last breaths, leaving two little boys and a devastated husband.

Mam kept the boys for a time, sharing the duty with Art's mother. Their confusion and sadness depressed the family. Shortly after Suzi's funeral, held in the Catholic Church as a consolation, Mam found herself expecting her twelfth child. Da was 'himself', the name John and I used to describe his tyrannical behavior, nearly all the time now.

I returned to Kansas for good.

CHAPTER 23

1901: PAULINE WEISSHAAR (1900-1993)
The Settlement Bethune, Colorado

A desiccating southwest wind parches Pauline's lips. Baby-fat hands splay open against the ground as she braces herself to stand. Her dress, thin and faded from lye scrubbings on a washboard, billows and slaps against stocky legs spread wide in a toddler's stance. She wears no pants or shoes. Though her feet and ankles are streaked with dirt, her fine brown hair is combed and tidy under a drooping bonnet.

A shrinking line of shade cast by the sod and stone house draws her forward. The sun climbs into a cloudless, brassy July sky and heat shimmers along the flat horizon. Dust, fine as silk, shifts and puffs as she pads around the corner of the house to its open door.

Inside, Mama is sweeping the packed earth floor with her broom and gently scolds Pauline for blocking the doorway. Silently, the little girl toddles to the water barrel that stands alongside the doorway and sits with the sudden drop of a year-old child to shelter against the oak staves. Less than a quarter full, it holds the chill of night; a cool spot to lean against. One hand traces patterns in the dust while she sucks on the middle two fingers of her other.

The older children are busy with morning chores. They know their jobs and need no one to remind them. The hen flock, pigs, sheep, milk cow and horse all must be watered and cared for. With no well nearby, watering is a burden everyone shares.

Pauline's oldest sister, Magdalena (Lena), has helped Mama clear the house of their mattresses – blue and white striped ticking bags stuffed with corn husks - laying them in the sun to air, shaking the linens and hanging them on a rope line that Father has strung for Mama's use. Sometimes Lena ties Pauline to it, too. She is fourteen years older than Pauline and very much the second mother of the house.

It is Saturday – water hauling and wash day – and as a special treat to celebrate Pauline's birthday everyone is going along to play in the creek. Mama feels children should play as well as work and she knows there's precious little time for fun on a farm in eastern Colorado.

Mama hangs the broom on a hook and closes the door. She scoops Pauline up, brushes dust vigorously from her bottom and gives her a quick kiss on the cheek. Settling her into a galvanized tin tub full of stiff, smelly clothes she hoists it and the baby into their wagon.

Mary, nine-years-old, settles in next to the baby to make sure she doesn't crawl out of her nest. Maggie, seven, holds five-year-old Jake's hand where they sit in the back of the wagon on the other side of the tub. Mama smiles at the two girls, thanks them for tending the little ones and tucks loose hairs under Mary's bonnet.

Everyone is quiet, not having energy enough to chatter in this unrelenting heat. The new decade has started out hot and dry. Now, in late July, the short grass prairie is crisp as burnt toast.

Tina, born Christina Margaret, is twelve and John Fredrick is fourteen. Together they have loaded the family's two empty water barrels into the wagon to be refilled while at the creek. Two loops of rope around each barrel keep them upright. An oak bucket hangs neatly from an iron S-hook on the wagon's sideboard. Inside the bucket a clean flour-sack holds cheesecloth to strain the spring water as it's poured into the barrels.

John has harnessed Blackie – their draft horse gelding – and backs him to the wagon's singletree. The Weisshaar family borrows their neighbor's Belgian mare to make a team when they work the soil, but Blackie pulls the wagon alone.

Foamy tan sweat edges his bridle below the blinders and trace-strap leathers that lie across his hips. He chews the bit and flings slobber, eager to be off on a water haul. A trip to the creek is the only time he is able to drink his fill.

Landsman (Lostman) Creek lies east of the Weisshaar farm. In wet years it flows steadily towards the Republican in Kansas and on into Nebraska to join the Platte, but it has been exceptionally dry since the Weisshaar family moved from Idalia to this new farm in the Russian/ German Settlement northeast of Bethune. The nearest big town is Burlington. The children have never seen it.

Father, John Frederick, has been away since the wheat was harvested earlier in the month. The crop was so poor there was very little to sell and Father had to save enough for seed and flour. After hauling the wagon load to Burlington for trade and have their year's supply of flour ground, he came home, staying just long enough to cultivate the corn. Joining other husbands and boys old enough to hire out, they traveled as a group to Denver to find cash paying jobs. The women and children remain to keep the farms running until they return.

Mama climbs onto the wagon seat with John on her left and Fredericka (Frieda), 10, on her right. She glances behind to be sure everyone is aboard, counting heads as they settle into place. She is proud of her children, valuing each as individuals and noting their differences.

She has borne ten – losing her firstborn son Johann Jacob in 1885, age one year twenty-two days – shortly before they fled Russia's change in political power. Like most of the settlement, the Weissharrs are part of a great migration of German Lutherans who believe they can practice their religion, raise crops and children and prosper on the Great Plains of America.

Christina's second child, a daughter, was born in Talmage, Nebraska in June 1886. When this baby was nine months old, they relocated to Idalia, Colorado; nearly four hundred miles of travel.

Pregnancy follows pregnancy with babies born every eighteen months to two years. When the Weisshaar family moved to Bethune early in 1901, their wagon carried eight children.

Pauline has reached her first birthday, giving no peace of mind to Christina Wilhelm Weisshaar, who knows the risks are many and whose religious belief is their only protection. That and constant vigilance.

It was not enough to save tiny Karl Frederick who was born in 1899 and lived a heartbreaking two weeks. Christina mourns her lost sons daily and deeply, imagining the graves she'll never visit. She cherishes every day that passes with no one injured or ill. A weight of impending dread lays heavy, but she knows the hand of God is in all. They will be reunited in His Salvation at the end of time. This is her comfort.

Lena and Tina sit behind the wagon seat where they can watch the smaller ones. They lean against the roughed grey backboard of the wagon, enjoying this brief time of rest. Lena has packed hard boiled eggs, coarse bread with soft cheese, salted garden carrots and crisp radishes wrapped in damp muslin for their lunch. She thinks about the pleasure of soaking her tired feet ankles deep in the creek.

The harness jingles. Blackie's hooves clomp rhythmically and his tail swishes steadily as he sweeps away biting flies. The trail to their washing place is clearly pressed into the curve of the earth and Blackie knows the way without guidance. Gusty wind washes through the short dry grass and rattles the brown/black seed pods of yucca. An oven of cloudless sky encloses the family group. Lena turns forward to squint against the glare, looking for the haze of green ahead which signals cottonwoods and water. She notices how Mama is slumped forward, her arms wrapping her lower belly.

"Jake, quit your fidgeting!" Lena snaps. She has caught him poking a finger in Maggie's ear, annoying his sister as he is wont to do. His nature is full of vinegar, loving to tease and then run for cover. Maggie is tolerant of him, but Lena is irritated by such foolishness and her worry about Mama puts more bite into her tone than she means.

Blackie's pace picks up as he smells the damp air of the creek. John gathers up the slack in the reins and slows him to a gentler walk. John has also noticed how Mama is sitting and doesn't want her to be jarred more than can be helped.

He guides the wagon down the sloped trail to a flat area along the stream bed. This far into midsummer, the grass has been grazed short by other horses and cattle watering alongside. Cattail heads wave in the swampy places that are too soft for the cattle to graze. Mama will want some gathered to make cattail ash for wounds. She has shown John and Lena how to harvest the early shoots for spring vegetables, how to use cut roots for a poultice and how to burn the heads to ash, then mix the ash with lard for an antiseptic salve. They are careful to never harvest more than they need to protect the plants for future years. The year of drought has reduced the size of the swampy area, John notices sadly. Range cows have intruded farther than usual, their droppings thick and fragrant along the freshly grazed ground.

With the wagon stopped, everyone climbs or jumps down. The air is cooler here and spicy with the scent of nettles and wild mint. Frieda calls to the small folk, "Jake, Maggie, Mary, come help me clear a place for the picnic. Be watchful for snakes!" She carries their basket of supplies below one of the bigger cottonwoods. "Put all those dry cow-chips in a pile and we'll load them later. Come on now, scoot! You can play in the water when we're done."

John unhitches Blackie from the wagon and leads him to the creek edge below their picnic spot. A cloud of midges rise from the damp earth. John waves his free hand to clear them from his face. He listens to the slurp and swallow of the big horse, the trilling song of red-winged blackbirds and the sucking sounds of Blackie's hooves sinking and lifting in the thick, fetid ooze. Behind him is the happy chatter of the children and Mama's even tones answering their piping questions. He loves this spot and believes it is one of the finest places on earth. Blackie lifts his head, water draining past his heavy lips, and sighs with contentment.

John knows the horse will want to roll so he takes time to remove the harness, stretching it along the wagon's side to keep everything in place. He unbuckles the bridle and slips on a grazing halter with a long rope attached so that Blackie knows not to stray too far. Blackie is broke to ground tie and unless something out of the ordinary happens, will remain in whistling distance of his family while he grazes.

Lena watches Mama settle Pauline on the spread quilt. She sees Mama wince and guard her belly as she straightens up. A frown of concern creases Lena's young face.

"Mama, why don't you nap while Tina and I do the washing? You feelin' poorly?"

"Sure, honey. I believe I will doze a bit after lunch." She pauses, considering. "Just my time, you know. I don't have them often, between the babies, but Pauline's not a baby anymore. My milk's dried up and so my monthlies have started again."

Lena's hot face flushes hotter. She hates this kind of talk. But she knows Mama is just stating facts she needs to prepare for. At fifteen Lena's body has reached womanhood. She is slender, but big boned, built for farm labor. Tina is heavy in the middle, but has the prettiest hair of all the girls, thick and walnut brown. Frieda looks more like Father, with a strong jaw and broad forehead softened by the waves in her hair. Mary and Maggie are will-o-the wisps, petite, fair and more like twins than two years apart. Little Pauline's character is a mystery: she never cries, not even when she teethed and her chin became so chapped from drool it bled; never needy, content to be alone while the older children bustle about.

Lena remembers the fright of a month ago when Pauline mastered walking and disappeared for an afternoon, slipping into the corn field where no one could see her, silent to their calls. It was Father who found her, curled below the green blades, the dappled shade and her dusty clothes making her nearly invisible against the turned earth. From then on, during times everyone was busy and couldn't keep an eye on her, Lena harnessed Pauline to the clothes line using quilting strips secured around her belly.

"Come have lunch everyone," calls Tina. She is orderly, methodical. Everything is lined up if Tina can reach it. She hands the food out. John gets two eggs and extra bread. He smiles at Tina, giving her a wink.

Mama mashes Pauline's egg with her finger, breaking it into small bites for her little girl. Pauline's eyes are deep brown, large and fringed with heavy lashes. She has high cheekbones and a sweet smile that lights a room. "Eat, eat, my little miss," says Mama. "You are a growing girl and soon to be running with the others." She sings softly and the other children are spellbound, hearing their Mama's sweet voice...

"Wie schön, dass du geboren bist,(How pleasant that you were born,)

wir hätten dich sonst sehr vermisst.(we would have truly missed you overall.)

wie schön, dass wir beisammen sind,(how pleasant that we're all together;)

wir gratulieren dir, Geburtstagskind!Uns're guten Wünsche (we Congratulate your birthday, Child!)"

Everyone claps and Pauline, watching the movement of the other children's hands, learns to clap herself – falling over with laughter at her own accomplishment. That sets up a rolling laugh from them all.

Then Mama quiets them, reaches into her apron pocket and brings out a special treat she's been saving – maple sugar candy shaped into leaves. The pieces are wrapped in waxed-paper and rest safe from breakage inside a tin. She has carried this with her since leaving Idalia. There had been so much sadness since the death of baby Karl, she'd not found a time happy enough to bring it out.

There are three precious leaves. She breaks each into three pieces; just the tiniest taste for everyone. Pauline has the honor of the first bite and sends everyone into rolling laughter again when her eyes grow round and fill with tears of joy. She does not talk, but her expression is of such wonder at the flavor no words are needed.

The children each give Pauline a birthday kiss and thank Mama for the fine sweet. The taste of maple will send them back to this day by the creek on the prairie for the rest of their lives.

After a short rest, each of the children go about their jobs: John and Lena to fill the water barrels first – Lena atop the wagon pouring buckets of water through a cheesecloth lined strainer as John hauls it from the creek at the spring head. Each barrel holds thirty gallons, but can't be filled to the top as much would slosh out, even with wooden lids. Each bucket holds about two gallons. At twenty pounds per bucket full, the total they will haul is about six hundred pounds of water.

The barrels are on either side of the wagon, centered between the axles to distribute the weight and maintain balance. When they get home, John and Lena will fill the house barrel first, take the empty barrel out of the wagon to the livestock's dugout and then fill that one with the remaining water, bucket by bucket. All told the water will be moved three times, the last time when it is given to the animals and used by the family. Every drop is sacred and much is used more than once: bath water shared, wash water poured onto the vegetable patch.

When they first arrived at the creek, John was careful to have the wagon turned toward home and on a slight downhill slope as he set the brake. This will help Blackie's first pull to get the wagon rolling. The hillside they must climb is gradual, but is still a heavy load for a single horse. Father has taught John well. Taking proper care of the animals is essential to the family and John has a natural instinct towards their wellbeing. He is sure no harm comes to them through his negligence or inattention.

Tina, Frieda and the smaller children except Pauline carry the clothes tub, washboard and lye soap to the water's edge. They remove the soiled clothes and sort them into piles: dishcloths, under garments, the girls' dresses, the boy's shirts and finally the pants which are dirtiest. Borrowing the bucket long enough to fill the tub, Tina adds soap to the water, stirring with her fingers, watching it swirl and clabber until she has it well mixed. The strong soap makes her hands burn and turns her knuckles red. It is made from rendered fat and lye and must be shaved with a sharp knife from a big bar. Mama had already shaved off the day's portion and put it in a lard can. She is careful about knives and keeps hers in a safe place on a high shelf in the kitchen.

When the soap has mixed well, Tina asks Frieda to bring her the dishcloths. Dividing the pile into two smaller piles she soaks the first in the tub, squeezing the water through and through and scrubbing any stains on the washboard. Then she calls Frieda and Jake to wring them out, careful to keep the soapy water in the tub. They put this pile on a nearby rock to wait for rinsing. When the second batch is done the same way, it is time for the next load. When these are done, Tina's arms are aching, but Lena has finished helping John and is ready to spell her.

Lena likes to sing when she works and the others join in. They have songs-in-the-round that she has taught them. Tina repeats one line off, followed by the rest. If anyone gets confused, they have to start over. Mary and Maggie like to sing with one voice and help each other stay on track. John's voice is still clear, more like a girls. Jake is too silly to stay serious and tries to get them mixed up, but a raised eyebrow from Lena sends him back to the creek to throw water in the air. He watches with fascination as the drops form into perfect spheres, sparkling in the hot July sun.

In no time, the laundry is washed, rinsed and laid in the sun on clean grass to dry. The wind is gusty enough to move a shirt sleeve, but it is Jake's job to place clean stones to hold the edges down. He has a 'rock safe' that he's made to store the rocks between wash days – a natural grassy hollow that is far enough above the creek not to be carried away in times of high water. Every visit to the creek he finds and adds more stones. Once he found a grinding stone and bowl used by Indians. These were examined closely by the family and made them feel ashamed, like intruders.

Mama and Pauline have risen from their nap and gone into the water to bathe. Mama is feeling stronger for having had this brief rest. It is lovely standing in the flowing stream, bringing relief to aching muscles and sticky, sweaty skin.

The others wade in, laughing and talking about how fine it feels. The creek's bottom is mostly sand and gravel. It shifts beneath their bare toes, tickling and scrubbing gently. In the deepest place the water rises to Mama's knees and she sits down in this spot facing upstream. As she lays back to soak her head, her skirts float up until they saturate. She holds Pauline in her lap, the cool water rising to her child's chest and Pauline slaps her hands into the water, blinking in surprise at the splash. Everyone is laughing and tossing water and getting thoroughly soaked. Using sand, they scrub themselves and their clothes. The water rinses away a week's worth of grime and sweat and odor. It washes over them, carrying their unspoken burdens downstream and away.

The sun's path westward brings this time of joy to an end. Together the family gathers and folds the freshly washed and dried clothing, places it into the tub and returns everything to the wagon. As they work, the south wind pulls the moisture from their hair and clothes, so that by the time John has harnessed Blackie they are only slightly damp.

No one rides the wagon except Mama. They all know Blackie is pulling enough weight up the hill without them. Lena, John and Frieda walk alongside the wagon to help push it up the hill while Mama clucks and slaps the reins. Blackie is well rested, too, though now he strains to take the water home. Mary carries Pauline while Maggie and Jake hold hands and walk up the hill at a safe distance from the wagon. John watches carefully to be sure no one is in the way should Blackie lose his momentum and the wagon roll backwards.

When the wagon tops the hill and is well along the flat, Mama stops Blackie and the children climb in. She takes a moment to retie her bonnet strings, notes the refilled water barrels, the clean tub of laundry, the fresh supply of cow chips and firewood. She gives her children a look of love and appreciation. "You are a fine lot, you are! Father can be so proud. God is good to have blessed me with you!"

Across the prairie the sun is dropping into the west, though it won't be full dark on a July night until well past exhaustion. Evening chores wait for them as they travel homeward. It has been a perfect day for the Weisshaar family.

CHAPTER 24

Mother's hen flock and Father's pigs need me. They are the foundation of our farm income, more reliable than the crops. I start early and end late. The days' labors give me satisfaction as I lay on my pallet in the lean-to behind the barn; satisfaction in my strong arms and back doing work I am meant to do. My part in the family is giving Mother her gathered eggs and sharing how many hens have gone broody, milking the cows and feeding the stock. My part in the family is putting animals on fields to graze and taking them off again. My part in the family is grooming the horses, harnessing and unharnessing them as needed.

There is satisfaction in knowing my jobs and getting them done with no one to bother me. Day follows day, month follows month. Boars mount sows, sows farrow litters, roosters pin down hens, hens lay eggs, chicks hatch and grow. Their food, their water, their bedding, their manure, that is what I do. I can see a problem before it happens. I can put down a sick or injured animal as easy as I can hold a new born. My strength is all I need. At the end of the day, I am mostly content. I know my place.

John, (he won't stand being called Little Jake anymore), works alongside Father in the auctioneering business. They have made a name for themselves and Father says the number of sales he's agreed to is growing like wildfire. The newspaper is full of his ads and brags. At least the auctions and hobnobbing keep Father away from the farm many days of the month. I believe that is a good thing. Tim travels with them as Father's 'muscle'. Auctions take lots of muscle and Father says Tim is better at spotting a buyer or a crook than anyone. In town they call Father 'Colonel'. Does that ever puff his chest! He cries sales in all the communities so his face and name are familiar all over.

Father is also known for his animal doctoring. He floats the teeth of horses, dehorns cattle and does hoof trimming. With George being a nearly grown thirteen, Father is able to ride away from the farm without a care. Mother does not go into Rexford often. It is easiest for her to give Father or one of the girls a list of what she needs. With the new phone line in place, she can call in an order, too.

The big talk at Sunday table is about Colorado land and a farmers' grain storage company in Rexford. Father is part of some wheeler-dealers who think they can make big money owning a grain elevator to hold the neighbor's crops for a fee. His work sheets filled with columns of numbers crowd the table in the evening and Mother has to be careful if she moves them.

There is new opportunity in Eastern Colorado and Father wants a piece of it. Many families are looking at this land as a way for their grown children to get a place of their own. Even older folks are getting bit by the 'land fever bug' and several families have already moved, taking all their belongings and starting over, just like our family did when we came to Thomas County. This land to our west is unbroken grass and requires only three years to claim. Father has decided; John and I will go first. John will get us signed up and leave me to start breaking the sod. We will go at the end of the year, to get rolling with spring. The Reads are homesteading again.

Sarah Lou, Mrs. Warner now, has got her hands full of babies and can't imagine moving till the newest girl is at least a year old. With May only five and Warden Wayne three she is looking a mite worn down. I would help out with May and W.W., but Sarah says, "Another time, Rich. Thanks, but not quite yet." She and her husband Arthur have been in Dresden for a while where he is starting out as a real estate agent with a man named Newton. I wonder how long that will last. Art is not much of a stayer. I see his eyes focus on Father when the conversation turns to Colorado land.

About the only thing I like about Art is his music. He's a playin' fool, leaving Sarah Lou to mind the little ones and keep the house while he travels to events. I listen when he visits, sitting on the porch while the family has pie and coffee inside. He's got some real pep in his tunes.

Now and then, when I know Art will be away, I ride over to their place in Dresden and weed Sarah Lou's flower bed. I like to see her with the small ones cuddled in her arms. May runs around like a colt and won't let Sarah catch her for washing up or hair brushing. She likes my mouth harp songs. One day I brought over my special music box to show her. She danced and twirled so pretty! Sarah watched awhile, her eyes shadowed and sad. When May leaped into my arms, wrapping her legs around my waist, Sarah called May inside and told me to go home. She sounded right scoldy. Her voice was tight and sharp. I don't know, but I guess I won't take the music box there again.

One day last week when Father and the boys were at an auction, Mother sent me to Rexford to take Attie Mae some eggs for the Hotel where she cooks. Attie Mae is mighty good at her cooking and all the folks like her. She boards there and enjoys the social whirl. I heard her speaking with Mother about her beau, Emery Owen Leach. She says his name like her mouth is full of syrup.

When I got to town, I saw posters about the 4th of July celebration that is coming soon. There will be trotting races, mule races and a dance. I don't suppose I will go. Father will want me for chores. He'll say, "Can't everyone go!

I work off the farm when a neighbor needs extra hands. They make arrangements through Father and he tells me who, where and when. When I get to the job, I can do most anything: plaster, husk corn, work the livestock, or plow a field. Folks know they can depend on me to be there when they need me and to give them a good day's work.

Tending our own animals is best, though. They seem to like me, but I suppose it's really just the food I bring them.

CHAPTER 25

Pauline jiggles Anna Dorthea's cloth dolly to make it dance, hoping to shush her little sister. The two-and-a-half year old wails with piercing screams, just as she has been doing all morning. Tears and snot glisten on her swollen red face. Pauline is six-and-a-half. Since Anna began walking Pauline has taken over much of her care, trying hard to meet her needs, but this baby is rarely content.

The household is in an uproar. Neighbors and cousins crowd the front room, stirring the air each time the door is opened. The noise of laughter and chatter is thick. Everyone's in everyone's way because this is Lena's wedding day. She is twenty-one.

Pauline watches Mama from under the table where she and Anna have tucked themselves. Mama weaves between standing guests, trying to sort out last details. Her mouth is tight, her lips thin and pale.

Two years and a month after the birth of William Christian (Bill), now a plump and happy little boy of five, Anna arrived. Christina was nearing forty years old and ill much of this, her twelfth, pregnancy. The Weisshaar family was in fear she might be too weak to deliver, but she proved strong enough. Just. Mrs. Adolf, the midwife, used all her skills to help Christina's labor be effective. Baby Anna was blessedly tiny and arrived squalling. For much of her life she has continued to do so.

Christina's health has not returned. She has lost teeth; her cheeks drawn in as though she's sucking on something sour. Her mouth turns down at the corners and her eyes are dull. With rounded shoulders she looks shrunken. Though this should be one of her happiest days, she is too exhausted to find much joy.

There are now twelve family members living in the two room house. Curtains divide these rooms into private spaces, but there is very little privacy for anyone. Tension and irritability, worse in winter, results. Slaps and yells between the children are frequently heard. Mama has given up trying to settle fights. Anna's continual fretting and screaming numbs her to all else.

Father and the boys began building an additional room last year, but were not able to start until late fall because of having to work away from the farm so often. Early freezes made it impossible to quarry enough rock to complete it. The walls are nose high to Pauline and she finds that if the wind is from the north and the sky clear she and Anna can shelter against an inner wall, playing and staying away from the hub-bub of the crowded house. It is the only place Anna is happy. Today is blustery, cloudy and too cold to escape the confusion.

Pauline sighs and spins a wooden spool to please Anna. The child won't even look, blubbering plaintively. The groom's mother, Margaretha Schlichenmayer, reaches under the table to gather Anna into a fleshy embrace and Pauline crawls out to follow, glad to stand upright.

Anna snuffles and rubs her face on the woman's bosom, leaving a sticky trail upon her formal black dress. Pauline is horrified, but Mrs. Schlichenmayer laughs and pats the baby's back, smoothing tangles of fine hair away from her hot face. Anna takes a shuddering breath, lays her head down and closes her eyes. Her scrawny legs straddle Margaretha's heavy waist, drawing comfort from the large woman's padding.

"This Prinzessin just wants schmusen!" Her kindness brightens the whole room.

Though he is one year younger than Lena, Gottlieb Schlichenmayer is a strong man. At age eleven he left South Russia with his parents and siblings, arriving in Colorado in 1890. The Schlickenmayer families are near neighbors. They are well established and respected. Father and Mama are happy about this match and especially glad to know Lena will not be moving far from them – just three miles northwest of the Weisshaar home.

The women of the Settlement have been baking for days, making Lena's special wedding feast. Cabbage rolls, buns stuffed with a meat and onion mixture, cakes of all styles and noodle puddings crowd the plank table. There are no fresh foods, but kraut, pickles and stewed dried fruits bring flavors of summer. Butterkuchen, everyone's favorite, is displayed on decorative plates. A great pot of green bean soup, made from dried garden beans, simmers on the iron stove ready for dumpling dough to be dropped into the rich chicken broth. Each family has brought at least one food item, as well as extra dishes and utensils to accommodate the gathering. The mixed smells bring sharp growlings to Pauline's empty belly and she places a hand over the sound. It has been a hungry winter.

Lena comes out of the back room surrounded by girl cousins. Her eyes sparkle and she is pale except for two bright spots of color on her cheeks. Wearing a dress made from soft white cloth and embroidered with row after row of fine stitching, she stands shyly while everyone gathers around.

As the first daughter to marry, she holds a high standard for her little sisters. Pauline has petted the dress many times, but always carefully washed her hands first. It is hard to keep anything white for long and the color is an extravagance. With care and some tailoring the dress may serve Tina and Frieda too, maybe even the younger sisters, before becoming swaddling-cloths for babies yet to be born.

Mama scraped potatoes and soaked them in water to make stiffening starch. The irons, heated on the stove, were checked carefully before applying to be sure there were no scorch marks on the pristine cloth. On his last trip to Burlington, Father bought a new pair of shoes for Lena. These are serviceable, heavy work shoes that she will wear daily, but the newness is something to behold and everyone knows the cost came dear to the cash poor family. Lena's glossy dark hair is enhanced by the brightness in her dress. Mama is awed by the transformation of her most treasured daughter and tears slip from her eyes.

Pauline thinks about the many ways Lena helps Mama and how she will be missed. Lena is more of a second mother than a big sister to Pauline. When William's birth ousted Pauline from the baby crib, she was placed to sleep between Lena and Frieda, while Tina shared the bed with Mary and Maggie. These thoughts make her nose burn and her throat tighten, but she knows this is a happy day for Lena and tries to hide her sadness. Suddenly Pauline determines to ask Mama if Anna can join her bed tonight. She is excited to share with her little sister the stories and songs Lena has taught her. She feels Mama will welcome the idea and this cheers her.

Tina has taken over some of Lena's jobs and Frieda is also carrying more of the household weight. Frieda does not like to be outdoors. She fights the wind and sun, a battle she can only win indoors, but her deft hand at making cheese is welcome in the family's diet.

Mary and Maggie work as a team in the garden and yard. They are in charge of the hen flock and do the milking, separating and churning. Maggie grates and squeezes small carrots to color the winter butter before it is put in pretty molds to be sold in Burlington for trade. This added effort helps bring in a good price.

For the past year John has made those trips to town almost weekly, taking extra eggs and butter and anything else the farm has to sell. He is twenty and courting Lydia Stahlecker, eighteen, the youngest daughter of Martin and Katherena. Because she is their baby, they are not letting John spend any time with her yet. They wish to see what type of man he will become.

Jake and John are responsible for the big livestock. Each day, weather allowing, it is their job to herd the cows and calves from place to place to feed. Boys from neighboring farms meet with their herds, some with only three or four cows, others with larger numbers, gathering them to graze. They take them to land that is not claimed by anyone – the last free quarters yet to be settled.

This provides opportunities of entertainment for them: mischief and foolery and sport, rough and tumble games that sometimes end in injury. When the sun drops into the west, the herds split apart, returning to their home corrals as the boys throw clods at stragglers and each other.

During the deep winter months if too much snow lies on the ground or the wind is dangerously cold, the boys must pitch stored fodder to the cows and horses kept in their corrals. It is a yearly challenge to feed them adequately while reserving enough to last until spring. In dry years the supply is desperately short and the herd goes into winter in poor condition with calves born weak.

Jake prefers to err on the side of caution, giving the herd a little less than they need. John wants the animals fed well, especially during times when the night winds howl and the day's temperatures don't get above single digits. He can't sleep for thinking of the miserable animals. A large stack of wheat straw gives them shelter and they eat their way into it during storms, but it has no feed value and gives the horses a dry cough that troubles John.

Keeping the livestock watered is brutal work. For weeks John and Jake and the neighbor boys have chopped heavy ice in the creek to reach running water. If the creek freezes solid the only source of flowing water is the spring. Then every mouthful must be hauled by barrel to the animals rather than herding them to the creek where they can drink along the pools. There is risk of the barrels splitting from expanding ice even as they are hauled homeward. The Settlement prays fervently for a February thaw and early spring rains.

Today the men and older boys complete morning chores while the women ready the household. The teams are fed, watered and hitched. The horses are tied to the wagons' sides, ready for single riders. Burlap sacks have been secured over the animals' backs while they wait. The younger horses paw restlessly at the frozen earth. Clouds of breath puff from their nostrils and drops of moisture freeze on their whiskers.

Now a line of wagons and saddle horses move in slow procession towards the Rock Church. Heavy woolen coats, buffalo lap robes, knit scarves and hide caps bundle the exposed riders, rounding them into bear-like shapes. Bitter wind bites exposed skin and the children huddle together in the wagon beds with heated rocks in their pockets and next to their feet. They giggle and tease and talk about the great feast they will enjoy when they return.

Lena rides between her parents on the wagon seat. Salt water leaks from her nose and eyes and she pats them with her wedding hanky, careful not to redden her skin any further. She is joyful, sad, excited and terrified. Mama takes Lena's mittened hand and tucks it between her own, but says nothing. Lena is aware of the smallness of her mother's hands, strong and bony, but full of love and understanding, fear and pride in equal measure. Father's eyebrows are frosted, nearly meeting above his nose in a frown of seriousness. He cares deeply for this daughter, but has no words to share his feelings. He knows Christina will grieve and he wants no further burden upon his wife.

In 1893 the Settlement families, with the guidance of Mr. Christian Dobler, a carpenter and wagon builder, labored to cut, haul and set stone to build a church home. Eight wagon loads of rock per family were required, while single members each contributed four wagon loads. Extreme drought, with no rain falling for eighteen months and a total failure of crops, did not deter them. Perseverance and faith brought the Rock Church to stand upon the dry prairie where nothing before had stopped the wind: twenty-four feet by forty feet by ten feet of stone, adobe mortar and wood, the Immanuel Lutheran Church. It would be nearly ten years before a thirty by thirty foot parsonage was added.

At the time of Lena and Gottlieb's wedding, over thirty family names call the Settlement home. Baptisms, Holy Days, communion, marriages and funerals occur in steady progression along with Sunday services. The Church is the hub for them all.

Reverend A. Stein will officiate today's ceremony. He has been the congregation's spiritual leader since the previous spring, replacing Reverend Robert Ackerman. As the third minister in the parsonage the Settlement families have made him welcome. They recall the challenge of religious study prior to having a church home and a residing minister to serve them. All acknowledge deeply the power of their common core faith to bind this community. Their personal survival often depends upon this cohesiveness. Today's wedding binds two family names more tightly and strengthens the Settlement's stability.

Over time this concentration of family ties will become problematic, but today the joining of Lena and Gottlieb is blessed!

Pauline, like her sisters, imagines herself standing in Lena's spot. Not too soon, but not too late, either, she hopes!

CHAPTER 26

1910: Sarah Lou Read Warner

Kit Carson County, Colorado

I think back to our first days in Kansas. We sure had nothing but hope and exhaustion and Father's unending drive. Nearly thirty years have passed since I played 'seeky-find', searching for eggs from nests hidden in the tall grass. I remember once, oh it's just too funny and sad, gripping the hem of my dress with my little girl hands and filling the hollow with eggs I'd discovered. While running to show Mother I tripped, landing atop and smashing them into a yolky-shelly mess all over my front. How I screamed! Mother and Richard came running, certain I was snake bit. Mother's face was so pale with fright I screamed even louder.

Richard helped me up, lifting my dress to see where I was hurt, but just then Father galloped up on Dancer because he'd heard my cries, too. Without stopping, he whaled off at Richard's head with his rope, striking and herding him away from me. Mother screamed and I screamed. Richard ducked and ran for his hiding place by the creek. Buster ran to and fro, going from trying to lick the dripping egg off me and wanting to be with Richard. Father was hollering and Mother was trying to calm him while trying to figure out why I was still screaming. I don't know why I screamed so loud. I guess I thought if I cried hard enough no one would swat me for spoiling the eggs.

Now, thirty years later I'm here on the Colorado plains alone with my three babies while Art shuttles back and forth to Selden to check on the store. What a dreamer he is! Sure, this land is free, but it's costing us dear. He's got big ideas, but can't seem to stay with anything long. I love him, I do, but I have to say I didn't think I'd be starting over again with no town in sight, no neighbors to speak of, and my family all east and busy with their lives. I surely know now how Mother must have felt those many years ago!

Oh sure, there are folks around us, but not our kind. I don't have any bad feelings towards the German Settlement folks. They are hard workers, good family people, but they keep Art and me outside their circle in a quiet, firm manner. I miss the social comings and goings of my home in Rexford and Selden. I surely do. Even Dresden had people who knew our people and we were made to feel welcome.

Here, well, here in Kit Carson County I'm not connected to anyone. I miss my sisters! Edna married, Villa married and both of them staying close to the home place where they can gather and visit. Here, well, here there's no one to fawn over the babies; no one to chat with over coffee and pie; no one to swipe away a few hard earned tears.

There's Richard, of course, with his homestead south and west of us. Sure not much help for me there though he does come by now and then when Art is away. I want to love my big brother and I do care about him. My feelings are mixed with heavy helpings of pity and worry. He is just so odd. An uneasiness settles just below my lungs when he is with the little ones; I feel gaspy, like the air has gone thin.

Father has always treated him so poorly, finding no use for him except the work he does. I don't think Father liked him from day one. I've heard so many times from Father, nearly every time a baby comes to a first time mother, the story of how Richard nearly killed his Kell. Father says it like Richard was to blame. A newborn baby! I don't understand his thinking, but no one can change his mind. He's never forgiven Richard and Richard has been measured and found wanting, according to Father.

Maybe it is good to have Richard this far away from Father and the rest. Maybe it will be better here and he can stand on his own. The time he spent in Republic City helped him learn a good trade in the cement business, but something went wrong. I never heard the details. Probably liquor again. That stuff is pure poison, especially for Richard.

Perhaps out here, away from Father, where there's less chance for him to get ahold of a bottle, well, maybe he'll do ok finally. Maybe he'll even find himself a girl who can see past his strangeness. Sure, he gives off something when he's around people, something that causes sideways looks and shuffling feet, but he's mighty good with farming and raising stock. He's real tender with little animals. Right now he's got a whopping good field of potatoes that he plans to take back to the Rexford market. He'd be a good provider for a woman who doesn't need much conversation. And who wouldn't mind that everlasting humming!

I miss my sisters! They always help me think more clearly when we talk about Richard. I guess, since there were just the two of us at first and I knew him as a child I have more kind feelings towards him. Attie and Villa and Edna won't let him near their children. The boys act like he's invisible unless they need some muscle. Then don't they go a'hollerin' for him!

It's hardest on Mother, I know. I watch how she looks so sorrowful at him when someone treats him rough. She only sees his goodness. He's her first born, after all. Any mother knows what that means. She won't stand against Father, though she tried in the early years. I think she saw how it worked against Richard, how speaking up brought him more harm. Poor Mother! Poor Brother!

Art wants to open a store here. He says there's no competition and the area farmers will be glad to have a place closer to their homes for supplies and a market for their goods. He's still sore about the partnership he had with Andrews, how it went sour so quick. I admit that was sure some dirty dealing and we all learned from it. Stick with family when doing business. Especially if its family with some capital to spend, like Art's father, the Judge. His family's been mighty helpful to us, no doubt. More than Judge Warner needs to be, but Art is a charmer and I think he's their favorite, though Ray's done pretty well for himself and Mabel is a diamond of a daughter with her teacher's certificate. Golly, I miss them all!

I wonder what Art is doing right now. Probably sitting at table with a crowd, telling Colorado stories and bragging on how soon we'll have made it big out here. They have no idea how lonesome it is. Makes western Kansas look like a well-watered land of milk and honey and we know that's not true! He promised me he's going to close out the store in Selden so as not to keep making these everlasting trips back and forth, leaving me alone on this empty land with nothing but babbling, hungry babies to tend. Oh, I'm sure it won't be long before he'll find a reason to head east, even without the Selden store to tend.

Well, next trip, I'm going home, too!

CHAPTER 27

1910: WEAVER/HUNTER FAMILY
Sheridan County, Kansas

A lovely name, Bow Creek. Just as pretty as Spring Brook. These are the township names where the Weaver and Hunter families settled and where Dorothy's parents spent their childhoods. These indicators of a well-watered land are sadly misleading if you base your image on rivers and streams of the East. In Sheridan County, Kansas imagined vistas are quickly adjusted by the sight of a bare earth ribbon cut in varying widths and depths through the surrounding land. Fed by the draws which slope at angles from higher elevations, the 'creeks' of this area channel run-off during spring snow melt and heavy rain. They are part of the Smoky Hill River watershed.

Before the prairie grasses were destroyed for crop production, these waters were filtered by vegetation and ran clear. By 1910 most of this protective barrier had been lost to plow and harrow. As a result excess water ate channels into the exposed earth removing silty particles of fragile loess soil to roil in a brown rush towards the lowest levels.

Springs, treasured by all inhabitants, wept into marshy pools. These seeps could be smelled and heard before they were seen. Cattails, adorned by joyous red-winged blackbirds, grew in full sun. Lush grass gave off a verdant odor when cropped by grazers. Animals that had eaten their fill lay shaded beneath gnarled cottonwoods and wispy red-willows, flapping their tails and chewing cud. Over time, grazed too often by too many for too long a time, these beautiful places became hoof-pocked, foul smelling, fly-plagued muck-holes. Disease carrying mosquitoes hatched by the millions.

For a few nights following summer rains, prairie toads sing. It is a lucky tadpole that stays wet long enough to hop free. Between rainy spells the beds bake dry. The silted flats crack into thin plates, lifting upward at the edges like rhino hide, but are oh so fragile. Winds scour and shift until a big blow sends the fine powdery earth skyward.

Polished grains of quartz sand reminds an observer that once there were mountains; fossilized fish bones and mollusks embedded in limestone outcroppings speak of a time when a shallow ocean covered this space; mammoth tusks and spear points honor long ago inhabitants. In 1910 Sheridan County this permanent damage was evident. The land of the central plains had been dishonored by its eager settlers.

Dorothy's parents spent their childhoods in these townships. Dorothy's mother, Jennie Lucille Weaver, was born in Van Buren, Iowa in 1905 to Fredrick Ray Weaver and Alice Duncanson. She came to Spring Brook Township when she was five and then, at age fifteen, moved with her family to Parnell Township.

Her future husband, Floyd Lloyd Hunter, born 1903 in Lincoln, KS was seven years old when his family came to Bow Creek Township. His mother, Rhoda Snyder and his father, Melvin Sylas Hunter had first traveled to Kansas from Centerville, Appanoose, Iowa. In 1906 the senior Mr. Hunter became a landowner in Sheridan County. A 1917 photo of the family farm gives evidence of his character: a well-built two-story home, a large barn with several outbuildings and an established orchard near a tall windmill.

Floyd, being the baby of the family, was perhaps spared the roughest part of establishing this lovely farmstead. His five older brothers, ranging in age from twenty to eight, and a ten-year-old sister surely buffered his childhood somewhat. Another brother was born four years after Floyd but did not survive, so he retained his privileged birth status.

Coming late in his parent's childbearing years meant Floyd did not know his Hunter grandparents who had passed before his birth, though they had also located nearby. It was unlikely he had much connection with his mother's family as they had remained back east.

The Weaver family was typical for the times: extensive. Jennie's siblings included her living older brother, Albert, two more brothers who had not survived, a younger brother Jay, born when she was one, followed by twin sisters Myrl and Pearl when she was three, a sister Irene at age eight, the birth and death in 1915 of sister Helen Marie who was one of another set of twins – the surviving twin given the name Ellen Maybell (Mae) and one more brother Orville Edmund. As the oldest daughter Jennie would have spent much of her childhood caring for babies.

Mr. Weaver did not own his land. He was a tenant farmer.

Hoxie, the county seat of Sheridan, is centrally located. Bow Creek, Spring Brook and Parnell Townships circle it as spokes around a wheel hub. In 1910 the town boasted a new two and a half story brick high school. Its modern court house was surrounded by a tree-shaded lot. Like other county seat towns, Hoxie rose above the other communities in appearance and attitude. Selden, the town Dorothy Eileen would call home, existed primarily because of the railroad.

Jennie and Floyd might have met at school and social gatherings. Though they shared Iowa roots, there is no evidence that the families knew each other before settling in Kansas.

Floyd and Jennie's wedding photo of September 28, 1921 shows the couple at the tender ages of seventeen and sixteen. Jennie's sad expression is disturbing in a new bride. Jennie's mother was still of childbearing age, becoming pregnant shortly after her daughter's wedding. This child was not to live.

The first eleven years these young folks were married, from 1921 to 1932, were likely wrought with lack and hard scrabble and disappointment. Offset by a strongly established family web there was evident love and happiness as well. Family photos of the Hunter children showed they were well cared for and lived in a good home. Then terror struck.

Dorothy's brutal death in 1932 left eleven uncles and fourteen aunts to rage at her mistreatment. At the time of the murder, Dorothy's mother Jennie was pregnant with their fifth child. Nationwide the Dust Bowl and Great Depression were cutting the tendons that held these farming communities together.

CHAPTER 28

1915: PAULINE WEISSHAAR
The Settlement Bethune, Colorado

The air is once again full of dust. A reddish-grey haze blocks the setting sun as I gather our cows in for the night. The cooling evening wind gusts against me, pressing my skirt between my legs. I cup my hands over breasts that ache in the cold. I am changing. It seems almost overnight the scrawny girl who ran rabbit races with the children is gone. I see the older boys at school give me sidelong looks. Father will whip any who come near, but it warms me to see them notice.

There are other changes, too. People have come. Many people. A trickle that became a flood. Most have come from Kansas; the grown children of the first settlers. Now every quarter of land is taken where once the farmsteads lay far apart. 'They' are separate from us.

With the ground being taken up and turned over at a furious pace the Settlement is in turmoil. It is thrilling to watch. I am tickled by the old folks' grumbles. At every meal it's the same, "Hordes, like the grasshoppers, coming and taking and tromping about!"

"It is no longer safe with so many wagons on the roads!"

"We must watch the little ones."

"Is there no stopping this? Will they try to take our lands, too?"

We have a bachelor neighbor who has settled on one-hundred-sixty acres adjoining our land. He built a small square home and plowed under grass for planting. He is the kind it's verboten to welcome. Father told us sternly we are not to cross his property when walking to school, even though it is the fastest way and had been our path. We are told to stay together; to not wander alone.

Father's heavy brows come down further all the time. I see him scowl at the horizon, watching the land to our west and south as though a wicked storm is coming. I do not understand his fear. It seems only right to me that someone uses the land, just as we are using ours.

Producing food is what our lives and the lives of our neighbors revolve around. Turn the soil, plant the seed, wait for the first little green sign of life, worry and worry about no rain or too much rain until harvest time comes and then store what we need and sell the rest. If there is a crop. If there is a market. If, if, if. Then we do it all again. Our livestock is the same: the rhythm of breeding, feeding, butcher and sell. Always the struggle, always the worry, always the prayers to God for His providence. Always lack and disappointment, while we pray for gratitude.

Father and Mother talk with fear in low voices. So much ground, so much planting, so much dust lifting into the dirty sky. If the crops come in will there be a need for it all? War talk has them frightened, too. Newspapers are read and heads shake. Dark looks are exchanged at Church. Men have special meetings after service.

The old folks have seen what happens when lines are drawn, sides are taken, loyalties questioned. They say that the Germans in Europe, those with names just like ours in the Settlement, are becoming America's enemy. The freedoms that brought us to Colorado are wavering.

These worries seem so far away when I hear the coo of a mourning dove or coyotes cry to each other in the evenings. Father's eyes fill with sorrow when he says, "Dottar, your thoughts and ideas are that of a young one. You do not yet know how hard life can be! You must turn to God for guidance, my Pauline. You must not look outside of what is right and proper."

I cannot see how life could be much harder than what Mother and Father have lived. For all these years they have worked relentlessly with nothing to show but worn out hands and broken down backs. I wonder if that is all I have to look towards.

The wind whips more strongly, snapping my skirt and slinging fine grains of sand against my cheeks. The cows, udders swinging side to side, pick up their pace as we near the night corral where they may rest securely, protected from the beasts. I can appreciate their placid natures, their desire for routine, while I long for something I can't name.

I do not believe the outside world is as fearful as I've been told.

CHAPTER 29

1915: RICHARD READ

Republic City, Kansas

Republic City has sent me packing. Once again I find myself moving on, moving away; alone as always.

Grandmother Cardwell died a couple of years ago. She was mighty brittle before she passed, living to over 90 like she did. The family gathered. Mother was here at the end and it hurt her something fierce to watch her old ma gasping for every breath.

There was a passel of babies to keep track of. My music box kept them dancing and twirling under the trees out back. It was cold, being February, but they were all rosy cheeked from the fun. Art played his music, too, but soft and easy out of respect for the sad times. Little ones don't understand sad unless they are hurt or hungry.

Mattie, my favorite Cardwell niece because she looks like Sarah Lou did when she was small, danced the hardest and went a little crazy spinning round and round until her lunch came up. That ended the fun and I went on home to my place at the Men's Hotel. When I was gathering up my things, I overheard Pinkie Cardwell, Mattie's brother, say to his mother, "Uncle Rich ucky, Mama. I afeared of him." She shushed him right prompt, but not before I saw the look she gave me. It was the kind that cuts.

For the last year or so the family travels back and forth from here to Rexford. I mostly stay put, but will be going west again soon. John and Tim and Joe are all working in Republic City. Edmee and her husband Will Gardner have their own place. Perhaps the Reads should have stayed in Republic City rather than gone on to Rexford so many years ago. Father had to have his way, though, and still does.

Now we've got that land in Colorado and it is struggling. That's a real hard country out there. Father set his mind to it and so it was bought, with no thought to how we'd manage. Sarah Lou's got the worst of it, alone much of the time when Art makes 'business' trips to Selden and to visit his family. I think about Sarah Lou at night when I can't sleep. I think of how her's is the only soft face other than Mother's that has ever turned my way. I wonder if she needs me.

I wonder if Mother is doing too much work on the farm since all of us except George have left the home place. Father's not cut back on his horse work and auctioneering, but he finds lots of reasons to 'go to town'. I'm sure she still labors with her garden and poultry. That's her way.

I've learned the cement trade here and it suits me well. Heavy work, it is. Wears me down and helps me sleep after a hard day. Leaves a solid job behind that I can take pride in. I built a cave for Mrs. Kier and she was pleased with it but cut my wage because she said I took eggs from her hens without permission.

She said, "Rich, honey, I'd have given you all the eggs you wanted if you had just asked. Taking them from me was wrong and you knew it when you did it. Are you that hungry?"

I couldn't answer 'cause no one had ever called me honey and I was thinking that through. So she got tired of waiting and handed me my money, shy of our agreed on price.

The County hired me because little brother John was already working for them and they needed more muscle. He spoke for me, though I feel sure it was to hand off some his load. I worked on a bridge during the summer. The coolness and shade the bridge cast, with the smells of crushed leaves and wet earth, made me think my hiding place along Prairie

Dog Creek when I was small. I get queasy when I think of that hole under the bank, hidden from everyone. I remember Buster and the man and then I quit remembering.

There's a man I met on the County crew who taught me to smoke Camels. It is odd how pulling smoke into my lungs helps me not feel so alone. A fresh pack sliding into my overalls pocket feels like a friend.

I buy liquor from him, too. When I see the clear golden stream pour into my mug, the biting sweet/sour fumes filling my head, and take the first hot sips, all my thoughts go away. For a time.

This fall Mother and Father came to visit Joe and his new wife Hannah Kelly. Mother thinks well of her. Though I wasn't invited to join them while Father was there, Mother stayed a month more and we met a few times at the Republic Restaurant. Once she bought tickets to the Navajo Theater, but I couldn't bring myself to go through the doors. So many staring faces, all looking our way.

Mother said, "Oh Richard, it's all right. I didn't really want to go anyway." She tried to take my arm, like I see other women do with a man, expecting to stand close and be together, but my skin crawled like ants and I knew she could smell the hot odor I give.

I was happy when she returned to the farm, but before she left she told me Father was thinking of putting the farm up for sale and buying something near Republic City to be closer to all the kids. My breath got short when I thought about him living nearby, making a name and parading around town like he does. I got a bottle that night after she'd gone.

Well, I won't have to worry. I'm in trouble here. I won't say what the trouble is, but there's a man who I owe some money to and other things that aren't as easy to recall. I'll go back to Rexford and maybe get cement work there. Or head on back to Colorado and watch over Sarah Lou when Art is away. She needs me, I think.

CHAPTER 30

April 14, 1916: PAULINE WEISSHAAR

The Settlement Bethune, Colorado

I have seen him watching me, our bachelor neighbor. I have felt his dark gaze. I wonder what he thinks when he sees me walking home from school or when I bring the cows along the fields between our farms. I wonder if he notices my shyness. At times we have been very close to each other, but I do not raise my head or hand in greeting.

His songs reach out. It is a lonely sound, like nightwind when a storm flashes silent on the edge of the world. It sends a thrill into places I am just now learning of. The other children make goofy faces when they hear the humming and put fingers to their heads, twisting at the temples to indicate crazy. I think they are mean!

I am curious about him and listen for talk. He has family nearby, I've heard, the Warners. She is his sister. They all came from Kansas to take up the empty land. The Warners live north of us, against the Schlichenmayer farm. That explains why I've seen him pass by our place, seen him slow his team. I admit, I watch for him, acting busy with yard chores or tending the garden. I think he knows.

This morning I am alone. Mother and Father have gone to see Lena, to take bean seed for their garden. They want to play with little Pete who is two and a half and loads of silly. I planned to go with them, but Father said someone was needed for the cows, to take them to graze. The others are helping the Bauders. They have a new flock of lambs to be worked. Karl, a demanding six year old, loves sheep more than anything and he squealed to go work and not "play with Baby Pete!"

I heard myself say, "Father, I can do it. I will take my knitting and watch the herd until evening. The moon will be bright tonight but I will be back before dark."

Before they left, just after breakfast, Father spoke to me again, "Keep them to the middle fields, Pauline. Do not let them graze into the oats. It is greening well and they will want to go that way. Mother has packed you a noon meal."

"I'll watch them close, Father. I can knit with one eye and watch cows with the other."

He smiled but I saw a shadow behind it. More and more his strength is leaving him. I've seen him grip his chest and rub his left shoulder. His face has a dusky color and I hear him cough thick phlegm during morning chores. It is a good thing his sons and daughters can do the big work so that he may enjoy his first grandson.

I gather my knitting bag. I am making a thick lap robe for Mrs. Arthur who has bad knees and mentioned in church that a cozy robe would be just the thing on these chilly spring Sundays. The wool is grey-brown which she will like. She is not one for bright colors. If I work hard today, Friday, I will finish before next service and I look forward to seeing her enjoy it soon.

My brown hair is braided and wrapped around my head, tucked under an everyday cap. The dress I wear is one of my favorites. It has a cream body with sprigs of red that make me think of ripening cherries; a smooth weave, softened by many wearings, that lays smooth against me as I walk to the corral. My feet are bare.

Our cows with their new calves stand at the gate waiting. They are as happy as I am that the long winter is over. The air smells sweet and fresh, the earth opening to awakening grasses. Jake has turned the big garden over and harrowed it. The potatoes and onions are in the ground and we've taken the first pie plant stalks for Sunday dessert. My spirit is soaring like the larks with the love of spring and life!

I take the herd, laughing at the little bucking calves, along the ridge and let them graze down a wide draw. Some of the early grass has gotten quite tall. They will be content for a time. I settle against a low bluff and take out my yarn. I am using a cable stitch which makes a heavy drape. As I knit I think about the neighbor.

He is tall and wide shouldered. He looks as strong as any of the men in the Settlement. I've watched his place go from open grass to tidy fields in a steady manner. For one man, working alone, he has done much since he first came four years ago, even with the times he's been away back east. I was just a child then. His place has changed, as have I.

When going to and from school, I've noticed his horses are shiny from care. He keeps his home site neat, the dirt yard raked smooth. There are a few hens scratching about. He has a small garden just the right size for a single man.

I unwind more yarn and my hands work the needles which make a tiny ticking sound that joins that of the black crickets moving about in the grass. I wonder what his favorite foods are. I imagine putting a big beef roast, sliced juicy with potatoes and golden corn, on a table for him some Sunday. I imagine him lifting his head to inhale the fragrant steam. I feel his calm gaze upon my face and hear his gentle voice calling me 'good wife'. Then I feel silly and scared and get up to move the herd again.

The sky is clear, the breezes light, the sun strengthening. Hiding my intent from myself I let the cows move further west, close to the southwest corner of our grass. There are no fences but we all know the edges of our properties. Before the man came to homestead our cows and those of the Bauders grazed these acres freely. Heads lowered to the grass, pulling up mouthfuls as they walk, they go that way easily.

There seems to be no one there, at his home. I am sad and relieved. I push the pairs back a bit north and east, keeping the herd securely on our land. A low area here, with twisted cottonwood trees and plum thickets for shade will be a good spot for lunch. The cows will rest and chew cud for a couple of hours.

I eat and knit and grow sleepy. It is so quiet I hear the cows' bellies rumble, the burps as they bring up cud. I think I can hear grasshoppers chewing blades. Doves call with a restful sound. I lay back and close my eyes, just for a bit.

A shadow comes across my face, chilling the air enough to wake me. I know I've slept too long and startle, looking quick for the herd to be sure I've not let them wander. Instead I see the man. He is standing above me, silently.

I see his wide jaw and full, well-shaped lips. His forehead is broad, his nose strong. A small dent divides his chin. His dark eyes are penetrating under his brows. They meet mine with longing and hunger.

My face burns hot and I drop my gaze to the ground. I brush my dress down and start to my knees saying, "Es tut mir Leid, I am sorry. I hope my cows haf done no harm."

I smell liquor. I know that smell from weddings and funerals and sickbeds. I know that smell from childbirths that have gone too long when a woman needs relief. I know that smell, sweet and biting and sour all at once.

I smell musk. I know that smell from bulls and stallions and the matings I'm not supposed to watch. I know that smell from the linens before they are washed, from my older brothers' and my parents' beds. I know that smell from some of the old men who do not bathe as they should and who want to hold the little girls on their laps at gatherings.

I smell myself, my fear. It prickles under my arms and breasts and between my thighs. I feel sweat break free and run along my ribs, tickling like ants.

I hear him hum, a deep sound that makes my scalp crawl. The hum of a wasp, the hum of a serpent's tail.

All these things and then he is upon me.

CHAPTER 31

1916: JOHN RICE (J.R.) RUBERSON
Burlington, Colorado

As most do in this town of Burlington, I wear several hats in addition to acting as sheriff of Kit Carson County. There are times I do feel I'm only acting the part. Though enforcing the law is an honorable job which I am honored to do I am often left with the sense of too little, too late. At least with my Real Estate and Insurance business I deal with solid entities and a promise I can hold onto. Folks here place their trust in me and I respect that trust even when it pains me. The company has sent terse telegrams to say I'd best not lose them money while taking a salary, but I put my weight with the man I've insured.

Oh, I'm on the watch for the flim-flam men. With those, I'll back the company. There's some in every crowd. I seem to smell them out before they cause too much trouble; the quick claim, the suspicious circumstance, the 'innocent eye'. Crooks are found on both sides of any money deal. They usually leave a bad odor.

Land sales have finally slowed. For the past five years it was all I could do to keep the papers filed at the court house. Lots of empty ground is now owned and being operated by folks spreading here from Kansas.

I've met some great families, the kind that will stay and not try to turn a fast buck. The investor types, the wheeler-dealers who come in to take advantage of volatile times, are less likely to prey on folks if there's honest men like me to keep an eye out. There's that trust again. That's something I can take pride in.

I've been in Kit Carson County now for nearly twenty years. I came here when I was just about that old. Funny how time does that…finds patterns where you least expect them. I've farmed, been a house painter, an odd-job man, and pretty much done anything that came my way. That's what it takes and everyone knows it. Sure keeps the men hustling and the women wondering how to string it all together.

Just recently the town of Burlington has exploded. Over eggs and coffee this morning I read a very funny editorial in the Kit Carson County Record about how the new city compares with the old written by an early pioneer who'd relocated to Iowa, a Mr. C. J. Eatinger. His words have kept me chuckling all day. Towards the end of his letter 'back home' he describes growing watermelons in the rich Colorado soil with claims that the vines grew so fast they wore out the melons by dragging them on the ground. To solve this, he'd heard the plants are now corralled by woven wire to slow them down. Knowing the droughts and winds and general wicked weather of these Eastern Colorado plains, I can't help but appreciate his hyperbole.

I am completing paperwork as late evening advances. Frequently I do filings and complete forms by lantern light so that my days are free for the working folks. Without wife or family I have no reason to hurry home.

Suddenly the door of my office bursts open. It slams against the wall, thrust hard by a large man who should be red faced by nature and exposure but who presents clammy and pale as a raw oyster.

"Hilfe! Hilfe! Sheriff! You are needed! Please, sir!" He gasps and removes his hat. It is one of the men from the Russian German Settlement. I don't know his name, but his dress and accent alert me.

"Yes, Mr.? What is your name, sir?" I ask.

"G. Adolf, sir. I am the Reverend of the Lutheran Church of Bethune. I, ve, need your hilfe, help, please, sir. There's been a vergewaltigen, an attack. On one of our tochters, daughters. A junges girl, not yet sixteen. She ist schlecht, hurt bad, sir. She darf nicht leben, may not live."

"Attacked? By what?"

"Nein sir, not by what, by whom. Ve have him, sir. He ist a nachbar, a neighbor to the girl's family. Her name is Pauline. She ist a Weisshaar. His name ist Richard Read, sir, from Kansas."

"You have him, you say?" I put my badge on the outside of my jacket and check my guns while he speaks, my eyes never leaving his face.

"Ya sir. Wir haben ihn gefunden, ve found him easy enough. He vas hiding like a hase, a rabbit. The men haf him at Bauder's barn. Wir müssen uns beeilen! Ve need to hurry, sir. I believe they nicht warten, vill not wait long."

"Wait?"

"Ya sir. I believe they vill handle this als Gemeinschaft, as community. I haf advised them to Folge dem Gesetz, follow the law and vait for your arrival. Sheriff Ruberson, sir, ve need to schnell gehen, to hurry!"

Reverend Adolf had more color in his face now, but his breathing was ragged. I was concerned for he was not a young man and obviously very distressed. I feel his urgency in the way my heart hammers in my chest. His need shortens my breath.

"We'll take my buggy. My horse is fresh. Deputy La Selle will care for yours until we return. Is that agreeable?"

"Ya bitte, sir. Danke, sir!"

I hand him a tin of water to drink while I hurry over to rouse my deputy who lives nearby. The night air is sweetened with spring damp as we drive away from town north towards Bethune. "Tell me what you can, Mr. Adolf."

"He is a Junggeselle, a bachelor farmer, this Mr. Read. His land lays to the west and sout' of the Weisshaar's. He has familie, a sister and her husband who live norden, north. The A. A. Warners. Gute folks, keep a gute farm. Ve haf not had any problems in the past, though wir bleiben getrennt, ve keep separate."

"Of course," I say, understanding the isolation of the Settlement folks even as the lands filled up around them; especially now with war sentiment turning neighbors into political enemies. His head drops low on his chest, turning from side to side as though to shake off an internal image.

"Pauline, mein Gott!, she iss hurt mighty bad. Like an animal, a wolf! She vas kühe hüten, herding the family's cows while the rest vere busy wit visiting and helping their nachbars, their neighbors the Bauders. The cows come home. No Pauline. They find her, the kinder did. In the dark, they find her. If they hadn't she surely würde sterben, vould haf died. She still may." He pauses, his head lowering further into hands which scrub his face, remembering sweet Pauline as a babe and a little girl; knowing so well how her life has been crushed today.

"Was Pauline," I paused, not knowing quite how to phrase the question, "acquainted with this Read man?"

"Nein! Nicht erlaubt! It vould not haf been allowed! Verboten! "

"And you are certain this is the man who hurt her? You are certain?"

"Sind sicher! We are certain!" Mr. Adolf is gathering his strength and his voice has become harsh, no longer desperate. His rage grows as we travel closer to his flock. I feel him trembling beside me and I feel stinging prickles in my fingertips. A passage from Macbeth comes to mind, 'by the pricking of my thumbs, something wicked this way comes', and I realize what a far distance I have traveled from laughing over watermelon vines.

I will be facing a mob, a mob of men with like minds and a clear purpose. I will be forced to stand on the side of law and that means standing on the side of what is likely a violent, abhorrent man. I will have to face the mob and control it and keep both myself and the prisoner safe back to Burlington. I wish I'd brought a few friends, but perhaps that would only have escalated the anger, increased the danger.

"Mr. Adolf. Sir, I will need your help, please. I will need you to help make it clear that I am protecting your community by taking this man into custody. I do not want any problems, any more than have already happened. Can you assist me in this, sir?"

"Ya bitte! This iss what I desire too, Sheriff Ruberson. This iss why I come for you. I tink they will listen. I do so tink."

A monstrous full moon rides high above us. It climbs into the sky like a cold flame as we turn into the Bauder's farmyard. A blazing fire leaps upward some distance from the barn doors which stand open. A group of men, fifty or more at quick glance, turn our way and then just as quickly turn back to the figure that stands with his arms close to his sides, hands tied behind his back, a rope wrapped around his neck and draped over the doorway beam, just taut enough to skew him slightly. His legs are tied together at the ankles with a leather strap.

I whoa my gelding who has worked hard to get us here so quickly and set the brake. "Mr. Adolf, will you please introduce me to your community?"

He stands, tall and accustomed to command as their church leader, but with respect and humbleness also evident in his bowed head and rounded shoulders. "Freunde, die ich geholfen habe. This is Sheriff J.R. Ruberson. He iss here to help us and to help our poor Pauline." I hear a catch in his voice when he says her name.

A low murmur and the scraping of boots on packed earth meets my ears. I clear my throat as if to help Mr. Adolf and stand on the buggy for a height advantage.

"Gentlemen, thank you for bringing me here. I am going to take this man into custody and place him in the Burlington jail where he will be tried as per law. I am here to do the duty of a county Sheriff and wish to relieve you of the burden you face in bringing justice to your community."

A man standing near to the prisoner grips the end of the neck rope with both hands. He raises his head to me and then lifts his chin to the prisoner. In that brief glance I see a shattered and unwell man, aged from toil and the night's terror. "Vit respect, Sheriff, it iss my daughter who this man hass harmed. Iss it not in my right to satisfy this justice here and now?" An agreeing rumble rises, lifting the hairs on my neck.

I step off the buggy to soften the tension surrounding this crowd. I remove my hat and slap it gently on my leg to dust it. The moon casts a pathway of light so thick I feel it could draw us all into the sky like a rushing river. It shines upon the face of the prisoner, who is weeping and keening in a steady flow of tears and sound.

The Settlement men's faces are cast in shadow from their hats. I smell anger and fear and the fire's smoke, a biting combination that burns high in my sinuses. The father of the ravaged child takes a tighter hold on the dangling rope and a mewling cry comes from the prisoner. There is a saddled horse standing nearby with a youngster holding its halter. I can almost agree the best course of action would be to let the horse lift this criminal into the air until dead. But no, I am sworn to law and law has a process.

"Sir, Mr. Weisshaar, do we need to bring a doctor for your daughter? Do you have someone nearby who could go for help. I am sorry I did not bring a physician with me!"

"Nein. The vomens are caring for her. Ve haf skilled ones here. Ve do not vish outsiders for this."

"Then, sir, Mr. Weisshaar, to answer your question. Your beliefs show a respect for all life and a hope of redemption. If you were to act now, though your actions might seem justified, they would harm you and those of your community. Each man has free will and yes, much badness occurs through misuse of that free will, but I urge you, sir, not to take action tonight which you will regret and for which you and your family might find them-selves punishable."

I hear murmurs and words in German moving through the standing men. I sense a rise and then a subsiding of energy from them. I walk over to the man standing roped and tied. No one approaches.

"Mr. Richard Read. Is this the name you go by?"

When he lifts his head at my question, I see his face is rubbery, slack and loose. His deep set eyes are shadowed, wet and terrified. I smell strong liquor and the foulness of vomit. The rope has burned across one cheek and his neck is raw. There is dry blood on his face and hands. I do not think it is his and this thought generates a strong urge to draw his blood myself.

"Yes... I am... called... Richard." I notice his words come with unusual spacing between them, each distinct and separate from the other.

"I am going to remove this rope from your neck and place handcuffs on you. Do you understand?"

"Yes... I... understand."

"Will you stand quietly now and not bring this mob down upon us both?" I ask this softly so as to keep the men from hearing.

"Yes... I... will stand... quietly."

I begin to wonder if this man has a slowness to him, a deficit in more than moral issues. His keening-hum only stops when he speaks. It grates upon my spine.

With care, I tug at the noose to loosen it and raise it over his head. The man is tall and powerfully built. But he seems as meek as an old plow horse long trained to work.

"Mr. Adolf." I do not turn my head away from the prisoner. "Mr. Adolf, would you and one other man please return to Burlington with me. You can retrieve your horse and assist with assuring we have a safe arrival."

"Bitte. Yes, I vill go. Mr. Dobler vould be a good choice for us." He waves over a young man, built like a brick fireplace, with hands the size of pork butts.

I place my cuffs on Mr. Read's wrists and he shuffle walks to the buggy. I ask Mr. Adolf to drive the horse while Mr. Dobler and I sit on either side of our prisoner in the rear of the buggy. I have tied a rope from his ankle strap to the buggy box to assure he will not jump, or if he does, will find himself being dragged behind us. He continues his wavering sounds, tears running freely. His odor is hot and metallic, as if wires have scorched.

Before I get in next to him I speak once again to Mr. Weisshaar and address the others. "I will return tomorrow to get details of what has occurred here today. A trial will be held speedily. I am assured you will have justice for your daughter, Mr. Weisshaar. I am so very, very sorry your family and community have faced this heinous act. I will do all I can for you! Please give my deepest sympathy to your wife and family."

CHAPTER 32

1916: EDWARD McGINLEY
Thomas County, Kansas

Da is gone. His funeral card reads:
"Old Settler Taken" July 5, 1916
"John McGinley, one of the respected pioneers of Thomas County, passed away at his home a few miles southwest of Colby on Wednesday of last week. Mr. McGinley came to Thomas County thirty years ago and was one of the pioneers that stayed by the country through the lean as well as the prosperous years. He raised a large family and lived to see them take their place in the busy world, and must certainly have been gratified at the success that attended their efforts. John McGinley was well known over the country and none could say ought against him as he met the requirements of a good citizen and neighbor. Friends of the family in this part of the county sympathize with them in their sorrow."
Schroeder's Funeral Card

Da had taken a cough when he was in Colorado, probably from poor nutrition and silica dust. It continued to plague him and he wasted down to a shrunken version of the man we'd been in such awe, and sometimes fear, of. At sixty-five he'd given Kansas and his family everything he'd set out to give. Da and I spoke, finally, at his very last.

In 1902 my world blossomed with love, but at a great cost. Stella Emily Harner, who I called Bess, boarded with my family while she taught school on the north quarter. I had my own place now and was twenty-seven years old; she a sweet eighteen.

Bess came into my life with a jolt. She was dark haired with brown eyes, small boned, soft spoken and refined. I felt my heart plummet and soar. Her smile made me breathless. When she stood near me, just seeing the crown of her head brought such a sense of tenderness and protection I was made a better man. Now I knew how Suzi and Art felt. What Da and Mam had seen in each other so many years past.

Besides her beauty, Bess was clever, smart and spoke well of my new hero, President Roosevelt. We were both Republicans and enjoyed a good debate at the 'literaries' that we attended. She was also a Protestant.

Da blew like a bull and refused to hear of my intentions. I was as good as dead to him. We were married by a Justice of the Peace in Colby. Da shut me out of his life, refusing to speak, calling me a fallen away Catholic not fit to be near.

I was not the last of his children to marry away from the family's faith. Hugh found his match with Ruby Johnson. She, too, was Protestant. Da cast us into a room of silent un-forgiveness and locked the door. Mam, crushed to see her family so mistreated by the only man she'd ever loved, was unable to change his heart.

My home was just a soddy, but Bess didn't mind. She brought joy and light into everything we did. Our firstborn son Donald was joined by Opal the following year.

The soddy filled quickly with the birth of Hazel Evelyn, then by Bertram and Glen Morris. Those first six years flew by with good crops and prices, love making and diapers.

Sadly, for many years Da continued his silent treatment of me though he'd visit with Bess and the kids when he knew I was in the fields. Such a stubborn man. Perhaps he drew lines he was then obligated to stay behind, but it broke my heart to not share my life with him. On the other hand

I was just as stubborn and refused to seek him out, feeling it was his role to 'chance his arm' or offer to make peace.

In 1911 it was so dry we weren't able to plant our wheat. With the drought came hungry jack rabbits that grazed on every living blade like a punishment from God. Rabbit round-ups were arranged, which I found abhorrent, but others believed was great entertainment with concession stands and dances. After one hunt, three railcars were filled with the carcasses of the bludgeoned hares. They were sent east to be ground into tankage. Farmers with hogs and chickens took their share home as feed.

Winter snow and spring rains finally returned, bringing life back to the plains. For Bess the spring of 1913 was tempered by grief over the loss of her father. His mare, usually placid as an old dog, had been one of the many to be hit the year before by an unexplained equine illness that devastated the area. Nearly every farm lost valuable animals vital for cash income and working the land. The sickness drove the beasts wild. Death came quickly to most. There was something about the horse plague that changed the surviving animals, making them untrustworthy and unfit for much labor.

When his mare reared and brought a fore hoof upon Mr. Harner's head, the catastrophic injury turned him into a madman unable to care for his own needs. Eventually Frannie, his wife, shut him up in a shed. When Bess discovered this, she was so horrified at the thought of her father housed like livestock that she asked me to assist her mother. I, caring deeply for my in-laws, did what I could, lifting him and bathing him and restraining him when fits of rage took over. Finally he passed out of his miserable state into eternal peace.

Now, in 1916 Da has passed, too. Seeing the end approaching I chanced my arm and went to his side hours before his death and we spoke for the first time since before my marriage thirteen years earlier. I am not ashamed to say the tears ran heavy from us both, though Da was so short of breath I hated to bring him grief. I felt each of his gasps and wished that by my own strength I could draw air to fill his wracked lungs. We recalled our journey to Kansas, our nights on the prairie as we came to our new home, the risks and the gains. At the end he said as clear as a soldier's command, "Do not lose what I have earned, son. Do not lose it!"

Mam, so broken by life's losses, has joined Alfred to live in a town home in Colby. Bess and I will stay on our own place. Young John remains on the farm and chooses not to marry. Ethel is a teacher and dating. Joe and Tom are sparking the Rowley sisters. Bill has joined the Army and will eventually go to France.

There is a heavy weight upon my shoulders to honor Da's dream. I will do the best I can to pull this load forward in honor of 'Himself'.

CHAPTER 33

1916: ADDISON ALANSON (A.A.) BACON

McDonald, Kansas

If anyone can make something of me, it will be Gladys. She is everything I could hope for but will surely fail to deserve. Her hopes are high though I can't understand why. I've got nothing to stand on but stand I will, if I can, for her sake.

She was a Smith from Cheyenne County and I met her one night at a dance after a week of hardscrabble work on the rail line. I'm not much to look at, pale blue eyes, light colored hair, on the short side with a slim build. I looked at all the real men lining up to whirl the gals and thought I'd be sitting out the show.

Was I ever surprised when this sweet sunflower stepped up and held out her hand like she'd been waiting for me all evening. I was so surprised I looked to my right and to my left to see if she meant someone else. She laughed a tinkling kind of sound and said, "It's just you, boyo! Now are you going to scoot me around the floor or not?"

Well I like to dance and Momma had taught me the basics before I left home, practiced with me till she giggled like a young girl and said I was ready for anyone, but I've not had much opportunity. The band was playing in a nice jumpy way though and I could feel the rhythm sliding through my bones like a good drink, so I took hold, in a gentlemanly manner, of this little sweetheart's hand and off we went onto the dance floor. And as they say on the radio, that's all she wrote!

I could waltz of course, but I knew the two-step and the fox-trot and this little thing kept up with me that whole night. I'd never had so much fun and I was head over heels in love. Never thought it would come my way, I surely didn't.

Gladys was like a turtle that clamps down on something (me!) and wasn't going to let go without her head having to come off. I kind of thought she was off her head to choose me, but she was determined I'm the one for her.

We married. Not long after she set me to learning how to barber since there was a real need in the area, what with all the men who work on the farms and railroad and no other barber in town. She's good at seeing opportunities.

I guess I'm ok at it, the barbering. No one's asked for their money back and I enjoy the visiting, the chatting that goes along with the job. Got a nice little space near Dr. Ott's office so I see the folks coming and going to get medical needs done. I see Mr. Edwin Lyman marching in and out of doors, too, always shaking hands and throwing his arm around the shoulders of someone who is looking mighty interested in what he's saying. Now there's a man who is a winner; no doubts there!

Often, I have time between customers to read the papers and when I hear the folks talk about the ongoing struggles of many I have to wonder who will hold on and who won't. Some seem to be in the right spot and know the right people to get a hand up. Some seem to be on the losing end of the stick, no matter what they try.

Like the widow Hoffenbeck whose only mistake was to marry a man who bought a farm and then died before he had it paid. Now she's destitute, enduring the shame of a sheriff's sale and through no fault of her own. Breaks my heart, it surely does.

Gladys says that's what she loves about me, my tender heart. But she doesn't know how terrified I am that I will fail her, just like Hoffenbeck did his wife. I am afraid I'm the losing kind.

CHAPTER 34

1924: WILLIAM L. THOMAS (1898-1986)

Menlo, Kansas

Pa left when I was three. Ma didn't last long after that. Neighbors took me in and I chored for 'em. At seven I got real work with a rancher and never stopped till I lost my eyes at eighty-six. Thought I'd go mad just sittin' there in the grayish dark with no one to talk to.

Tater Pie was always off tending folks and she weren't used to me hangin' about the house with nothin' to do so she got those talkin' books to occupy me. I liked the romance ones best and that made Tater Pie laugh. After listenin' to a dozen or so, I told Tater Pie that I had a better story to tell. I got a bit of steam in mine, too. She says I'm a feisty old cuss, but I can hear the smile in her voice and I recalled her sparkly eye when she was feelin' frisky.

So here is me and Tater Pie's story.

The oil fields went bust and folks were out of work. Lots of folks. Even the ones willin' to do anythin'. Some crookedness happened in that business, but I weren't smart enough to know what the dirty dealings was. I just figured I'd go home. I'd been roughneckin' it for the last five years, having moved into oil field work after bronc bustin' my way through three ranches in Kansas, two in Oklahoma and finally my last outfit in Texas. That's where I got tied in with the well boys. I started out as a ginzel, the lowest paid and least trained man on the crew and worked my way up to being a worm. Being a bit on the mechanical side it weren't long a'for the toolman moved me into the job of floorhand.

I put back together what the boys tore up. I couldn't do much for the boys what got tored up, though. And man, that was dangerous miserable work. I guess I weren't too unhappy when the job went tits up.

I've always carried gear with me: saddle, blanket, rope, bedroll and my canvas canteen. Oh and my mouth harp kept in a pocket, wrapped in a clean hanky to keep the dust out. I like to breathe a tune of an evening. It helps fill the lonely hours. A horse, good or bad, can be found most anywhere you go.

Didn't need one on the rigs, course. Those boys came and went in wild fashion in their autos. We'd get hauled to a site, start laying out the pipe, raise the derrick and off they'd go, leavin us to make the big boys big money. Everythin' else I owned, I was wearin'. It was simpler for a strong man then. You didn't own and you didn't owe.

Well, like I said, the job were over, I had no place but home to go because no one was hiring.

I got on the train purposin' to see my brother and his wife with their new little baby that was already two-and-a-half and I'd yet to meet her. She was named after our ma who'd passed and I just couldn't wait to get acquainted. Robert had hitched up with his school sweetheart and got into a good spot that way, her daddy being a big wheat farmer and all. He was always on the lookout for the best of everythin' but Robert is good hearted and earned all his licks.

I'm younger by three years and seem to take the hard road ever' time. I recalled once't he pulled me out of a pig wallow where I'd got stuck trying to catch one of the runt pigs thinkin' I'd have me a pet. He said Ma would thrash me good for getting my clothes so dirty, but then he took another look at me and really laughed, cause I had taken 'em off just to keep that from happen'. I never did catch that little pig. He'd squirted out of my hands ever time I got close enough to snatch him. I was chucklin' over that memory as the train left the Texas station and headed north to Kansas.

It were midnight when I stretched my legs and rubbed my back at the station in Menlo. The sky was bustin' with stars and I filled my nose with the damp fresh air. Nowhere else ever smells like home and western Kansas has its own perfume. I left my gear at the depot and walked two blocks to the hotel. The town weren't much changed from what I could see. Dusty streets and grey, wind scrubbed buildings. I noticed the grain elevators glowing in the starlight and towerin' over the rest of the town. Looked like there might be a new one or two, but everthin' else was just like I recalled.

The hotel lobby was quiet and dark with just a bulb hangin' on a twisty wire to light a sign alerting the folks who arrived late which rooms were empty. Moths that came in with me through the screen door thumped on the hot bulb and I hated that I'd let them in. The notice board said "Be quiet when you go up and pay in the morning - we ain't meeting night trains no longer - The Management".

Crossing off a number on the chalk board to show I'd taken that room I climbed the stairs to a hallway of doors, found my room, shucked off my outerwear and went to bed. Early next mornin' I heard some stomping about through the wall beside me, so I figured it was time to get up. The wash basin were full and the towel clean. That weren't always the case in a little town hotel and I 'preciated the kindness. After I shaved and did the best I could washin' off my smelly parts I stepped out the door into the hall and nearly run over the cutest little gal I'd ever seen. She had curls down to her waist and couldn't a weighed a hunner pounds. She was carrying a big pile of wrinkled linens.

I said "Hi, Tater Pie."

She looked up at me and said, "Now who are you?"

I told her I had family here 'bouts and named my brother and his wife. I told her I was going to meet my new little niece before she got growed up and that I'd been in Texas a spell, but was ready to be home now. She walked alongside me as we went down stairs to the dining room and her head wasn't much higher than my elbow. I watched her curls bouncing, shiny as a spring colt and the color of pecan wood. I wanted to lay my hand just under that fall of hair.

She told me her name was Ellen and that she was earning her board by working in the kitchen and that she also worked at the hospital over at the county seat. I'll never forget her soft voice, just full of perk and fun. Bouncy as her curls. She made me mighty glad I'd come home to Menlo.

Breakfast was grab and git what you can. Folks were hungry and it seemed there was just enough to go round. I finished fast, hardly tasting my food. Risen' from my chair, I gathered up any used and empty dishes. I found Tater Pie, (I kept thinking 'bout her that way: sweet and good for you), in the kitchen leaning into a deep tub of suds.

"Let me give you a hand," I said.

She turned her head, little curls of hair all around her face specklin' with steam drops, and reached a forearm up to brush it away from her eyes. Even with a load of plates and bowls balanced in my hands, I almost tried to help her. I wanted to touch her so bad!

"Well, ain't you the helpful one! I don't know if I ought to let you back here in the kitchen with me... but Mrs. is gone for the morning, so I 'spose she'll never know. Just don't bust nothin'!"

I set the dishes I had down on the collectin' table and saw how she scraped them in a scrap bucket underneath before putting them in the sudsy water. I went right to work, having done plenty of dishes in cow camps. I didn't mind washing up. I always liked leaving a place better'n I'd found it. Just somethin' satisfyin' 'bout that.

We chatted awhile, gettin' to know one another. I'd heard of her family name, but didn't know them well. She was the youngest of three girls and her Daddy wasn't about to pay for their weddin's. He'd made it clear they had better carry their own weight 'cause one man could take care of only one female and that was his wife. Ellen laughed when she said that. She loved her Daddy, but "he really only looked after himself and it took all four of his females to keep him out of trouble."

That made me a bit mad, thinkin' how someone as little as Ellen shouldn't have to burn her hands on lye water and scrubbing, but I didn't let on. No need to come between a girl and her Daddy.

They was eighteen boarders at the hotel, some who was staying while they got set up in business or searched for a land deal. A few of the early settlers had given up and were moving back east, others were getting too old to run their homesteads and were looking for a quick sale. Land was trading on both sides of the railroad. Folks was hoppin' in this prairie town. Menlo had just celebrated its first quarter century and feeling mighty big to have lasted so long.

Eighteen boarders meant lots of dishes and lots of cooking. It meant lots of wood hauled to the cooking range, lots of bedding to be washed and lots of sweeping up after. There was a boy to haul the water, but Ellen was busy all the time. I liked working alongside her whenever she'd let me. She was quick and easy with her work. Somehow, just watchin' her scrub the scrap bucket after she'd given the hen flock their share seemed a joy to me. I spent three days at the hotel, until my jingle ran out, just to be with her as long as I could. Then I had to leave for my brother's place, ten miles northeast of town. The mail route man had promised to tell Bob that I was comin'.

"Don't you be forgetting me," I said as I gathered my kit together at the depot. She had walked alongside me to say goodbye.

"I don't believe I will, Mr. Thomas. I don't believe I will." Her gray-green eyes looked deep into mine and I thought I'd never seen such life in anyone.

Then she stood on the toes of her shiny little boots and gave me a sweet kiss on the cheek. I saw several heads turn in our direction, some shaking at her boldness, some with knowing smiles. I touched her cool, smooth cheek with my hardened fingers and felt a tenderness in my gut that nearly brought me to my knees.

She spun about, skirts swishing against my legs in a final farewell, and walked in her brisk manner back towards the hotel. Those shining curls filled my head.

Robert and his wife, Hattie, were set up in a foursquare frame house alongside the Prairie Dog Creek. Wild plums and chokecherry bushes grew thick on its banks. A cottonwood, the trunk split into three sisters, shaded their home from the western sun. All around them were the sloping draws of short buffalo grass that ran southeast towards the creek. They'd done a good job of using brush and branchy logs strung with bob wire to fence the range cattle from around their homestead. I'd passed a well-tended garden near the windmill and saw how the tank overflowed into a trench system. That was just like Robert, take what's there and make it better. I guess Ma gave both of us that lesson during our short time with her.

Their baby girl's name was Addie, just like Ma's, and she was a splinter from the same board. Her dark brown eyes shot fire at me when I came walking into their yard with my saddle over my shoulder and the dust knee high on my trousers.

"Daddy says NO BEGGARS 'LOWED! If'n you want to eat, you's got to work!" She had been trotting a block of wood, shaped something like a pony, along the bottom rail of the yard fence before she'd spied me approaching.

"Hello, Little Bit," I said. "I'm not a beggar. I'm your Uncle Will."

She squealed sharp as a stuck piglet. "Oh, Momma, oh Momma! Come quick. Unca Willum is here!"

From around the corner of the house came Hattie. She'd thickened since I'd seen her last, but it had been almost ten years and I 'spose I'd changed lots, too. I guessed she might be settled with another baby, but I didn't want to say out loud 'til I'd heard it from her or Robert. A woman could get mighty huffy if you pegged that wrong.

I took off my hat and swatted the brim to free the dust. Then I reached down and whacked at my pants' legs to do the same. It didn't help much, but I made the effort. I remembered how Ma just hated the dust that crept into everything, wind or no wind. She wouldn't speak of it, but I'd seen her lips squeeze tight if a visitor failed to brush off his road dirt and came inside with it droppin' off at every move. I was sure, from the looks of things, that Robert's wife kept a clean house.

"Hello, Hattie. Robert around?" I didn't want the discomfort of a woman alone to mar our reunion.

"Well, for Heaven's sake! Come in, come in! I'm sure you've walked all day to get here and you must be worn to a nubbin." Her smile was full and sincere. "I've got some fresh coffee made, thinkin' you might be here 'bout now and supper'll be set on the table 'for long. Bob will be along any minute. Our milk cow just freshened and he's trying to settle her into the routine. She's a wild thing." Hattie's hands wrung her apron and her head dropped a bit as she spoke. "I don't know how I'll ever get her milked, but come harvest time, I'll have to do it. Bob'll be too busy in the field and I guess I'll just have to manage."

She was talking and moving so fast that I was a bit reluctant to follow her inside. I'd got so used to the quiet while walkin' to their farm that it took me a moment to switch into all this activity. I felt like I'd gone from workin' a plow horse to a newly broke colt. Addie eased her way past me into the house and then ran for her mother's skirts. She poked the head of her wooden horse around first, to test for danger, and then she looked at me with round eyes. Her boldness was gone now that her Momma was near.

I suddenly saw myself, my own home and my own child, with dear little Ellen waiting on me to come in for supper and I felt a hunger for something I'd never tasted. It pained me not to turn right back to town and gather her into my arms.

Robert hallooed from the yard, milk pail sloshin' in his hand.

"William! Oh my dear brother! Gosh, it's been a coon's age. Look at you! I can't believe what a man you've grown up to be!" Robert was grinning fit to bust.

He set the milk pail down and we hugged. I don't know that I've ever been so close to tears and my throat ached like a fist had a holt of it. We'd always been close. Ma had kept us friends, even when we tried to beat on each other like brothers will. She'd told us, "You boys only got each other and me. And someday it'll just be each other." I think she always knew she'd not live long. After Pa left us to follow the corn harvest and never came back, she'd started to shrink. Inside and out. Whenever my mind turned to Pa, I only recalled a large hand cradling the back of my head. Robert remembered him better, but he couldn't figure out what had kept Pa from comin' home. I think he'd blamed hisself for not being a better son to Pa and had always tried to make up for it. Since I'd been on the road from age 13, I knew how many things could happen to a man. I meant to try to tell him this, if I could.

"Golly, Robert. Look at this place! You've got it all. A beautiful wife, a little punkin' girl smilin' up at you, stock, crops, everything. I'm mighty proud of you!" I meant every word I said. I also wanted the same thing, though five days ago I had no idea this was my dream.

"Hattie, I smell chicken. Am I right?" Robert was grinning at his wife with pride and confidence.

"Well, old Mr. Rooster that's been waking us so early won't be crowing tomorrow." She laughed as she said it. "We've got some early garden goods and nice biscuits. I think I've got a jar of plums left from last fall if you and William will go to the cellar for them. Give that milk pail over and I'll get it strained. There'll be sweet milk to wash down that chicken." I think she needed her space just as much as we did. It was thick with feelin' in that small room.

Robert led me to a storm cellar dug into a bank. "We lived in this awhile when we first married. Don't know how we did it, but it sure was cozy. I think Addie likes to play in here 'cause this is where she got her start." The wooden stairs were soft with damp and cobwebs made the dirt walls fusty, though the floor was swept clean and the shelves built solid. I saw bins for potatoes and pumpkins, but most everything was empty waiting for this year's harvest of garden crops. A few canned beets and pickles stood alongside the fall plums. Dim light from the ground level doorway shown purple and pale green on the glass canning jars. I suddenly recalled the moist heat from Ma's big canner as she pulled a jar of precious food from it with her tongs. It was a memory of both security and fear; knowin' we had this much to eat, but not enough for the winter ahead.

"You doin' all right, Robert? You have enough?" I felt the pinchin' of an empty stomach both past and present. It had been a long walk from town and I hadn't had much appetite at breakfast, my last one with Ellen. I remembered how long the dark days of late winter were before the early spring crops had started coming in; when Ma had been frantic to feed her boys.

"Call me Bob, Will. Ever one does now. Oh, we're great! It makes all the difference to be part of Hattie's family. They're real well off. They're real generous too. I feel good about what we're doing. Every year gets better. Next winter we'll have our second baby, if God is willing. We're talking about building onto the house. We'll need the space. Will,

I'm so glad you're here! Can you stay? We've got room in the cow barn for you, if you don't mind bunkin' with the stock. I could sure use a hand if you can stay on a while. There's always more work to get done in a day than there are hours. Hattie's folks even asked if you thought you might settle back in your home town. They think a lot of me and I told 'em you work even harder than I do. Can you stay?"

"Whoa, Bob." It was hard to give up my habit of calling him by his given name and I stumbled a bit. "Brother, I got nowhere to go and I'm in no hurry to get there. I'm so happy to see you in such a good state. Sure, I'll help out. Whatever you need, I'll stand by you. I've seen enough country for a lifetime and none of it looks as good as right here in this county. For the first time I feel like I'm home and I like this feelin'. To tell the truth, Robert... Bob... well, I met my own little gal this week."

"William L. Thomas! What are you tellin' me?"

"At the Menlo Hotel...I met her the mornin' I come in. She's the cutest little thing you ever saw. Her name's Ellen Rains. You know the family? She's the youngest of three girls and she's a hard worker. She's holdin' two jobs and talkin' about being a nurse. She'll do it, too. She's that kind of go- getter!"

"Will, I couldn't be happier for you. I know just what you're thinkin', too. Its how I felt and still feel about Hattie. The day's brighter, somehow, than before. Well, dadgum it! We got to git you your own place soon as we can. I got some ideas you might like, too."

Bob took the plums down and put his arm around my shoulder. "Baby brother, I got some big ideas!"

It was 18 months before I saw Ellen again. Bob got me working with Hattie's father and there was no end to his jobs. When I'd pull in for an evenin' to wash and swallow supper, hardly drawing a breath, it'd be time for Bob and me to work on his place.

First we built an add-on to the east side of their house, a room that would hold the new baby and Addie's bed with space for more when they came. We used sod for the walls up to the window height and it was a tight room with nice morning light. Bob and Hattie's bed was just on t'other side of the dividin' wall so they could hear the little ones easy if they fussed at night. I liked that idea and put it down on the notepad where I was keepin' all my dreams for me and Ellen's home.

The summer months kept us away long hours, Bob especially, 'cause he was in charge of plantin' the corn and keepin' it cultivated. He'd come home covered everwhere with dust 'cept the whites of his eyes and the circle of lips where he'd been lickin' them.

I rode fence lookin' for breaks and moved the cows and calves from graze to graze. It'd been a wet spring and the grass was thick. In Texas I had learned about keeping the herd together so they didn't spread out and take only the best grass. This way they had to grub down half of everthin' before I'd let 'em move to the next patch. It kept the pastures fresh. By the time we came back to a spot, the good grass had recovered and gone to seed, assurin' there'd be more next year.

Mr. Schmidt liked the idea and sent extra riders out to help me get the herd trained. After a week, the cows seemed to understand and stayed in a bunch. Then I could relax and dream about me and Ellen's fine herd that we'd build a few head at a time.

The wheat crop was good. Heavy yields and no rain to spoil it. A threshing crew came in with their big machines. I got to visiting with those boys, learning the ways of a harvest crew that went from farm to farm, how the divi-ing up was handled, how much for the farmer, how much for the crew boss, how much for the labor. The crew boss liked my interest and showed me the figures in a little black book he kept to record all the pertinents.

One fellow, a man who was a hell of a worker but stayed off by hisself at meals and water breaks, caught my eye. I noticed he was always a'hummin under his breath, a sound sort of like wind in the grass or through a window screen at night. I saw him watchin' when I'd pull out the mouth harp and play a few tunes after dinner. I saw his fingers tappin with the notes, his head down-facing but turned so that his ear were directed towards where I sat. I made it a point to set down near where I thought he'd take his spot. We became sort of partners on the job, just natural like, without either of us saying we would do so.

The crew boss called him Rich, but no one really spoke to him, or he to them. His deep set eyes would now and again meet mine, but then slide off liken he were afraid of what he'd see reflected. I allus tried to meet his looks with a smile. Figured everone needs a little friendly.

I was made to be the grain wagon driver. When one were filled, I'd head to town to unload the grain at the elevator. I hauled wagon after wagon to Menlo, but I never could meet up with Ellen. The hotel owner told me she were taking nursing classes back east; that she were one of their best students ever. I were sure proud of her. I tried to send her letters, gave them to the minister to give to her mama at Sunday services, but I don't think she was gettin' them or else she couldn't get an answer back to me. I missed her fierce and had to keep remindin' myself that I'd only spent three days with her and didn't have a claim. But my heart wouldn't listen.

Hattie's new baby, born right before Christmas, were a boy, red faced and fat as a gourd. I started callin' him Dipper, 'cause he'd tuck his chin down just before he'd start squallin'.

I'd say "look out, the little Dipper's fixin' to holler" and sure enough, he gave good warnin' ever' time. Hattie were doing all right by him, but she seemed to lose a pound for ever' one he gained.

I tried to get most of the mornin's small chores done afore we'd leave for the job while Bob took care of the big stock: milk the cow by lamp light, turn the hens out to scratch and haul water to the stock what couldn't reach the windmill tanks, but I knew she only sat down when the baby wanted to feed. Addie were big enough to help and I made sure she knew what could lighten' her Momma's load. She always did her jobs and tried to do extra. I looked at her little self, stretching to reach something or pulling hard on the chore cart and tears filled my eyes.

"Your grandma Addie would'a been so proud of you!" I told her. "You make me remember her more all the time."

One morning real, real early there came from the corrals a terrible commotion. Bawlin' calf and momma cow bellerin' like I imagined a dinosaur might sound. I didn't bother to pull on pants, just shoved my cold boots onto bare feet and ran out, meeting Bob in the same state of undress. He'd grabbed his .30-06 Springfield and a lantern. I had my Eveready and an ax.

Eyes flashed green in our lights. The momma cow was circling and throwing her head at some varmint while her newborn calf stumbled about wet and wobbly. "I got him in my light, Bob. You take a shot when you can!" A poor coated coyote crouched low, its glaring eyes locked in the beam. White foam flew from its snapping snout. "Bob, that's a mad one there. He'd of run off by now otherwise! Shoot him clean and quick. I've seen plenty of hydrophobe in the south. It's a terrible thing!"

Bob fired true and the mangy beast jerked high in the air before landing on the hard earth. The cow and calf had moved off to the far end of the pen and momma was licking her new one steadily. "Don't touch it bare handed. I'll pull on my pants and get a shovel. We need to burn the carcass." I felt the cold night wind drying my sweat. "Stay put just a bit, Bob, so's nothing comes close to it. I'll start a fire in the fire ring, but we'll want to bury it deep after. Man, I am sure afraid of that hydrophobe!"

"Whew! What a thing! That's some good advice and I'm mighty glad you were on hand to help. You've a clear head in tough times, William. I'll tell you, I'm shakin' like a weak kitten right now!"

"Sometimes you just got to act, Bob. I've seen men who froze up and I've seen men who can't make a decision, but there's times you just got to act. Hydrophobe's one of those times."

CHAPTER 35

1924: RICHARD READ

Rexford, Kansas

On July 2, 1922 I step off the train in Rexford. I don't expect I'm welcome, but I have nowhere else to go and the Pen did the arranging when they told me I'd done my time. I won't say the last years have been easy, but they've been no harder than what I'm used to. I'm as strong as ever and they give me a set of clothes to go home in.

In just a bit of time, stepping along the storefronts of town I decide folks must not have known where I've spent the last six years. I got greeted just like usual with no more side-eyed looks than what I'm used to. In fact, when I passed by the newspaper office, Mr. Gillispie, the editor, welcomed me back to town. I guess he's thinking I've been on the Colorado farm all this time. Last I'd seen him I was delivering some potatoes from there. I'm not surprised Father hasn't told folks about what happened. Sure not something he could brag on.

I was going to walk to the home place, but a neighbor saw me on the road and gave me a ride in his Model T. I'd not ridden a country road in one before and was surprised at how wild it was, lurching back and forth across the ruts.

I likely smelled a bit from my travels or maybe it was the suit I'd been given when I left the Pen, but Mr. Claar seemed ill at ease. I tried hard not to hum the way I do, but the more worried folks get the more it oozes out of me. He quit asking questions pretty quick and just said "Give your ma and dad a hidy-ho for me. Tell them good luck on their harvest."

Father and Mother did not expect me. Mother's expression was forlorn. She stood on the porch, her hands rising and falling like she wasn't sure what to do with them. Her mouth was twisty and her eyes full of tears.

I felt the lack of welcome from Father right off. Father said, "We've not got much use for you here. I hear there's jobs in the western part of the county for someone to work on a threshing crew."

So after a couple of days I took my kit and went on my way, leaving the suit behind. I went from job to job and as one finished another opened up. I didn't mind sleeping rough. It felt good not to have walls around me and eyes on my neck all the time. I didn't come home again until the corn crops were done and winter cold settled solid.

Not long after I got home, Art came from Colorado. He'd left Sarah Lou on their place like always. I'd hoped to see her and the small ones. It was just after Thanksgiving. He took me aside and spoke pretty straight. "Rich, your Colorado land went to the Weisshaars' for what you done to their girl. Your dad made the deal and that's all I know. Far as I can tell, you got nothing to work with and no one wants you botherin' them. The farther away you stay from your folks and kin, the better we'll all feel. Good lord, man! Didn't they break that damn humming while you was in the joint?"

I didn't have a thing to say to Art. I'd of left that day, but until winter broke I needed a place to sleep. My lean-to behind the barn was about how I'd left it. Someone had brought my things from the Colorado soddy and piled them in the corner. There wasn't much I cared about except my music box. I cried silent listening to those beautiful sounds.

For Mother I chopped wood and broke ice and fed stock. It was easy to see what needed done around the place. There weren't so many pigs now and Mother's flock of hens was a size she could manage.

It was terrible how she'd changed. She had peeled down to bone and stretched skin during the six years I'd been gone. She was as shriveled and droughted out as the land. She'd lost so many teeth her cheeks were drawn in like she'd sucked chokecherry juice. I watched the way she walked stiff and bow legged, taking careful steps like she feared sudden pain or a fall. It was sad, the way Father and Kansas had used her up.

Soon as winter gave up its hold and the ground could be worked Father gave me one of the English Bull pups he had raised. I think it was his way of sending me off. "Here, boy. Train this pup up right. Maybe he can keep you out of trouble."

I tucked the little guy into my denim chore-coat pocket, put a bundle behind my saddle and rode south towards Oklahoma. Butch and I would catch up with spring and then follow it north. He and Rowdy, a horse Father let me take, were fine and quiet company. I liked the feel of pup flesh under my palm as we rode together.

I joined up with a crew in Texas. We moved from place to place, running the sheaves of wheat through our machines to separate the grain from the straw. It was work that suited me. There was so much noise I didn't have to talk to folks and the boss appreciated my strength.

By late July we'd gotten into Kansas and were working for a man north of Menlo. This was a farm not too far from home. No one knew me, though. I was careful not to get too friendly.

A real kind fellow sort of paired up with me. He had a mouth harp that he could play fine and I was drawn to the nice sound. He wasn't pushy or nosy. He nodded at me when I sang along, as though he was ok with the partnering. I liked working alongside him, he gave a good day's work, and I was sorry when that job was done.

After that I went by the home place thinking they could use a hand but saw that John and the rest of the boys had come to help Father and Mother bring in the wheat. Some of girls with their kids were there, too. I stayed just one night and kept my distance. The next day I moved on north again, rejoining the crew I'd signed on with.

There were some rough boys on the harvest crews. More than me had been in the big house at one time or another. I stayed clear much as I could; hating the times we had to hole up while waiting for a rain to pass.

Liquor was more plentiful than water. At nearly every farm some fellow showed up peddling a trunk full of bottles. I had a taste for it. It was best if I could get a bottle and hide out. I had visions when I'd had too much and spells where things happened I had no memory of. Once I started a bottle, though, I couldn't quit till it was gone. I heard voices and songs and traveled down roads that weren't there when I came back to myself. Sometimes I woke to Butch's whimpers of hunger, knowing I'd been away somewhere for too long. I'd tell him I was sorry, that I wouldn't do it again, but I knew I was lying.

Early winter, when the corn crop was mostly in, I met up with a crew that had been through Colby. One skinny old coot kept watching me, like he knew me from somewhere. When he heard my name, he asked me, "You one of the Rexford Reads? I met your brother. I think, it was... Joe? You got a brother Joe Read?"

"I... do."

"Well, by gum! He told me he's moving to California and the other brother, John I think he said, was heading to Ioway. Sounds like the Read family is scatterin' like BBs from a broken shell."

I knew George was still in Republic City, working in a store. I wondered who was helping out Mother. So I made my way back and got home after the first of the year, 1924.

For the first time I think Father was glad to see me, but all he said was, "Pup sure turned out nice. Well Rich, we could use some help around here and that's a fact."

Then he headed off to town to put an ad in the paper for auctioneering again. I was back to being his unpaid hand, but he'd called me by name.

CHAPTER 36

1931: EDWARD McGINLEY

Thomas County, Kansas

Most of my family are living nearby; those who have not passed. In 1920 Hugh, Joe and Tom returned to Thomas County from Nebraska. Hugh and Joe settled on farms near Levant and Tom took up a plumbing business in Colby. Brother Elmer, who'd become a butcher in Sterling, Colorado comes to visit often, but his home is now east of the Rockies.

In '24 my sister Minnie lost her husband Clarence to cancer. They had been farming in Missouri when the illness took him. I drove to bring her and her six children home to Colby where they settled in as best as they could under tough circumstances.

That same year Opal, our oldest girl, married Cleo Miller. They got right to work having babies of their own, making Bess and me grandparents. Imagine!

Hazel caught wedding fever and found a strong husband in the son of the longtime Colby merchant James Donelan – a good Irish family we've known since coming to Kansas. Hazel was welcomed into their clan with warmth.

As time does its work, babies are born and the old folks pass. Mam's health failed the year after Hazel's marriage and she left this earth in 1926. Her kind and gentle hand had nurtured three generations with grace and love. The Church, while defining much of her life, never created barriers with any of her children whether they stayed in the faith or not. Instead, her beliefs allowed her to find goodness and forgiveness in all things. She was only sixty-eight, but had weathered much in those years. She lies next to Da in the Catholic Cemetery and I have no doubt he met her in Heaven with a twinkle in his blue eyes.

Our son Don stays on the farm and is a valuable ox of a man, standing over 6 feet and heavier than any of the other children. Bert and Glen school in Levant, staying with their Uncle Hugh and Aunt Ruby. Hugh has continued to be a cheerful, pleasant natured man and the boys find him full of wild antics.

When they come home for visits, Bess says "Don't tell me those things, boys. You know how I worry!"

Billy, born so late after Glen, who we'd thought was our last, is only six and a pistol of a boy. His favorite pastime is racing his pony along the ditch to match its pace with any auto that goes by. The roads are being paved at a steady rate, giving some folks good cash-paying jobs, but taxes rise every time I turn around.

Everyone wants improvements, but those don't come free. Landowners take the brunt. Seems the farmer is getting squeezed from all directions. Between the loans I took out a few years ago, property taxes rising and dropping grain prices we are struggling!

Bess tucks her arms around my middle and once again I look down on her dear head, greying a bit, but still my own sweet lady. She says, "Ed, I don't need anything but you and my children to be happy. No matter what happens, I'm content to be with you. We have so much to be proud of. What happens next is not through any fault of yours. Don't carry your father's guilt on your head."

I shudder with an intake of breath. She knows me so well. She knows that as the eldest son, the weight of my Da will never leave. I am glad he is not here to see these changes. Even though this looks like progress I fear something will give. I fear it will be the landowners who will go down first.

In a moment of desperation I file for the position of sheriff. When I tell Bess of my decision, she beams, "You are perfect for the job, Ed. Born to it!"

I feel a thrilling mixture of excitement and trepidation at the image of wearing a badge and representing the legal authority for Thomas County. I am stirred by the thought of stepping into the role of my old hero, Buffalo Bill Cody, long forgotten these many years.

CHAPTER 37

1932: JENNIE LUCILLE WEAVER HUNTER
Selden, Kansas

"What do you think about the new factory in Colby?" Mae asks as she scrubs the bean pot with a wire brush. "Scorched beans are pure devilment," she scolds gently, the flesh under her arms tight from her vigorous rubs. "I'm sorry about that pot, Mae. I was hanging clothes and let it burn dry. Sure caused a stink in the kitchen!" Jennie smiles wanly at the recent small disaster. "What factory?" Her hand absently rubs the tired muscles in her lower back. It aches all the time from this pregnancy, her fifth in under ten years.

She is glad her 'baby' sister had time to stop by this evening. Mae was one of Momma's second set of twins but where both of the first had lived, Mae's birth-mate Helen Marie had died when the cord strangled her. Mae carries a bit of loneliness with her and Jennie knows how important their sisterhood is to them both.

The Weaver girls are vivacious, folks say. Mae is especially pert and always boosts Jennie's spirits. Jennie hasn't felt too attractive lately. Mae has promised to give her a shampoo and set when the babies are in bed and she is looking forward to some pampering.

Dale Dean, typically an exuberant four-year old, has a spring ear ache and has been fretful and feverish since Tuesday. He sits on Jennie's lap, sucking a thumb noisily. He's old for thumbs, but Jennie is too tired to try to fight him about it. She sets him down and raises herself with a grunt. Dean starts to whimper, but she hushes him softly. "Here, little pup… let's put you in the scuttle near the stove. The heat will help your ear." She dumps the last of the coal dust into the range and swabs the blackness out with a sheet of newspaper then lines the bin with fresh sheets, making a nest for the little boy. Placing Dean's rump into the base she watches him curve his back into the scuttle's tapered front and rest his head against the wooden handle. His eyes, shiny with fever, droop half closed in minutes.

Mae answers, "The new egg cracking factory. The paper claims 30 girls will be working there when it opens. I heard tell 20,000 eggs are going through that place the first month. Gracious, I didn't know we had that many hens in the country."

Jennie brushes supper's biscuit crumbs from her bosom. She sees how stained and thin her apron is and thinks about cash money for things. A job cracking eggs all day sounds peaceful. She imagines herself sitting on a tall stool, eggs rolling past while she and the other women chatter about their families; how a paycheck would buy all those nice things they'd done without. Well, she thinks, taking a deep breath, it won't be me there. Who would run the house and children? Mothers don't leave their babies. She unties the apron ribbons from below her swollen breasts. What has happened to her? Just yesterday it seems she'd been a school girl with nothing to fret about except spelling.

"Do you know anyone who'd work there?" Jennie asks, toweling the shiny bean pot dry and hanging it above the range.

"There's talk all over, but most of it is just talk. Mercy sakes, can you imagine how the men would holler if supper wasn't hot and ready on the table when they stomp in? Maybe some of the single girls will sign up. I'm sure their families could use the extra."

"Do you think the price of eggs will climb? I could keep back some of this spring's hatch and raise more pullets than

I usually do. That old shed would hold a few more hens. Alice is a big help with the chicken chores." Jennie takes a damp cloth from the sink, swipes down the worn oak table, dries it well and settles a yellow rose print tablecloth over it. Crumbs from supper are swept into a dustpan. Having Mae with her has halved the work and conversation makes the cleanup hardly noticeable.

Jennie pours weak coffee from the glass percolator into her cup and sits at the table again. Springy wisps of hair frame her smooth face. All the Weaver girls have good hair and her little ones are following suit. She can't wait to enjoy a good scalp massage from Mae.

"I suppose everyone is thinking the same thing and we'll have a scarcity of fryers and a glut of eggs that no one will pay for. Sister, I don't think anything we do in this little town is going to make much money. You are blessed with a hard working husband. He's got that good job with the Highway Patrol, after all! That's about all a girl can hope for. That and health!"

Mae has her eye on Julius Diederich who has a steady job with the city, but she's in no hurry to tie herself down. Mae knows how to enjoy life and Jennie admires her for that. Being married at sixteen sure tied her down in a hurry, but once she met Lloyd there was no waiting.

"You're right, Mae. Things are going to be pretty bad, worse than we've ever seen I'm afraid, if this drought doesn't end soon. Old Mr. Hotchiss said he'd read in the Almanac the worst is yet to come. Can it get worse?" Jennie reaches down to place her hand on Dean's forehead, gauging his fever. His skin is damp and seems a bit cooler, thank the Lord.

She sips the tepid coffee. She hates to imagine worse times. All the town businesses rely on farmers doing well. That trickles down to those who work for the businesses, too. There is nothing else much to count on. Everything they have comes from their own efforts. The Hunters and

Weavers are hard working families, but nothing can grow without rain. It has been a dry winter, with just a few spring showers to sweeten the air, and the winter wheat looks grey and shriveled in even the best fields. Drifts of dust, soft and fine as China silk, pile against the barns and yucca plants. Snow fences, meant to slow the blizzards, have caught blowing dirt instead. Despite daily dusting the house is fuzzy every morning.

Mae sighs and says, "Well, the sunsets have been mighty red. We'll just have to see what the Lord provides and make do. Just like always." Shaking her head gently, she changes the subject. "Where are Alice and Dorothy? Shouldn't they be giving you a hand?"

"I've quit trying to get Dorothy to do inside work. It is just not worth the fight. She doesn't like outside work much either, but at least I don't have to listen to her pitiful moans and sighs if she's outside. That child thinks she was born into the wrong family, thinks she's a European princess or should be a pampered young actress in California." Jennie chuckles at the thought of her precocious eight year old and continues to speak.

"Oh, I let them go to the program in Colby: Edna 'The Kansas Wonder Girl'. You know, the one who claims to be a psychic? They went with the Muellers. Mrs. Mueller bought two extra tickets as birthday presents for the girls and I just didn't have the heart to say no. Dorothy was so excited! She is just sure this is her chance to find out her destiny. That's the word she used…'destiny'! What a child!"

Mae's expression hardens and then softens again as she looks at her sister. "My! That is a treat for the girls, though I hope such foolishness doesn't make Dorothy any more feather-headed." Mae knows how challenging Dorothy has been for Jennie and Floyd to raise. As soon as she could talk she spoke her dreams of flash and glitter. From being a tiger trainer in a circus, to having a chariot drawn by six white horses, her imagined life was more real to her than the hand me down dresses she hated to wear. "She'll likely come home quoting some extraordinary prognostication. There are times I almost believe her when she claims fame is in her future, she's so sure of herself. "

"It's true, so true. We get a kick out of her imagination and no doubt she'll outgrow it soon enough. Life will ask enough of her without me pushing. In time we all face reality and if she's lucky it won't come as too much of a shock. I'm sure someday she'll find a good husband and have a bundle of children to love and that will be enough for her."

"You are such a good mama! Maybe now that she's finished third grade and learning to read so well, she'll find her adventures in books. The Colby library is putting in some new sections for young readers. I'll take her as soon as I can. We can make a day of it and go to the Lyric for a show. I saw in the paper that a Jean Harlow movie will be playing next week, but I'm sure that wouldn't be suitable. Something else will come along soon. It would please me to have a special day with her."

"You're a dear, Mae. I'm so glad you can visit and lend a hand! I don't know what I'd do without you." Jennie's eyes shine with tears of exhaustion and gratitude. She reaches out to hug her sister, but has to turn to the side because of her bulging front and they both laugh, lightening the suddenly heavy mood.

CHAPTER 38

1925 -1932: RICHARD READ

Prairie Dog Creek

The world is changing around me. The old ones are dying; those tough men and women who knew me as a boy, the friends of my parents. "ANOTHER PIONEER GONE" reads the headline in the Rexford News. I see Mother and Father sliding into the ground soon, too.

In January 1925 Father convinced Mother to take the train with him to Catalina Island. The sunny coast of California! They invited Edmee to go along and she jumped at the chance. They stayed about a month and when they returned Sarah Lou came to hear their travel stories. There's talk that Joe and his wife are homesick and want to return to Kansas.

With all the visiting back and forth it's up to me to keep the farm going for Father. The wheat harvest was very good and I knew every acre like my own hands. I'd worked them, planted them and repaired the 'combine' that Father had bought last season. A machine that cuts, threshes and bins the grain, combines have replaced many of the harvest crews, putting men out of jobs. In the cities it is real tough, we've heard.

Now that the crop is in the bin, Father fumes at the prices. His face goes dark when he compares this year's price to that of the high just five years ago.

"Almost half value, but my costs haven't dropped, no siree! No call for this! No call at all! People still eat bread, don't they?"

I'd heard Mother tell Tim that a loan had paid for the combine. That meant a mortgage, she said. Their faces were long and they shook their heads together like sheep.

When the elevator in town burned, Father and the other owners had taken a bad hit. He's out of that business, but the damage was done. He always thought someone set that fire out of jealousy. He carries that anger like a rough stone to rub and polish at will.

Father 'lent' me out with the combine to cut a few of the neighbors' fields. He got some cash for my work with a promise for the rest to come after their grain was sold. Every day that the price drops means a year's effort loses value and he expects some of his due won't get paid.

Art had done what he promised and opened the Warner Store on a crossroads next to their place. Sarah Lou does the orders and accounts while keeping house and farmyard. Art has always worked hard at looking busy, but Sarah Lou has the backbone that all his dreams need.

Everyone agrees that this should be a big Christmas, now that Joe and Hannah are moving back to Kansas, leaving California to be with their families.

*****

Christmas Day the table is full. It is the first time that all of Mother and Father's children have been together in twenty-five years, or so I hear as I bring fire wood in and carry out ashes. It is a cold December and I have cut a good supply for the stoves, though with all the cooking and water for baths, the pile is dwindling fast.

Faces look up when I enter the house, but quickly drop back to their noisy conversations. Joe tells of the new place he's bought from Cal Fringer, how he's glad it is so close to the folks 'so he can watch out for you better' and his two children can help Mother in the garden . Villa has come from Ft. Morgan, Colorado where she describes irrigation channels that water acres of potatoes, onions and carrots from the Rocky Mountain snowmelt. Attie left Oklahoma early to be here to help Mother get the house ready and she bustles about refilling water glasses and carrying dirty plates to the sink. George is here from Franklin, Nebraska, and John from Father's old hometown of Gladbrook, Iowa. Edmee brings love from all the folks in Republic City.

Tim and Joe have been back and forth all week from their homes in Rexford giving me instructions on what to bring in from the smokehouse and root cellar. I'd helped Tim do some butchering early in the fall to have plenty of smoked pork for the meals.

Not all the husbands and wives could come for this gathering. Some of the grandchildren stayed back, too. This is something that has given Mother great pleasure, to have all her children around one table again. I see her looking younger and happier than she has in years.

Mother says as she passes me at the woodpile, "Rich, I'll bring your plate out soon as we've all had dessert and coffee. Looks like there's plenty of extras."

*****

April 1927 the skies have turned black with blowing dust. There is so much electricity in the air that folks drag chains behind their cars to keep them from stalling. There have been several suicides blamed on the unnatural heat and never ending dirty winds. Things are worse than 1912-1913, the old-timers are saying. Of course, in those years the whole prairie hadn't been turned upside down and cultivated to pieces.

Father turned seventy-seven this year and put on a boast for the paper about how he shucked 40 bushels of corn in six hours. I know the truth of it, but he needs his glory. It hurt him real bad that his auctioneering days ended with all those 'upstarts' taking his place. His glory years are behind him but he won't admit it.

In '28 Joe's wife became the family's poultry gal. Everyone is looking for a way to make some cash. She's incubating chicks for herself and a bunch of customers. Her favorites are the golden colored Buff Orpington breed. She says they are so quiet they could be pets. They lay well in winter and the cockerels make a solid meal. Real dual purpose, she says. She has me deliver cardboard boxes of the day-old peepers to nearby farms and gives me a few dollars for gas.

I like driving around the country in Father's sedan. I like seeing the roads that run seeming without end. I especially like the few that curve along the creeks with the pools of shade from overhanging cottonwoods flickering light and dark through my windscreen. I like seeing the different farmhouses and barns that folks have put up over the years. I sip from a bottle and think back over the time I've lived in this country; all the seasons and changes that root me here. I hope rains come soon. I can smell the farmers' desperation.

In August Father takes to his bed for several weeks. He has lost something, like a cornstalk broken at the joint, still showing green, but browning fast. So much dust pneumonia, whooping cough and influenza is in the area, but that's not what took Father down. It was something vital inside of him.

By October he rallies and he and Mother take a trip to visit Sarah Lou. The A.A. Warner Store north of Burlington is barely hanging on during this low time. If possible, it has been even drier in that region. No one even talks about the weather anymore. That alone says how serious things are.

Father has sold most of the pigs. There's no corn raised and the alfalfa fields went dormant and stayed that way. The swine had no value since there's no money and everyone is selling everything they can. We've only kept back enough for the family to use. I work hard on the garden to keep the pumpkins alive for winter feed. Chickens and pigs both enjoy those and they store well.

In January 1930 Joe and Hannah gave up their farm and bought the old Farmers State Bank in Rexford to start a café. They hear all the news as they pour coffee and serve up scrambled eggs from our flock.

The Thomas County Sheriff's race is running hot with several men who've lost their farms and want a steady income. These new made politicians come to the towns, meeting and shaking hands with everyone they can. They put up flyers and head on home. According to Joe, the word is that an Irishman named McGinley has the best chance.

August the town was rocked by a gas explosion. One of the new fueling stations blew and took out several buildings. If the wind had been blowing the other direction, the whole town might have gone up in flames.

So many folks are dying or horribly injured by automobiles. Every week the paper shows another 'gone turtle' event where a rut or a blow out or an unexpected curve in the road sends a vehicle wheels up. Young and old alike are victims. The paper says that this year alone there were 450 deaths in Kansas from autos. Used to be it was horse wrecks. So much is changing.

I have always liked to read the paper. In the evenings when the day's work is done I have a smoke while I read and re-read the Rexford News from front page to last. I do not read quickly, but I remember well.

In January 1931 Governor Woodridge vetoed the Muir Bill. His decision was unpopular. He claimed there was no money to install an electric chair, so there was no reason to have capital punishment. The vote in favor was 28-11, so you know that his name is being drug in the dirt around here. Banks and stores are hit nearly daily by robbers and Father raises his fist at the lack of capture of those 'foreign and criminal types'. I listen to the talk. I don't share my thoughts and no one asks for them, though when the subject gets on to prisons and such I see the side-eyed looks.

March 26 is Mother's 79th birthday. We have a fierce spring blizzard, but her brother Doug from Republic City, Sarah Lou and the girls, Edmee, Joe, Tim, and George are all able to be here to celebrate. Doug slips out to my room behind the barn and gives me a bottle of hootch. He said folks in Republic City are keeping their supply pretty tight. More and more stills have been destroyed. What used to be looked at with a wink and a nod now earn serious jail time and fines.

"Same...thing...'round here...Uncle... Doug. I'll...sip this...real...slow." I struggle to make my tongue work.

"You do that, Rich. I'll stop back in before we leave. Maybe have a snort with you. Are you always out here alone?" He had been a help to me when I lived in Republic City, setting up jobs and making sure I had enough to eat. I thought real well of him and didn't want him to feel sorry for me.

"It... is the... way... I... like things. I... like... quiet. I... don't... mind. No one... to bother."

Uncle Doug raises his hand to pat my shoulder, but when he sees me draw back, though I don't mean to, he drops his arm and just nods real friendly. "I'll see you, Rich. You're doing a fine job for your Mother. She's mighty happy you came back to the farm."

I read in next week's paper about Mother's birthday gathering, blizzard and all. Just like Christmas a few years ago when it was such a big deal that all the Read children were together, my name isn't part of the list. That cuts deep. Father puts these 'family pieces' in the Rexford News. He's a bud with the editor and if he says boo, the paper prints it.

In June Father slips on the windmill platform. I'm below him, holding the brake solid so the blades don't turn while he adds oil to the gear box. His yells and curses fill the air and bring Mother as quick as she can manage. She holds the brake while I climb up to bring him down. I've not touched Father in so long I feel shock at the softness in his arms, how I can feel the long bones in his legs with no meat to cover them. I only remember hardness and strength coming from him.

Doctor says he'll need a cane for several weeks while the ligaments behind his kneecap heal. A month later the old man puts a notice in the paper, another brag on himself: 'Jake Read, age 80 cultivates 60 acres of corn in 7 days'. Well, he did stand along the field rows making sure I kept the lister straight so as not to take out any of the barely living plants. Even the weeds have failed to grow this year.

Father gets to make another newspaper headline in September announcing the big watermelon day in Gladbrook, Iowa on John's place. John had grown so many melons that he hosted a festival, with special awards for the youngest, the oldest and the person who'd traveled furthest. One melon weighed 33 ½ pounds.

"Yes siree!" he says. "Little Jake's a son to be proud of. He is indeed!" He is sure to say this around me many times, slapping his leg and hooting with glee.

In 1932 Tim and his wife Millie move onto the Dible property. Dust drifts are so high in places the road has to be cleared same as after a snow. Mother's cough, left over from a winter bout with the flu, keeps her hunched over and weak. She's not able to help much with the move but insists on packing lunches for everyone.

I stay at the farm to clear the garden. It's ready to plant if we just get rain. I look around the farm as I straighten my back, rubbing the curved scar behind my ear, humming to echo the whining wind that blows fitfully out of the south.

I remember the little bags of seed beans that Sarah Lou played with. I remember the watercress with fresh bread and churned butter sandwiches Mother fixed for a quick lunch. I remember the beginnings.

What was once new and freshly built is sagging and grey. The hog pens are near empty. The hen flock puny. The cattle, once so many and so fat on the thick prairie grass, stand with their heads low, coats eaten by lice. The corral is falling apart faster than I can mend it. The price of wheat, if any can be grown, is less than half a dollar a bushel.

So much is changing. I smell desperation in the dry wind.

CHAPTER 39

1932: DOROTHY EILEEN HUNTER (1924-1932)

Selden, Kansas

Standing in the center of Highway 83, Dorothy raises her arms to shoulder height and reaches east to west, feeling her thin arms, her wrists, her fingertips reaching and reaching, joining herself to the road's journey. Her feet are placed heel to heel and she holds a ballerina's pose, toes pointing the same direction as her fingertips. Head rolled back acutely, cropped dark hair curling under at the collar of a simple school dress, she stares upward into the April afternoon sky; a day warm enough to break open the buds on Grandpa's Russian apricot trees. Soft breeze slides along the tender skin of her arms and beneath her dress; gentle hands of spring air.

Freezes could still come, she knows, burning those same buds into brown death, but today the air is full of blossom scent and promise. A sense of adventure and excitement beyond her little Kansas town life sweeps through her. Squeezing her eyes until only sparks shine through her black lashes, she wills her body to fly away, to join the meadowlarks looping over the tops of the last year's Indian grass, to float into the brush stroke clouds and 'dissipate', a word she just learned and holds in her mouth like sweet candy. To melt away, spun sugar on her tongue, never to feel anything again; she craves escape from the dirty dullness of her northwest Kansas home.

Edna... Edna the Kansas Wonder Girl saw her! Chose her! Out of all the other boys and girls and the grown folks, too, Edna picked her! Dorothy's arms roughen with goose bumps and a shiver passes over her skin like a horse twitches away a fly when she remembers the 'communication' she felt when Edna's eyes met hers. Dorothy spins in a slow, dancing circle. She spins in the center of the highway, in the center of her dreams; spins and spins and spins.

She is eight years, one month old.

*****

I can tell that Mrs. Mueller, my friend Sarah's mother, is startled when Edna points a red tipped finger at me. She grips my hand tightly in hers, leans down and whispers, "Dorothy, I don't think your mother would approve. You stay with me, sweetie and let someone else go up on stage."

But nothing is going to stop me! I pull free and march right up those steps to stand before this special lady who has picked me! I reach out to shake her hand, but she pulls back with a slight shuddering that makes me think I might have a stink. I'm confused and hurt. I think she would want me to introduce myself proper and all.

Then she explains in a breathy voice, "Miss," she says, "Miss, please do not touch me until I am prepared to receive the spirits. I must pass through the veil of the unknown before I connect physically with you. It is clear to me already that you are set apart from others." Her voice reaches across the great space of the auditorium but is not loud. I feel like we are alone, like a small room is around us, one without walls. Her voice is as silky as Mama's bed gown and her breath puffs into my face. I smell spice and sweet and bitter herbs.

"I see today. I know tomorrow." Edna's patter helps her regain control of her breathing which had been stopped in a gasp when the little girl with a fat bow tied in her hair seemed to lift out of the crowd, spotlighted when there was no light to shine upon her. This is not part of Edna's planned show. Instead, her hand, with index finger pointing imperially, rose without volition and bound this little girl's soul to hers. She grieves for what she foresees.

Edna is terrified. She does have a gift; she's known it since she was a child no older than this one. Or, as her mother and her grandmother and the ones before called it, 'the eye'. Edna is a Romany, a gypsy. With puberty she'd acknowledged the sight. Womanhood brought a career. While the flow of energy often takes a toll on her it is usually harmless entertainment. This little girl, though. This little girl is going to hurt!

CHAPTER 40

1932: ADDISON ALANSON (A. A.) BACON

St. Francis, Kansas

To become a sheriff in a small town one has only to put their name on a ballot and wait for the community to show confidence with their votes. In some cases there may only be one candidate to choose from.

When the position opened up in St. Francis for Cheyenne County sheriff I was a janitor at the court house. Like the years I spent barbering I listened to folks' chatter, watched them come and go and observed there didn't seem too much to the job. I told Gladys about it at lunch that day and she did just what I expected. She insisted I put my hat in the ring.

Oh, she was planning our new future in a heartbeat, brimming over with ideas and finding more and more reasons I should jump on this opportunity. There was no doubt in my mind she felt some embarrassment at my title of janitor, though she would have never said so to me. I took pride in keeping our nice new court house and grounds running smooth. It was steady work and secure, but Gladys wanted more.

Gladys was certain that with this job I could make enough for us to buy a home. She thought folks looked down on renters. More than that, she hated having to answer to Mrs. Fritz who owned the house. It wasn't that Gladys didn't take good care of the place. That she did, maybe even better than if it were her own. The problem was Mrs. Fritz was so tight that things needing repair went undone unless we paid for them ourselves. That made Gladys hot! I felt it all balanced out, us not having the taxes on the place or having the risk of ownership, but Gladys fumed.

"Addison, I do swear you have less gumption than a box turtle. Listen to me. You can do this as well as anyone in the county. You are good with folks and have a real level head. These are your neighbors. You know practically everyone already and they're not likely to give you any trouble. You can do this just fine, Addison, and think of what it will mean for the family. Why I'd be so proud of you!" Gladys sure knew how to push me along.

"I'm not much for size, Gladys. Don't you think a sheriff ought to be a bigger fellow?" I imagined the snickering behind my back as I tried to break up a cowboy brawl.

"Now, Addison. You have always been too sensitive about that and for no reason at all. In fact, I think you might stand a better chance of taking charge because you aren't all big and threatening. You'll know how to calm folks down and prevent things getting worse. Why you're just the right size for sheriff! It's the position that holds the respect of the people, Addison."

I wondered if maybe Gladys ought to run in place of me. There'd be no one who could stand against her forceful nature!

"Well, I'll think it over."

"What's to think over, Addison? You wait and some other enterprising person will step right in front of you. I want you get listed on the ballot today and I'll stop in at the newspaper office to put the notice in. Why, I'll start calling my club ladies right now and let them know the exciting news!"

That is how I found myself in the wrong place at the wrong time.

CHAPTER 41

April 14, 1932: DOROTHY EILEEN HUNTER

The last day of school was so exciting! It was just pure fun! We cleaned our desks, scrubbed the board, sang all the songs we'd learned through the year, had a water balloon fight on the playground and ate treats that Miss Ruth brought. We had a multiplication race and signed our year books, the ones we'd made during Christmas holidays, for each other. It was just the best day ever!

Alice, Wanda and I started for home. "Sister, do you know what I'm going to do this summer? I have so many plans! I want to swim at Brookwood Park and I want to build a treehouse and I want to plant a whole big patch of sweet peas. I just love sweet peas, don't you? And I want to make a bean tipi. And I want to get a new kitten and I ..."

We'd walked a couple of blocks when Alice looked at my hands which I was waving in the air and said, "For goodness sake, Dorothy, you Dodo Bird! You've left your dinner pail. Again! With school over for the year you can't get it tomorrow. Hurry on back, we'll wait for you here."

Laughing at my silly head I turn around and run as fast as I can back to the school. The doors are closed, but Mr. Tompkins is still there sweeping up. He tugs my hair a bit, like he is ringing a bell, when I told him why I needed into my classroom, but he wasn't angry.

"Thank you, Mr. Tompkins! See ya next fall!"

I hurry back towards Alice and Wanda. My mouth is dry now and I am out of breath so I have to slow some. I am still on the main road when I hear a car rumbling up behind me. It is a brown car. When it stops alongside, me I see a man is driving. He has his window down and his elbow is resting on the frame, his fingers holding onto the steering wheel real casual. He wears farmer clothes.

"Hey, Mister. Are you gonna to give me a ride?" I don't know why I say such a thing. I've never been so bold, ever! I think the fun of the day is still racing around in my blood and with imagining a whole summer ahead I feel wild inside. Since the day in Colby with Edna the Wonder Girl I've been expecting something really stupendous to happen. Maybe this is it!

"I… can… do… that." The man answers. He talks funny, one word at a time, sort'a like when Dale was first learning.

So I run around the car and hop in the front seat. It is a real nice car and I smell the new of it. I can smell the man, too. Kind of strong, like a big dog, but I don't mind it. His clothes are clean. Looks like someone irons for him. I can tell because of the creases in his sleeves. He is wearing a hat that shades his eyes. He has a real pretty mouth for a man.

"My sister and friend are waiting just up the road a bit. Can you take me just that far? My sister is Alice. My friend is Wanda. I'm Dorothy, but sometimes my sister calls me Dodo Bird and I don't like it much. Sometimes she makes me feel real dumb and that's not nice! Is it?"

"No. It… is… not… nice… when… someone… laughs …at you."

"Today's the last day of school! Did you know that?"

"No. It… has been… a… real… long… time… since… I was… in… school. I… didn't… like it… much."

"I love school! I see my friends. I read books. I color and cut and paste and I get to write stories! At recess today we had a water balloon fight. It was so much fun! And we had treats, too! I got so excited I left my lunch pail and had to go back for it. That's why I was walking when you stopped."

"Uh… huh."

"Oh, oh…I think my sister forgot to wait. She should be standing right there on that corner with Wanda! Well, dang! I guess you can let me out here anyway. Thanks awful much for the ride. I was real hot and thirsty!"

"I… have a… Coca… Cola. Would… you… like… some?"

"Oh sure! Mama hardly ever lets us kids have pop. She says water and milk are fine for growing children. But sometimes on a real special day we get to share a bottle. I guess this is a special day!"

The man handed over a bottle that he had between his legs. I hadn't noticed it. I feel funny drinking from his bottle, but he is so nice I don't want to make him feel bad, so I take a good drink.

This is the strangest Coca Cola I've ever tasted. It is the same stuff that I've had before, the way the bubbles burn the back of my throat when I swallow, but it has a different flavor. Reminds me of Mama's cough syrup.

"Is this something new?" I ask, looking at the bottle. Its curved sides and narrow neck seem the same. The glass is the same and the writing on it looks like what I remember. But the taste is richer somehow. Better sort of.

"Do… you… like… it? You… can… finish… it… if you… want. I've… had… a plenty."

I suck on my tongue a moment, trying to decide if I like the taste or not. Maybe another sip will be ok.

It is good and before I know it I've finished the whole thing. I feel pretty silly, too. "Oops! There it is. Bottoms up!"

I look around and see we've driven a ways out of town. The man isn't going fast and it doesn't seem like he knows where he is headed, but I think, uh oh, I need to go home and he's going to have to turn around in the road.

"Mister. I should go home now. I have chores, you know. Mama wants me to water the chickens first thing when I get home every day. She'll be 'specting me to do my chores."

My words don't come out like I expect them to. They are slushy.

My mouth feels funny and I lick my lips, tasting the sweet pop flavor. It seems like my head is dizzy, too. "Mister, I need to go home now. Can you go back to town? We just live near town."

I am real glad when he slows down and makes a big loop in the road. But he keeps looping and looping and I start laughing as the car turns round and round, pushing me against the door like a ride at the fair. I feel really silly! And really, really dizzy.

He is laughing too. A friendly laugh, like a friend makes when you're having the best time together. I like his laugh and it makes me laugh harder. "Oh Mister! Oh Mister! You are a silly man!"

When the car finally quits going in circles, I don't even know which way we are driving and I don't care anymore. I start to sing. "Yankee Doodle Went to Town". And the man hums along real nice. He has a pretty sounding hum and makes all kinds of extra purrs and burrs and trills with his mouth closed. He keeps tune with me. So I keep singing, one song after another and he keeps humming along just happy as can be.

The sun is getting lower in the sky. The man says, "I… am… hungry. Are… you?"

My stomach is growling a bit and I have hiccups. They make us laugh, too. "I am, Mister. I could eat a horse!" That makes me snort and laugh even harder.

"I… will… get… some… food. Then… you… can… go home."

There is a little store at a crossroads. Big trees stand around it. The leaves are spring leaves, little and shiny. I bet in the summer they make it real cool and peaceful. I feel kind of sleepy, so when the man tells me to wait for him I lay down on the front seat. The soft upholstery is fuzzy like a kitten and I start thinking about a summer kitten to play with. I like grey ones best, especially ones with little white paws. They look like they stepped in a saucer of cream. My eyes close and I pet the seat.

When the man opens the car door, I wake up from my little nap. He has a sack and I hear bottles clinking. We drive some more and then he parks behind an old shed that stands by itself. He has potted meat, soft white bread, potato chips and two really big dill pickles. I love dill pickles! He had bought more Coca Cola, too.

"If we're going to share a meal together I should know what to call you, Mister. What is your name?"

"I... got... my... first name... from... my... grandfather. It is... Pleasant. You... can call... me... that."

"Now that's a right good name, Mister Pleasant. I think it suits you fine!"

He says, "I'll... open... these... sodas... outside. They... fizz."

I feel bad for him, how hard it is for him to talk. I think he might have more to say.

He opens the trunk and I see him fiddling with a blanket. He puts that in the back seat and then gets in behind the wheel again. He gives me another bottle of Coca Cola with the top off. I see the liquid swirling and swirling as the setting sun shines through the glass, bubbles rising up and popping like fireworks out the top. Now isn't that something!

I take a long drink. It is so good after the salty meat and chips and pickle. I smack my lips and Pleasant laughs real soft. He makes me feel like everything I do is special. His smile is just for me. I have never had anyone except my mama and daddy look at me so warmly. It makes me feel shy and good inside.

"Mister Pleasant. I'm sorry, but you will have to excuse me a moment. I need to find a privy. All this drinking's got me in a bad way."

"I... will... stay in... the car... Dorothy. You... can... go... behind... the shed."

When I step out, the ground rolls under me and I stagger sideways. It is so funny! "Oh my goodness! What happened to my feet, Mr. Pleasant? I sure do hope I don't fall over!"

I laugh all the way to the shed, do my business and laugh all the way back to the car. Then I see the sun has gone. It is suddenly dark.

"This has been the best time ever, Mr. Pleasant! But I should go home. Its night time and I feel kind of strange. Can you take me back now?"

"Yes... Dorothy. We... will... go back... now. I... have... had... fun... with you. You... are... real... nice."

I put my head on the seat and Mr. Pleasant lays the blanket from the back over my shoulders. I smell dust and wool and Mr. Pleasant's man smell. I fall asleep.

Sometime, I don't know when, I wake and we have stopped again. It is late. I can tell from the stars. I feel a little sick and get out of the car to pee. I don't even worry about going very far away.

There is grass waving in the wind and when I look up high, putting my head back, there are two moons shining down. Two big, bright full moons. I blink and blink, but there are still two of them. If I close one eye they come together and behave, but when I open both, there they are again. They are so beautiful! I squeeze my eyes almost closed and a white pathway comes down from the moons to me and I think, this is a road to heaven. I can walk right up to heaven on this silver white road. It made tears tickle my nose so I wipe them with my dress. Then I feel real cold and lonely for my mama.

I crawl, shivering, back into the car. Mr. Pleasant has his head against the door. I think he is sleeping. I can feel his warmth, so I snuggle up to his big leg and put my head on it, pulling the blanket around me, tucking myself in as well as I can.

The next time I wake we are parked in a ditch and morning has come. My mouth is dry and my head aches. When I sit up, Mr. Pleasant lays his hand on my leg and says, "I... got... lost... in the... dark."

"Oh. Have we been driving? Where are we?"

"I do... not... know. We... are... out of... fuel. Maybe... someone... will come... by."

Mr. Pleasant looks like his head hurts, too. I try not to cry, but I want to real bad. I am sick and missing my family. I've never spent a night away from home. I know Mama and Daddy must be wondering where I am.

A humming starts up. Then it becomes a song with words. It is Mr. Pleasant, singing a real sweet, sad and beautiful song. His words come easy, without any funny gaps between. It sounds just like what I am feeling. Tears drip from his chin and I am crying too. It seems just fine for us to cry together.

"Going home, going home
I am going home
Quiet like, some still day
I am going home
It's not far, just close by
Through an open door
Work all done, care laid by
Never fear no more
Mother's there expecting me
Father's waiting too
Lots of faces gathered there
All the friends I knew
I'm just going home
No more fear, no more pain
No more stumbling by the way
No more longing for the day
Going to run no more
Morning star light the way
Restless dreams all gone

Shadows gone, break of day
Real life…
There's no break, there's no end
Just living on
Wide awake, with a smile
Going on and on, going on and on
Going home, going home
I am going home
Shadows gone, break of day
Real life has begun
I'm just going home

I crawl up against Mr. Pleasant and he pulls the blanket over me tighter and lays his warm hand atop me. He sings and I sleep until I wake to the sound of someone talking.

"Yes, I have fuel. Wait here and I'll bring enough to get you into town. Atwood is just a few miles on south. You almost made it."

"Thank… you," said Mr. Pleasant. "We… thank… you."

"Are you going to take me home now? Now that it is day and you can see where we are?"

"Yes… in …a bit."

I have trouble keeping my eyes open. They are gummy and my mouth tastes real bad.

The farmer came back, put some gas from a can into the car and waves us on our way. We drive over some railroad tracks and cross a bridge, then turn left and go into the town of Atwood. I see a sign that says so. Mr. Pleasant drives slow and when he sees a lady with bags in her arms asks, "Is… there… somewhere's… we can… get… breakfast?"

The lady bends her head down to look inside the car. She smiles at me. "Yes. Just on up the street there. The big building on the left. It's Shirley's Opera House, but the Owl Café is on the main floor. They serve a good breakfast." She shuffles her bags while she speaks and points ahead.

"Thank… you… mam."

"We are going to have breakfast?" I'm not sure I can eat. My belly is real unhappy. But I am thirsty and think maybe some tea and toast will settle ok. That's what Mama always brings when I feel poorly.

"Yes. Then… I will… take… you… home."

We park the car in front of the pretty Opera House building. There are stairs going up one side and two doors that open in front. I wish I could brush my hair and teeth before we go in, but Mr. Pleasant smiles real nice at me and makes me think I don't look too bad. Mama would have washed me up good first, though.

The place is busy and the waitress is in a real rush. She looks like my friend Wanda's mother. I look at her real hard to see if she knows me, but she just puts glasses of water down for us and says she'll bring coffee quick as she can. She didn't hardly look at me at all.

Mr. Pleasant has eggs and toast and potatoes with ham and he eats like it is his last meal, like my grandad Weaver says if someone rushes at dinner. I have toast and drink water. I felt too puny to ask for tea and coffee isn't for little girls. The jelly is good, though. Real plum jelly like Granny Hunter makes. Mr. Pleasant gives me one of his triangles of toast when he sees I've eaten all mine.

I use the bathroom and wash my face and hands a bit. The roller towel is too high for me to reach, so I dry with my dress. It is awful wrinkled and I feel ashamed.

Mr. Pleasant is standing by the front door when I come out. When he sees me, it is like I am the only person in the room. His eyes catch mine and something takes my breath. I can hear his song in my head, deep and moving and I feel tears fill my eyes. My nose is hot inside and I swallow over and over. The noisy dining room gets real quiet in my head. I look at his eyes and I walk right to him. Then we are inside the car again and driving up a hill towards the morning sun.

The road curves to the south and I think, 'now I'm going to go home'. This has been a very strange adventure, like Dorothy in the Wizard of Oz or Alice in Wonderland but I've had enough. I am ready for a normal day.

Mr. Pleasant reaches under his seat as he drives and takes out a bottle of dark golden liquid. It is the color of honey. He pulls the top off with his teeth and pours the drink down his throat. He wipes his lips with the back of his hand and drinks again. I watch big bubbles rise as the liquid gets lower and lower.

Just before it empties he looks at me. His eyes are glassy. They can't seem to find my eyes.

"Would... you... like a... soda? It... might... help."

"No, thank you. I want to go home."

He doesn't answer me, but tips the bottle up, swallowing the last inch. He puts it back under the seat and begins his humming sounds. They don't sound so nice now and I feel like something is changing. It is like a kettle of thick soup that gets hotter and hotter until the surface blisters and heaves. His odor got hotter and hotter too; like scorched fabric when the iron is too high.

I slide closer to my door and look out the window. The ditch is going by fast and makes me feel sicker. Mr. Pleasant drives from side to side, going faster and faster. It is a good thing there are no other cars on the road.

"I think I'm going to throw up," I say and look at his face. He is staring straight ahead and his mouth is all twisty. It doesn't look pretty at all. His jaw is clenching and clenching and his hands are holding the steering wheel real tight, squeezing and squeezing. His humming sounds more like growling.

"I need to get out! I'm going to throw up!" I start crying and beg, "Please, stop the car. I am sick!"

There is a little road going down towards some plum bushes. I can see their creamy white blossoms against brown branches. It is more of a path than a road, but he turns the car onto it and slows to a stop. I can hear his humming, louder and higher and coming in a gasping sort of pattern. The door opens and I nearly fall out. I take a few steps and lean over to heave, plum jelly toast and water running down my chin and out my nose. My tummy is sour and my throat burns, making me cough. Tears mix with it all.

I feel his hand, big and hot and strong, grip my arm. I think Mr. Pleasant is going to help me, like Mama does when I'm urping, holding my hair back and wiping my chin with a wet cloth.

His one hand takes my arm and the other slips under my knees and he lifts me up as easy as I would scoop a little grey kitten with white paws. I looked into his black eyes and he says, "My name is Richardson."

And I knew. I just knew.

CHAPTER 42

April 14, 1932: RICHARD READ

A flower, a jewel, a spark of light dances ahead of me as I drive Father's car along the main road through Selden. Pale arms swing, thin legs step up and down, up and down with a sweet rhythm that lifts my heart. She moves like music is playing. I hear her music.

I slow the car alongside her, my arm resting through the open window frame. Her bright face grins at me openly.

"Hey, Mister. Are you gonna give me a ride?" She speaks to me real friendly.

"I… can do… that." I answer and she skips around the front of the car, her shiny dark hair bouncing up and down, up and down. When she slides onto the front seat, she grins and I grin back. The doctored soda between my legs is about half gone and I am feeling the cheerful loosening that comes from a first drink.

I start the car rolling forward, real slow, holding on to this time. I delight in her little bird voice. She is chirpy as a baby chick.

She tells me her sister Alice and a friend are waiting for her. When she says her sister sometimes makes fun of her, my heart squeezes tight. Should no one tease this little dolly! I am of a mind to tell the sister so.

She chatters about school, what fun her last day has been. I don't have to say much, she is so free with her words. She's just like a robin singing a morning song, so many notes, so much joy.

I look at her bare arms and legs, all knobby at the joints. The fine hairs on them shine golden in the afternoon sun, palomino color. I want to smooth her skin, brush away the dust around her ankles.

When we get to the place her sister is supposed to be, no one is there. She says, "Oh, oh… I think my sister forgot to wait. She should be standing right there on that corner with Wanda! Well, dang! I guess you can let me out here anyway. Thanks awful much for the ride. I was real hot and thirsty!"

I hate to think of her going on home thirsty when I have this nice soda so I offer to share it. Her big brown eyes gleam with excitement. I am pleased to make her happy.

She looks puzzled when the bottle lowers after her first swallow. She tastes the corn liquor. I think she likes it. I tell her she is welcome to the rest and we drive on west, real slowly, following the railroad tracks, while she sips and talks. Her little girl voice washes around the car like a sweet breeze. I notice the smell of soap and laundered clothes and her own freshness. The freshness of young life.

"Mister, I need to go home." She says. Then she goes on about chores and folks expecting her and all so I slow way down and turn the wheels in a big circle. Something gets into me then and I keep spinning the automobile round and round, round and round driving in big circles down into the ditch and up again until we are both laughing real, real hard. I feel so happy! When I pull out of the last turn, we are heading into the sun.

She starts to sing a silly song and I feel the music bubbling up from deep and join in, following her high notes with my low ones and it feels like we were meant to sing together. When we finish one song, she starts another and I keep driving and we keep singing.

The sun is setting. I am losing my buzzy feeling and getting hungry. I thought she might be too. So I tell her we will stop and get some food at the Cumberland Store.

She has hiccups and giggles after each one, pats her mouth and says, "Oh, pardon me!" Every now and then she gives a big yawn and then she smiles at me like it is a good trick. She's slumped in the seat, real relaxed, her knees wide apart under her thin cotton dress. When we get to the little crossroads town of Cumberland, I park under big trees where the shadows are dark. I ask her to wait in the car.

I buy canned meat and a loaf of sliced bread, some potato chips and more Coca Colas. A big jar of dill pickles floating in brine catch my eye and I buy two of those. For a treat I get her a cherry Tootsie Pop.

We drive north awhile and then east until I find a little pull off spot with an old machinery shed tucked in a draw. I drive up alongside it, park and step outside. I open the trunk and remove a lap robe Mother keeps in there for 'just in case'. The two bottles of hootch that I'd bought in Hoxie are wrapped in the blanket. I put one under my seat and pour a good dose into the two soda bottles from the other. I don't have a plan. Each step just seems to follow the one before.

It is a fine picnic supper. We leave the car doors open to let the night air swirl through. A near full moon is rising from behind the black edge of the earth. I have a sudden flash of a full moon long ago when I was a boy. Then I have another flash of a bright moon shining on the bare skin of an older girl. I am stirred in a bad way so real quick I stop thinking about those things.

I listened to Dorothy's sing song voice telling me about kittens and books and some woman in Colby who had told her fortune. She drinks her soda and smacks her lips so cute. Then she has to relieve herself. I stay in the auto, listening to the night sounds and watch the moon climb higher and higher. I take some straight swigs from the bottle, washing them down with sweet cola. It is a beautiful night and I have someone to share it with. Someone sweet as a sister who seems to like me, too. This is a real new feeling!

When Dorothy gets back in, she spoils the nice time by saying she wants to go home. I guess it makes me a little mad that she doesn't want to stay, but she says it so pleadingly that I tell her I'll take her back. She lays down, such a small shape lying next to me, and I cover her with Mother's lap robe. With the sound of the engine and the movement I guess she falls asleep. No reason to take her home, after all. So I drive and drive, watching the moonlight paint the roads into silver ribbons.

Sometime in the night I pull off and sleep. When I wake, she is curled against me, her head on my leg. I touch her soft hair and a few other spots, but don't want to wake her. I put my hand, real gentle, on her chest. I feel her ribs rise and fall, faster than my breaths and my breaths come faster to match. I drive again, on and on with no memory of where we've been or any plan of where we are going. In the early grey of dawn the auto runs short of gas. As it slows I pull off into the ditch heading south. With my hand on Dorothy, the span nearly as wide as her, I lay my head on the doorframe. Then I sleep some more.

A man, he says his name is Rudy Horinek, has offered to help. He doesn't ask us any questions. Dorothy was asleep when he knocked on the car window.

"Yes, I have fuel. Wait here and I'll bring enough to get you into town. Atwood is just a few miles on south. You almost made it."

Our voices wake her but she stays real still, lying under the blanket. I can tell from a change in her breathing and how tight her body got after the softness of sleep. I keep a hand on her shoulder, just in case.

When Mr. Horinek drives away, she asks, her voice muffled from the blanket and my leg, "Are you going to take me home now? Now that it is day and you can see where we are?"

"Yes... in... a bit."

Once we start driving again she sits up, combing her matted hair with her fingers. Her voice has lost the joy from last night. She sounds lonely and scared.

I think she just needs some hot breakfast. I do.

The folks at the Owl Cafe take care of us. No one suspicions a thing, it seems. I keep my eye on the door, just to be watchful, but breakfast goes just fine. I savor the flavors of egg yolk and salty ham, potatoes fried crisp on the outside and soft in the middle.

Dorothy's face is pale and she has dark places under her eyes, but she eats her toast fine. I wonder if folks think she is my girl.

When she leaves for the bathroom, I get a real scared feeling she might not come back and I watch real close. When I see her little shape at the end of the long dining room and I know she is looking for me, well the zing that goes to my groin makes me grunt aloud.

We drive east on Highway 36 and I follow when it curves to the south and then east again. We are heading back towards her home and mine.

I reach under my seat and take out the second bottle. I open it and begin drinking, just pouring it down my throat like a man in the desert. When the bottle is empty, I feel the liquor hit my brain like a freight train. Wham!

My face heats up, my lips go numb, my hands clench and unclench the wheel as I hear the voices of my life. Ape boy! Monster! Rapist! Fiend! I remember the beatings from Father, the cruelness of my brothers, the way Sarah Lou and Attie and Villa keep their little ones away from me. I feel it all! Wham! Wham! Wham! And the heat goes from my face into my groin.

Why shouldn't I have love? Why shouldn't I have tenderness? Why shouldn't I share the comforts of family?

Dorothy begins to whimper, "I need to get out! I'm going to throw up! Please, please stop the car. Mister Pleasant, I'm real sick!"

I see a road that leads into a thicket of plum bushes with white blossoms fighting to survive. As I pull next to them their sweet smell sickens me and takes me back to a time of unbelievable pain, of loss and grief, of pure terror. Then, wham, Richardson is here. He is in my head with his smooth voice. "I am here Pleasant. I am here now."

There seems to be two men with me. Both are angry, both are hungry for touch and flesh. Both make sounds that echo through my brain like boars and bulls and tearing wolves. Then, somehow, the men are gone. I come back to myself and see how hurt my little girl is, how battered and torn. Her frail body is naked and fouled, bloody and ripped. I put my hand on her chest. It moves up and down, up and down in shallow gasps. She is hurt mighty bad. I have to stop her pain like I've done for sick or damaged animals my whole life. I can do that for her.

Nearby is a lister plow that had been pulled aside for repairing. A heavy piece of metal, a sub-soiler, lies alongside. It fits my hand like an ax. I bring it down on her head, twice. The sound makes me retch. Her chest moves up and down, up and down with a raspy wheeze. I have to stop that sound.

My solace, the humming that blocks all thought, is not enough. I put my hand on her throat and lean atop her. She shudders and spasms. The smell of piss and shit and vomit and blood rise with the morning sun. My own stink is strong.

Of a sudden I see how bright the day is, as though a blindfold is lifted from my eyes; as though a dark room has suddenly been flooded with light. I see that someone could drive by at any time and we'd be right there for them to see. I pull my coveralls up and latch the twist loop. I see stains of blood on my pants, my shirt cuffs and deep under my nails.

Richardson says, "She must be hidden. She must be hidden and we must go home."

I gather her into my arms, patting her and tending her as gently as I can, and put her into the back seat of Father's car. Oh Father will be mad, I think. Oh Father will be so mad at me again.

Just a short way ahead I see a straw stack behind a gate. I open the gate and drive through. Dorothy does not take up much room under the straw. She is easy to bury. I drive out, close the gate and go on south.

I need water real bad. My mouth is foul with blood and breakfast and the parched feeling of a black out time. In the town of Achilles I see a woman hanging clothes on her line. She brings me a glass of water and she says, "You look a fright. You been punching it out with someone?"

"Yes… mam. I… think I… had… a rough… spell… last night. I'm… just… trying to… get… home."

I drive on, trying to figure what has gone wrong, what has happened. I drift in and out. I am confused about where I am and pull into another farm yard. The lady there gives me more water and says Colby is 10 miles south and 10 miles west. So I drive that general way and get to town.

I go to the jail that is near the courthouse. I need to report the strange men I've been with. A big man is sitting behind the desk, thumbing a magazine. He gives me the look I know means 'what are you doing bothering me?' I tell him what I can remember and he tells me to go home and sleep it off. So I go home.

I park Father's car in the barn. My head stabs something fierce and I want nothing more than to sleep. So I drink more water and climb into bed.

Car doors and voices and Mother's wails wake me. "Not again, oh please, not again!" I hear her cries.

The door to my room is wrenched open and a sheriff stands beside Father. Another man stands just behind. "Richard Read, I am Sheriff Beaver. This is Mr. Clark, the Sheridan County deputy. We would like to take you to Colby. Will you come with us?"

I look at Father, meeting his eyes. They are empty as a poured out sack. He has shrunk to nothing. I have done this to him.

"Yes. I… will… go… with you."

I hear the humming rise inside me and I remember singing with Dorothy. Her voice mingles with the sounds that come from my chest. I feel tears sliding past my nose, running down my neck.

The sheriff locks my hands together behind me and puts me in his car. I think about the night before, spinning round and round in the car, eating dill pickles as the stars came out. I hear Dorothy's songs tinkling like bells. I have trouble getting enough air.

The Colby men, the McGinleys, do what they have to. It takes them a while. My slow speech makes the deputy really angry. He says, "Spit it out, for God's sake!"

Richardson shuts me off when they ask about Dorothy. He lets me tell them about the two men. I know it doesn't make sense. Nothing makes sense and I want to shut it all out. After hours and hours Richardson gets tired and goes away.

They put a heavy vest over my arms and cuffs on my ankles and drive me back to Rawlins County. I try to find the places where the two men had taken me. I try hard, but what I can't explain is how it had all been black; like I'd been blindfolded. I did remember silver roads and a bright straw stack and I remembered the two women who gave me water. I guess that helps. I sleep in the Colby jail Saturday night and I hear lots of yelling and cars speeding up to the jail.

Now it is early Sunday. I know because the church bells are ringing, sounding like angel songs. Sheriff Ed McGinley and his son Don do a lot of yelling into phones and to each other. They seem afraid, but want to hide it. I am afraid, too. And sad, so very sad.

They put the vest and ankle cuffs on me again and drive me for about two hours to another town. St. Francis. They take me to the new court house, right in the center of town. The sheriff there, Mr. Bacon, is waiting. He looks like a child in front of the McGinley men. He takes us up three flights. The stairs are hard with ankle cuffs on. The McGinleys help heave me up from step to step and they shove me into the new cell.

"He'll need to go to Lansing. I'll make the calls tomorrow morning," says Sheriff McGinley, but his tired face has a peculiar look like there is a joke somewhere.

Deputy McGinley snarls at me. "He needs to go straight to Hell and burn for eternity. He's a fiend and a monster!"

Sheriff McGinley says, "He's here now and justice will be done, son. Let's let justice be done."

Sheriff Bacon stands with his arms folded and looks at me. "Well, sir. You will remain quiet and there will be no trouble out of you. Is that understood?" There is a quaver in his voice and I can tell the others hear it too.

Deputy McGinley claps him on the shoulder with a hard hand and he loses his balance a bit. "Don't fret Sheriff Bacon. This will all be over soon enough."

"Not soon enough." Sheriff Bacon answers.

The older McGinley says, "We appreciate you holding him here, Bacon. Things are just too hot in our neck of the woods. The little girl's funeral is today and I pray that will calm folks down. I'll make those calls tomorrow and see if we can't get some state support out here."

"You don't think we should request help now?"

"Not a bit of it. You know those state boys don't work on Sundays. We'll have this all wrapped up and ready to hand over tomorrow. I have to admit, it's been a real tough weekend and I've got to get some sleep. Thanks again." Then Sheriff McGinley and the big man Don give me a last look, grimacing real big like dogs about to bite, and move back down the stairs..

I am alone with Sheriff Bacon. He is breathing real hard and fast. Sweat beads like blisters on his brow. "I don't like this," he says softly, speaking to himself. "I don't feel good about this at all." Then he, too, goes down the stairs. I hear metal doors clang and then all is quiet.

In my mind I see Dorothy standing like a star, a jewel, a bright shining spark of light. Then her dear little hand waves me down for a ride.

CHAPTER 43

April 15, 1932: SHERIFF EDWARD McGINLEY
Colby, Kansas

While I carried no credentials for the position of sheriff, Bess's words echo in my heart. I do feel I was born to it. Perhaps the farm's loss to unpaid taxes was a blessing I could never have asked for, freeing me to attend to the role without distraction.

In an effort to see beyond my lost identity as a Kansas farmer, I put this one on like a pair of shiny new boots. Indeed, I took a portion of my first pay and purchased an outfit to match the dignified role. My natural height and bearing are favorable. I look the part, I feel the part and folks seem to see me that way, too.

Da's reputation with the people of Colby went a long way in helping the 1930 election results, but I've risen to this job on my own merits. In the past year I've been the one determinedly seeking justice and protection for the citizens.

The current national crisis has criminals and scoundrels aplenty trying to take advantage of simple folks. Anyone with that bent has found I am serious about defending my people. With diligence to the law I will make my name one that carries into the future of Thomas County.

We are living in Colby; Bess, Don, Billy and I. A small house next to the jail became ours when I was elected. Bess cooks for the prisoners, full meals she takes great pride in and they are lucky for it! Don is our Under-sheriff. His powerful build is an asset to subduing belligerent prisoners. I suspect he gets a little too much enjoyment from the task. Upholding the prohibition law keeps us hopping. It seems a shame that possession of beverages we've all enjoyed turns decent folks into criminals, but that's the law and until things change I've got to enforce it. A farmer can turn his corn into gold by making a mash, converting it from feed to drink. Lord knows income is desperate hard to come by. The 'thirst that wants to be quenched' is universal to man so there's a steady market. Confiscated liquor, the decent kind, sometimes finds its way beneath Don's bed. I don't ask questions when he pours me a tipple of an evening.

Unfortunately, many of the folks making the stuff have no conscience. They don't care what goes into the brew, including foul items that turn the strongest gullet or worse. Deadly, some of it.

Of course, the intentional poisoning of liquor by our government is a known fact. Criminal indeed! I've seen enough of the jake leg disease in wandering hobos for me to feel pure sorrow. When one of those boys gets picked up, they go in our cell overnight and are given a couple of hot meals. The Mrs. will even do their laundry if they'll let her. The next day I drive them to the county line; whichever direction they were headed. Those boys are in mighty sorry shape and haven't much hope.

We stay busy most days. Seems outlaw-ing climbs when folks are hungry and can't find work. The whole country is rootless. Added to the nation's problems is the local drought. I guess it's not so local really. The dad-burned center of the country seems to be on the move. One day it blows from the south and the Oklahoma dust, red as the Cherokees themselves, settles in a fine powder. The next day it comes cold out of the north where Nebraska's sandhills lift free and take to the clouds. Our own soil drifts so deep across sidewalks we use shovels to clear it. Static electricity is fierce. It snaps and cracks and rolls along the bob wire fences at night like the banshee of old Ireland. It is unsettling!

We've had some rough crimes committed in northwest Kansas. A few were solved, but many not. Several brazen bank robberies across the country bring a sense of uneasiness to small towns. The banks that failed, those that closed their doors on the trusting populace whose hard earned cash is lost forever, gives these hooligans a celebrity that irks me.

From time to time I must remind myself that the majority of people are family oriented and law abiding. I suppose being a sheriff is like being a doctor when all you see is sickness. You begin to think that's the condition of everyone.

No, we've got a great community here and I am proud to serve it. If it takes a little head busting now and then, well Don can provide any attitude adjustment needed.

******

Friday, April 15, I had gone home for lunch and dozed off. Spring fever had infected this year's high school seniors, turning them into rascals bent on devilment the night before. I'd been up until the wee hours answering complaints of jalopies tearing up the city streets. I hadn't caught any of the fools, but maybe my presence helped keep worse from happening.

The phone startled me awake. It was Don calling from the office to say he had something I needed to come over for. His voice alarmed me. I splashed cold water from the basin on my face, got my boots and hat and walked next door.

"What have you got, Don?" I asked. I could sense his chagrin.

"Dad, the strangest thing. Not too long ago a man drove up in a brown sedan, came in and told me the wildest tale of being kidnapped by two men last night who forced him to drive way the hell over the country. He was real odd, that's for sure. Well, I could tell he'd been drinking. He smelled something awful! I told him to go home and sleep it off. But Dad, while he was telling this crazy story he mentioned a girl from Selden. So I called over there and spoke with their deputy, Carl Clark. He confirmed there is a child missing. An eight year old who didn't show up for dinner yesterday. They've been searching all night, he said."

"Well God-dammit! Why didn't they alert us yesterday?"

"I asked that too, Dad. He said they thought they could handle it locally and expected her to turn up before now."

"Jesus H. Christ! What was this feller's name, the one who came in?"

Don looked at his boots. "Well, Dad. He was such an odd ball and he smelled so bad, I sent him on home without asking a name. He just seemed like some fool coming off a tough drunk."

"Oh, God almighty, Don! Get that Selden deputy back on the phone and let me talk to him."

In a few minutes Don handed the phone to me and then made himself scarce.

"Carl, this is Sheriff McGinley from Colby. I understand you've got a missing girl? What can you tell me?"

"Sheriff, the news is bad. I was just about to call. We're bringing a man to you now. He's from Rexford. He has a record. Richard Read. You know the name?"

"No sir. I don't believe I do. Rexford you say?"

"Yes, Sheriff. The family of the little girl, the Hunters, well, the grandfather on the mother's side is a Mr. Weaver and he's real good friends with the sheriff of Logan County, Sheriff Beaver. Ernest L. Beaver? Anyway, Mr. Weaver called for his help and he got some information that led him to the Read farm this afternoon. He's on his way to Colby with Read now, sir."

"Lord help us all! Do they have the little girl?"

"No, sir. She's not turned up and this Read fellow has got some cockamamie story about getting kidnapped last night. He's admitted to getting booze in Hoxie, but it starts getting real vague after that. We thought it best you took over since he's a Thomas County man and all."

"Deputy, can you tell me what Read's record is? Does his history pertain?"

"It surely does, sir. It surely does. Spent six years in the Colorado pen for raping a fifteen year old. Nearly killed her from what we've heard. He's been living off and on with his folks northeast of Rexford since getting back about ten year ago. The family's been real quiet about him all this time."

"Holy Mother of God! Why weren't we told of this? Colorado had no business sending him back here! Least of all we should have been warned. Of course, ten years ago, maybe this office was told, but it failed to get passed along. There's been a lot of that type of thing, I guess. Well, we'll handle it from here, deputy. Thank you. You can expect I'll be in Selden and will stop by your place."

"Yes, sir. Thank you, Sheriff McGinley."

While I waited for the prisoner to arrive I spoke with Don. "Listen, son. We've got to get the truth out this fellow and get it quick. Folks are going to be on the warpath and we've got to get the truth and keep him safe, both. Tell me exactly what Read told you!"

"He said he was coming back from Hoxie where he'd got hisself a bottle and two men stopped him in Selden, took over his car and made him drive all over the country. He said he was in fear for his life. He wanted to report it and all. But, Dad, he looked like an old farmer had too much to drink and got the hoo-dos after him. He didn't make enough sense to pay a mind to. Oh he was a mess, all right. Had blood on his coveralls and man did he smell!"

"Blood?" I raked my hands through my hair and wanted to smack my son atop his thick skull. "What do you mean, blood?"

"I asked him about that. He said he'd been skinning rabbits. Made sense to me. It would have to you, too, Dad. You'd a done just what I did. Sent him home to sleep it off."

"What did he say about the girl? You said you called Selden because he'd mentioned a girl."

"I almost missed it, Dad. He was just rambling away with the bizarre story, he talks real slow and odd like, and somewhere in the middle said 'the little girl got in the car' and then he just kept on about how he'd been kidnapped by two men and didn't know what had happened."

I felt like screaming and I know my voice was raised pretty loud. "And you didn't jump on that? My God, Don. Don't you have any sense?"

"Dad, I'm tellin' you. He made no sense and was such a strange case. His speech is real slow, like I said, like he's got something wrong upstairs. I was just tryin' to get him out of here before he scared some citizen wanting us to find their lost kitty."

I was so disgusted with my son I could hardly speak. Remembering how hard my dad had been on me, I tried to calm down. "Well it can't be undone now. You be ready when Sheriff Beaver pulls in to help get that prisoner inside. Let's make it quick and keep it quiet. We don't want the whole town to notice!"

In a short while the Logan County sheriff's car pulled up to the jail. Don and I went out and helped escort the prisoner in, shielding him from the public eye. Don was right, this man did have a mighty strong smell about him, noticeable as soon as the car opened. He was near my height, but there was an added bulkiness about his shoulders and neck that took up more space than his size warranted. His eyes were set deep beneath heavy brows, the whites bulging in a way that gave him a wild look. His clothes were soiled and looked like they'd been slept in. I noticed brown stains on the cuffs of his long sleeves, his fingernails rimed dark and, though he did not have much facial hair, I saw flecks like dry tobacco spittle in the creases of his neck where whiskers had trapped it.

He moved like a sleepwalker, slowly putting one foot in front of the other as though the earth might betray him. I could see what Don meant. This man was different and not in any good way. But he didn't resist. He seemed in a trance.

We put him in the back cell. I locked it tight and left Don to watch while Sheriff Beaver and I went to the office.

"Sit down, please. May I get you a coffee?" I needed it too.

"Coffee would be fine, Sheriff McGinley. It's been a real tough night!"

I called over to the house to have Bess bring us a pot. She was good about adding something sweet to soak up the brew whenever I needed mid-day coffee. I guessed Sheriff Beaver could use something of the kind and was grateful when I caught a whiff of apple fritters when she came through the door.

"What do I need to know, Sheriff? Call me Ed, please. Your name is Ernest, is that right?"

"E.L., most folks use. Ed, I'm telling you. There's no way this is going to turn out good. I think…." He paused, swallowed hard, fought for control and said, "I think we're too late. I think Dorothy Eileen Hunter won't be found or if she is won't be found alive. I think this beast has done his worst and the only thing left to do is try to find her; give her back to her folks for burial."

"Good God! Did Read say anything to you on the way here?"

"No sir, just hummed and whimpered and scratched at his self like he's got a demon running through his head. Which I believe is the God's truth. This is a man who is not fit. You know he's done it before, went to the Colorado pen?"

"I don't know more than that. What are the particulars?"

"He had a homestead out north of Burlington. Him and a few of his kin took homesteads when that ground opened up some twenty years back. His dad's a real go-getter. Family's been here from the beginning. Well-respected in Rexford and all. But Rich, I guess he's never been quite right. The other kids are all fine folks, though.

"Anyway, seems he'd been watching a neighbor there, one of the German Settlement girls, for a while. In 1916 he caught her alone and did her over right mean. Nearly killed her they said. Local men were going to string him up, but the Kit Carson County sheriff got him to trial and he went to Canon City for a time. I think he got out lots sooner than his sentence. Colorado's got some strange formula for good behavior and all.

"Anyway, he came back to Kansas and has been doing farm labor of all kinds in the area and for his folks. I don't know if there's been any other problems, but considering what I've heard and seen of him, I'm guessing he's done some other wicked stuff."

"Ok. Anything else?"

"No, that's about it." Sheriff Beaver paused, cleared his throat and began to speak in a strained voice. "You know... me and my wife... well this little girl means a lot to us. This is kind of personal and all, what I'm about to tell you, but it's why I'm here, out of my jurisdiction and all.

"Anyway, I want you to know. Me and my wife, we've had a real hard time with our babies. Lost one after another after another. Most of them hardly draw a breath before they're gone. No reason anyone can explain; they just don't live. Well, a year before Dorothy Eileen Hunter was born we had us a little girl. Happened to be in Kansas City when she came. They've got some real good hospitals there and my wife, well, she wanted to be in one for this birth instead of at home. Good thing, too. They had some way of getting our baby girl past the critical time and she's nine years old now. We named her Dorothy Eileen. She's the only baby we've been able to raise. We've lost two more since." Sheriff Beaver paused for a swallow of coffee, his eyes desolate.

"Anyway, the Weaver family, that's the missing girl's mother's people, they are real, real good friends of ours… so good, in fact, that when Jennie Hunter, that's Floyd's wife, had her second girl they named her Dorothy Eileen after our little one. So you see that's why I'm here, Sheriff McGinley. And I'd appreciate staying on until it's over."

"I'm glad to have you, Sheriff Beaver. I'm mighty grateful for your help. And I'll do all I can for the family! Let's go see what this monster has to say."

Don had been 'warming up the prisoner' during our absence. He used a piece of pipe to strike the cell bars while he paced back and forth firing off verbal threats. It was the game we played with those we put in the cage. Folks we needed information from. Don scared the living daylights out of them and then I would come in real calm, send Don away as though I was protecting the prisoner and then I'd start asking questions in a friendly, off-hand manner. The method had worked well for us.

Rich sat on the bunk with his hands dangling between his knees, his head drooping low on his heavy shoulders. A slight rocking motion made the cot creak. He looked whipped already. An odd sound came out of him. Like a teakettle boiled dry or grain pouring down a spout. And his odor filled the whole area.

"What's this commotion, Deputy? That'll be enough of that. Go on out and see if you can't find this man some supper. I reckon he could use a plate of something warm. While you're at it, see if we've got something clean for him to wear. Underclothes and all." Don knew I wanted his soiled clothes for evidence.

That's how we usually started and typically the prisoner would perk right up, looking forward to some grub and kindness. Most of our 'guests' were folks who'd made a stupid decision or kids or petty thieves who caused no real harm. This was different and serious as anything I'd ever faced. Richard Read sat as though he'd not heard a word. Sat and hummed and rocked himself.

Sheriff Beaver sat down on the single folding chair in the hallway that separated the two rows of cells. We could hold six individuals or more if we doubled up. The other cells happened to be empty today and I was glad of that. He took off his hat and ran a hand over his face. His color was wan. Pouchy yellow-tinged skin hung blister-like below his eyes. He looked like an old man, though I believe he was more than twenty years my junior. All those losses in his life, all those babies hoped for and grieved over. It's a wonder his wife had any sanity left.

"Will you please state your name, age and address for the record." I start with facts that should be easy for a person who is under the strain of incarceration. I feel their discomfort and try to use it to my advantage.

The strange sounds stopped long enough for him to answer, "Pleasant... Richardson.... Read... Rexford, KS – we live... north east... of town... on... the Prairie... Dog. I believe... I turned... 53... this year." After stating this, the odd humming resumed.

His phrasing was broken with pauses between each word, pauses just long enough to sound mechanical. His voice was flat and monotone. I shook my head trying to wrap my mind around what we had to work with.

"Do you go by Pleasant or Richardson?"

"Rich... will be... ok."

"OK Rich. You've had a rough night of it. Would you like to tell us about it, Sheriff Beaver and me? My name is Sheriff McGinley. Sheriff Ed McGinley. We're here to listen."

The humming stopped again. Without raising his head or meeting our eyes he began with the slow pace of an old horse plodding down a road. "I come... from Hoxie.

In... Father's... car. Had me... a good... big... bottle... or two. Shouldn't... have... bought it... but... I did. Come... through... Selden and... stopped. Two... men in... suits got... in. One... on... my right... and one... on... my left. I was... in the... middle. They... was drunk. They... took me... all... over the... country. I... don't... know... where all. They... told me... not to... tell... anyone... what we... done. Then... they left... and... I... was alone. I... come here... to... report it."

It seemed to take an eternity for him to tell us that tall tale. "What about the little girl, Rich. Tell us about the little girl?"

"One... man... put her... in... the car. I... don't... recollect... what... happened."

"Rich, you know, this little girl is missing from her home. Her parents and her family are all real worried. She didn't come home from school Thursday. Folks have been looking everywhere for her. Tell us about the little girl, Rich."

"I'm... real tired... Sheriff. I... need... to get... some sleep."

"Not yet, Rich. I need to know about the little girl. You can help us find her, Rich. Then you can have some food and sleep. Tell us about the little girl. Her name, Rich. Do you remember her name?"

"I... I. I'm... real tired. I... need... to lie... down. I don't... feel well. My... head... is hurtin'... real bad." He reached up to rub behind his right ear. It seemed an action well practiced. His fingertips traced an old scar visible through his close cropped hair, following the curve of a pale ridge.

My voice was not so calm now. I could feel the heat of frustration rising in my face and I looked over at E.L. wondering if he wanted a go at the brute. I had to be careful that this man, the only man who knew what had happened to Dorothy didn't shut down on us.

"Sheriff Beaver here, he knows the family real well, Rich. He is here because the family, the little girl's mom and dad, are desperate to find her. Can't you help us on this, Rich. It'd mean a lot if you could give us something that would help us find her. Her name, Rich. Did she tell you her name?"

I was trying hard to hold in my anger. I wanted to take Don's lead pipe to the man's head. If he didn't say something soon I'd send Don back in to do a little persuading.

"I... I... I think... she... told... the man... her name was... Dorothy... but... I don't... know... if that's... right. I... might... of heard... that... somewhere... else."

Bingo! We had him now! He knew her name and that meant we had the right man for sure. Sheriff Beaver gasped.

"Rich, that's great. That's real helpful. Yes, that's her name. She's not very old, Rich. Only eight. Just a little thing. Where is she, Rich? Where in hell is she!" Sheriff Beaver looked up sharp then, wondering if I was going to go in the cell and beat the truth out of this man, but I knew we had to go easy. I'd just slipped a little.

"Help us, Rich. Tell us the real story. Tell us what really happened. You were in Hoxie. It was Thursday. Just yesterday afternoon. You got a bottle. You started towards home. You went through Selden. Then what, Rich. What happened then?"

Don came back to where we were. He'd brought cuffs and a restraint vest we used for transporting tough characters. He brought our leather sap.

Earlier in the evening, before his confession was gained, a crowd had come storming up to the jail, scaring Bess mightily.

I met them outside with my gun in hand, pointing at the ground, but clearly visible. "Gentlemen. Listen closely. If we're going to find Dorothy you've got to let me do my job. I know how you feel. I feel the same way. But you will not, do you hear me, you will not force yourselves in here. The only one who knows where we can find Dorothy is in my protective custody and will remain so. I call upon each of you to let me do this job correctly so that we can find the little girl. Now go home and stay there. I will let you know when we need your help."

"We heard he might of taken the little girl to Atwood." I knew the speaker. He was a hothead I'd seen before. He carried rumors of domestic violence.

"You hear that, too? You been up there to Atwood to look?" This came from a Rexford store-owner that I felt might be less volatile. He'd been one of the big promoters for me during the election.

A large man, one I didn't know, but figured was from Selden, stood to the front with his fists clenched, his eyes bright in the moonlight. His voice was raw with emotion. "Some of us are heading up that way to search. You got anything you can tell us, Sheriff? You know anything, you better tell us now or we might just come in and get those answers for ourselves!" A roar of angry voices rose from the crowd in agreement.

I brought my gun to chest height and said firmly, hearing my Da's commanding voice in mine, "I will shoot each and every man who tries to step through this door." Then I went back inside and locked us in.

Eventually Bess reported by phone that the crowd had gone. I was not certain how long we had before their fury would rise to a breaking point. I had no doubt that Richard Read would soon be a dead man.

We took turns, the three of us, until about midnight he finally broke. He told us the truth in his slow, word by word manner. But we had it. We still didn't know where she was, but we were closer. We were closer to finding the girl child who'd trusted this monster.

This is the confession of Richard Read as recorded by the Thomas County Sheriff's office:

"I am 53 years old and live with my parents north of Rexford in Thomas County. On April 14 I went to Hoxie in my father's Ford. I came back thru Selden and a small girl about 8 years old was in the middle of the road in front of me and waved at me and asked if I was going to take her riding. I told her I would and she got in the car in the front seat with me, and I cannot remember where we went that night as I had been drinking. We slept in the car and drove into Atwood about 10 o'clock in the morning and had breakfast. Then we drove east from Atwood several miles and then south on a side road. Then a madness overcame me and I don't know just what went wrong. Then she had a gash on her head but was not dead. Then I choked her to death and carried her body about 100 yards and buried it in a straw stack. Then I went south to the creek and went into a farmhouse and took a drink of water and then on up the hill and got another drink at a farmhouse and inquired the way to Colby, and was told it was ten miles south and ten miles west. Then I took that general direction and came into Colby. I make this statement of my own free will and without promises or threats on the part of any person."

With his signature we had him.

His confession gave us a definite area to search and we loaded Rich into a car, vested, handcuffed and reeking. To protect him and ourselves we didn't take my official car, but one that might not be so noticeable. We drove north and east onto the moonlit prairie following in reverse his reported return from the straw stack to Colby. Despite the brightness of the near full moon and repeated turnings up and down roads, Richard could not identify the exact location in the dark.

"The... plums... they had... flowers. I... smelled... them." His keening, moaning hums were interspersed with odd phrases. His blubbering sounds made us sick! "Sings... so... sweet. A... peeping... chick."

Just after dawn, our strength and the auto's gas running low, we returned to Colby. I called the Atwood sheriff and some of my 'boys', the ones I could trust, to let them know the direction their search should take. Sheriff Beaver drove back to Selden to stay with the Hunters, to give them what we knew and to prepare them for the worst. We were all shattered.

As morning light filled the spring sky a flood of cars began searching the suspected vicinity north of the Sappa Creek. Others would finish this gruesome task. My job and that of Don's was to remain with the prisoner.

Just before noon a call came to the office. We were told that Dorothy's body had been found by Albert Hase. Just as Rich had stated, she was hidden in a straw stack on the Victor Carlson farm north of Achilles. Mr. Hase and Dr. G. T. Reinert, B. R. Hamilton, Irvin Nicholson and C. L. Pope stayed with her corpse while H. L. Smith, the driver, had gone to a nearby farm to phone the Rawlins County officials. Calls went out to the surrounding farms and as cars traveled past they were hailed and instructed to return home, the search was over.

The child was examined briefly in the field by the Rawlins County coroner, Dr. Henneberger, and then taken into Atwood for complete autopsy. Dorothy Eileen had been viscously abused.

Hugh came for Bess and little Billy. They would stay in Levant until this was over. I didn't believe anyone would bother them, but I felt better they were with family.

Don and I barricaded the front and back doors of the jail and stayed there through the night. More than once we heard the sound of revving engines and pistol shots, then towards dawn the town grew quiet. It was Sunday.

We knew it was time to get Richard Read out of Colby. Now, before the mob of raging men and women returned for him.

"Listen, Don. We've got to find a safe place for the prisoner."

I didn't want to even call him by name any longer. "He'll be torn to pieces if they get in here and we might just get the same treatment. I'd like to take him back to Colorado and hand him over to the idiots who let him out, but I think our best plan is to get him to the prison in Lansing or better yet, the Topeka insane asylum. But for now, we've just got to get him out of our jail."

"Goodland's too close, Dad." Don's brow was furrowed with thought.

"Get the car gassed, Don. We're taking him to St. Francis."

"Really? I've seen Sheriff Bacon, Dad. He's a runt! If the boys find out Rich is there, there'll be no protection at all."

"Do as I say, Don. I'm not going to be the one folks remember who 'lost' a prisoner. You get my meaning?"

"Yeah, Dad. I get it. I might let it slip where we're headed."

CHAPTER 44

April 14-18, 1932: WILLIAM L. THOMAS
Menlo, Kansas

It were some time, all right, but me and Tater Pie stuck out the wait and got to marry. I didn't have all I wanted for her, but once't I had Tater Pie alongside me I had all I needed, ever. We set up just south of Menlo in a little frame house so's Tater Pie could get to the Colby Hospital easy for her nursing shifts.

I were still helping Bob's in-laws some, but had also started farming with Tater Pie's dad when he had work for me. Just a week after our wedding I were going to hitch up a team of mules to take to the harvest field. I 'spose my mind were on all the snugglin' we'd been doin' and I weren't paying close 'nough 'tention to my business because all of a sudden I were in a pile of trouble.

A rope which I should'a secured proper got 'tween my legs and wrapped itself round me when the mules started a'circlin and before I know'd what were happenin' my face and the mule butts was in kissing distance. I guess one of the mules, not wantin' to be so friendly with a feller, lashed out with a back hoof and the explosion of pain put me clear out. I was lashed to those dad-burned animals and a draggin' behind.

I were lucky, 'cause there were a corn crib not far off from the barn and the mules stopped there to sniff the good stuff. Mr. Rains found me not too long after the event, got me untangled and off to the doctor.

Dr. Smith, our local man, said, "Will, there's not much I can do but exam your injury and give you some pills for the pain." I had a glossy pink rope burn cross't my hip and my business parts were swole up like melons, only they was the queerest purple-red you ever saw. Dr. Smith told me cold compresses would take down the swelling, but it'd be some time for me and Tater Pie could resume cuddlin'. He also said something that just broke my heart!

"I can tell you this," he said real matter a fact. "You will never raise a family." Now I know'd he weren't tryin to be cruel, but he didn't know how much my Tater Pie loved the little ones. So for a time I held onto the hope that maybe she was already in the family way after all our fun this first week of her bein my Mrs.

I had a restin' up spell after that. Tater Pie liked carin' for me, puttin' all her nurse's know how to work. She and I spent a fair 'mount of time just talkin' and sharin' our dreams. In a way, I think back and am glad for that time. Otherwise we'd have just worked and worked like we knew we had to ifn we were goin to get somewheres and missed that good startin' out conversation.

By late summer I'd lost my limp and night times were back in business, but month after month, no little one showed signs of comin. One of Tater Pie's old beaus had married a friend of hers and they already had a baby that we went to visit often, just so she could get what she called her 'cozy' time. I liked to have tears ever time I saw her holdin' that little fellow against her breast, gazin into his eyes and tapping his rosy lips to make him suck, cooing and a singing to him.

One evenin' as we laid in bed talkin' the way we do I put forth the poor orphans that were coming out to Kansas from back east. There were a society that matched abandoned children with farm families, bringin' em out on the trains. I'd been studyin' on this after readin' about it in the papers.

Tater Pie, bless her heart, well she listened real quiet and I could tell she were a'thinkin on it. In a bit she sighed real deep. I know'd she just wanted one of her own so bad. She said, "Will, those little ones need good homes too, so maybe someday, but let's try just a bit longer. It's not been all that long. I am hopeful, aren't you?" And her sparkly eyes and little curls framin' her sweet face made me want to do anythin' she wanted.

There were so much sickness in the farm families. The country'd gone through the Spanish flu when I were still on the road and I'd seen plenty of sick folks down south. The cities was the worst for that, where too many people was crowded like cattle in a corral. Out here, though, it were too many babies in a home and not enough clean water or sanitation. That's what Tater Pie said, anyway. Typhoid, something that closed up babies' throats that she called diphtheria, infantile paralysis, scarlet fever, measles, small pox, whooping cough, well there seemed to be a baker's dozen ways for a small person to get sick and die. Almost overnight it seemed. Of course, there was those terrible accidents that happen on a farm. Horse wrecks, mad bulls, machines that tore off'n an arm afore you say jack. I'm not sure why we was a'wantin' a baby so bad anyhow.

Tater Pie hated the way there weren't more help for the little ones. Usually, by the time the farm families got one of their children to a doctor it were already too late. She said time after time, "If they would only come sooner!" But knowing how tough these folks was working I understood the difficulty of it all. And how to keep the animals tended and the crops cared for and the other six or eight children fed while someone were in hospital. Well, it just weren't an easy thing.

She blustered about sayin' the state o' Kansas ought a be shamed in how little they spent on health. She said they was preventatives! But they wasn't getting to the farms, no siree.

Tater Pie made sure I paid special attention to washing up well before visiting anyone with babes in the home. Especially Bob and his family. Tater Pie sure got along well with Hattie and we tried to go out near ever Sunday if she weren't working in Colby. She shared all her trainin' with Hattie about boiling water to rinse dishes, about using Clorox to sanitize the linens and underthings and milk equipment. Hattie were thrilled at what Tater Pie taught her. The newest thing coming, Tater Pie said, were somethin' called vaccines. She promised Hattie and Bob's kids would be first on a list when those got to Colby.

Another thing Tater Pie hated and broke me of mighty quick were spittin'. She said spit, 'specially the hawkin' kind, is packed full of bad things that folks can track in or breathe in when it dries. She said men are just fools about dirt mostly anyway. Not good soil dirt, she'd point out. That weren't the problem. It were the human dirt and the animal dirt that spread disease. And coughin'! Don't let her get started on the need for a clean hanky in everone's pockets. "Cover it up!" she'd say firmly with her feisty eyes flashin'. "Cover that cough, cover that sneeze!" She were a nurse on a mission!

Time passed and so did her dad. Seeing her mom living lonesome with no one to care for, we invited her to move in with us. That were an adjustment, but I were just as happy to do it 'cause it meant when Tater Pie got home from a tough day nursin' Ma would have a supper all set for her, the house tidied and the tea kettle on the boil. She was a mighty good help growin' garden sass, too. We played cards of an evenin' and they both liked my mouth harp playin. All in all, even without little feet tapping to my songs, we was happy.

Well, that peaceable time came to a sudden end in the spring of 1932. I were workin' on turning last winter's horse bedding into the garden when an auto come tearin' past the yard heading into town, horn a'blarin. The driver's arm were out the window, waving at folks to follow.

This were a Thursday evening, just getting' on towards sunset. Tater Pie were at home for her three day in a row break. The nurses worked long shifts at the hospital so her usual pattern were four on three off and sometimes she did nights the same way. Well, she come out on the porch when she heard the commotion and we got in the car to see what it might be. I didn't smell smoke, though it'd been terrible dry all winter with bad dust storms choking out the crops. Folks was real concerned we'd have no harvest a'tall this year.

A crowd was gathered by the depot. The town whistle were blowing by this time, letting the area know they's trouble somewhere. We got out and joined the men and women who was talking fast, wearin' expressions of fear and anxiousness.

"A girl missing, I heard," said one man.

"Didn't come home from school," another said.

"Selden way. Little second grader, name of Dorothy."

The man who'd driven in raised his hands for quiet. The whistle wound down like a howlin' dog. We stood side by side, Tater Pie and me, with folks crowding behind and before. I took Tater's hand and felt how small and cold it were. She was tremblin', so I patted it with my other hand, trying to settle her some.

"Folks, listen up. We got a missing child, Dorothy Hunter. That's Floyd and Jennie's second girl. She's eight. Her sister says she went back to the school for her dinner pail and never came home. We need your help to go lookin'. Probably nothing going to come of it, she might have just gone visitin' a friend we don't know about, but folks, the family is asking for help and we can do this for them. I need anyone who's got a car and the time to join in the search to step up here. We'll divide up the places she might have gone and try to get them covered before dark. Who can help?"

There was some who either didn't have a car or had too many little ones of their own to leave alone, but about ten drivers stepped up, me included. "Tater, I want you to go home and wait with your Ma. If the little girl needs nursing, someone will come get you. But if you go with me and she's found elsewhere, they won't be able to find you as quick."

"I understand, Will. Makes sense. I can walk home, no problem. I'll put a bag together with things I might need. You be careful! And find her!"

Well, dark came and we searched all night driving the roads, knocking on farm house doors, shining our lights under bridges and into basements. I'm afraid we scared several of the farm wives with our stompin' and door bangin', but there weren't no time for politeness. Ever barn were checked, ever chicken house between Selden and Rexford, north-east to Dresden, south-east towards Hoxie. Found nothin' but skunks, coyotes, monkey-faced owls and jack rabbits.

It were a sad bunch of men who come in worn and hungry for coffee and biscuits. Ever'one met up at the church basement. The ladies had scrambled up eggs and cooked a mess of bacon, sausage and hotcakes. Tater Pie were with them, pouring scalding coffee into empty cups. Seeing her familiar face so distressed jist melted my heart.

"I'm mighty worried," I told her. "A whole night gone and not a trace."

"Some of the gals have heard that the Sheridan sheriff talked to Dorothy's school friends and her sister Alice. They said they waited for her awhile when she went back to the school, but then had to go on home. That lady over there," Tater Pie pointed at a plump grey-head gathering up plates, "said a couple of girls told the sheriff a strange man tried to get them in his car a few days before. I don't know if I believe it, sometimes girls will make things up to get noticed, but oh Will! If she's been taken by a man, I shudder to think."

"We'll find her. We ain't quittin' til we do."

The men returned to their cars, filled their tanks with gas and then we all drove back to the same routes we'd driven before, hoping daylight would give us reward. There was just too many roads to try, too many ditches and gullies. The lively conversations that we'd started with was over. The cars held silent, grim men.

Nothing of the little girl were found, no sign at all, but when we gathered in Selden for a late lunch great news awaited us. A phone call from Atwood had come in, saying a little girl that matched Dorothy's description was seen eatin' breakfast in the Owl Café with an older man. She seemed to be fine. The two had left in a brown car. The Atwood sheriff, Mr. Jennings was interviewing the café owner and anyone who might have seen the pair.

We was told to go home and get some rest, tend to chores or whatever. The whistle would blow if we was needed again. I felt empty, like it had all been a waste and the child still missing, but I did just that. I went home, washed up, changed into fresh clothes and sat down for a short nap. I'd planned to finish the garden later as full planting time were a few weeks away and the manure needed to mix with the soil afore then. That was my plan, anyhow.

I slept through the day and about evening Tater Pie brought me a heaping bowl of warm milk toast, buttery and peppered just like she knows I take it and we went to bed. I slept without dreams. It would be my last dreamless night for many a year.

Saturday about noon the phones started ringing all over Menlo. Ringing in all the towns and out to the farm homes that were on the line. Dorothy had been found. Left crushed and broken and brutalized under a straw pile east of Atwood, near the town of Achilles. The murderer was caught. The funeral for Dorothy would be the next day, Sunday, in Selden.

Outrage! Fury! Sickness and fear! How could something like this could happen in one of our communities? Was no one safe? Who? Why? Plenty of opinion, but no good answers.

After a time, the name trickled out; Rich Read from Rexford. My ears rang when I heard the name. I know'd that name. Oh God! I'd met the man, had worked 'longside him during wheat threshing. He were the one who hummed, the one who were partial to my music. My knees buckled and Tater Pie screamed when I fell to the floor in a dead faint.

The funeral were the saddest thing I ever saw. The little tyke was holding her doll in her arms, dressed in an outfit that matched hers, even down to shiny black shoes and pink anklets. A ruffled bonnet covered her hair. Whispered talk told horrid stories of her injuries: a head bashed in, a strangling, bite marks, oh, it were just too much! The bruising on her cheeks show'd, though the mortician had tried his best. Her child's coffin was not much bigger than a peach box.

The school auditorium were so crowded there warn't room to breathe. Tater and all the ladies and many of the men cried through it all, nearly drownin' out the preacher's words, but towards the end there were a change in the mood. A change that raised the hair on my arms and neck, a change that brought a chill wind whispering 'round the room.

Somehow we joined into one mind. We was no longer men standing as individuals. We become a force, connected in a like purpose. A neighbor of the Reads, Mr. Osborne, took charge. His face was purple with held in fury. There would be justice for Dorothy. Primitive justice.

A whole bunch of cars left after the funeral, driving fast to Colby where we figgered Rich were bein' held. When we got to the Colby jail, we found we was wrong. Sheriff Ed McGinley, well, he knew there were a pretty good chance something like what we had in mind would happen, so he and his deputy and some others, we were told, had taken Rich to St. Francis, to their new court house jail.

When this was discovered, some of the men backed out, it being getting on toward night and there were chores and family to think of. I think they had cooled off some too, but one of the men said, "Boys, its better this way. No one knows us in Cheyenne County."

Seven cars drove north to Atwood, turned west and went through McDonald, Bird City and Wheeler before getting to St. Francis. It were a good road, that Highway 36 west of Atwood and we could go a fair speed. At Wheeler we'd pulled off and made a plan so everone know'd his job. Even with all the time it took us to get to this point there weren't a one of us wantin' to back off.

The big new courthouse were in the middle of the city, easy to spot and in plain view of homes and businesses. But being it was late on a Sunday most folks were safe in bed and we felt invisible somehow. We parked by the jail and about a dozen of us went in. We had one real big guy with us, a man with a Russian last name, the rest of us bein' just average size. The sheriff there, now he were a real small man and looked mighty concerned, met us and, knowing what we'd come for said, "Yes, I have this man in custody. Now why don't you all go home to your wives."

I know'd there was guns in the crowd, but we was all real quiet, no one threatenin' or anything. I didn't carry one myself. One voice said real clear, "We've not come all this way to go home to wives. We're here to end this now. You can give us the keys and step aside willingly or we can do it the hard way."

I asked the sheriff, "Sir, what is your name?"

He had to clear his throat to answer and it took several swallows before he could say, "A. A. Bacon, Sheriff Bacon. I want no trouble tonight."

"Sheriff Bacon, do you have a gun on you?"

"I do, but with permission I'm going to unload it right now and put it in my desk drawer."

That's what he did, broke open the cylinder, cupped the bullets and put everything in the desk drawer. His hands were shakin' mighty hard, but so were ours. I could feel my teeth clenchin' so's not to chatter. Then he unclipped his keys, handed them to the Russian fellow, pointed up the stairs at the back of the room and stepped outside into the night. Leavin us to our task.

The stairs going up to the cells was narrow and went up three flights. The whole crowd of us couldn't fit, so we divided up, leavin' some in the front room and one man on each landin'. Three of us, me, the big Russian and one other stern man who I didn't know went to the top.

When Richard Read seen, us he let out a high shriek, something like a rabbit does when a hawk pierces its spine. Gave me chills worse than I'd ever had. Then he starts this keening, blubbering kind of a crying. I felt ashamed for him. I wondered if he recognized me, but he didn't seem to be too aware. He were whimperin' and blubberin' like a child after a belt's been put across his backsides.

When the door lock clicked open, the Russian man took a'hold Richard's arms, clamped them behind him and slipped a piggin' string round his wrists. With a grip on Richard's coverall's waist the strong man kind of hopped him down those tight stairs, his legs being floppy and loose and his ankles bound in leather. He looked beat up some and I wondered how things had gone for him since his capture. His odor were fierce, enough to make my eyes water, biting and sour and hot like a rubber belt that were about to fly off a shaft. It weren't the smell of shit or vomit.

It were a chemical smell, almost like the oil rig chemicals I'd worked around. An electric smell.

He were put into the back of my car. A bunch of men piled on top and I didn't envy their closeness. I took several breaths of cold night air to clear my head before getting behind the wheel.

We drove east out of town, the original plan being to take him back to the place he'd murdered the little girl, but someone had called Mr. Carlson upon whose land she'd been found and he begged us not to do it there. Enough sorrow for his family already, he'd said.

None of us was real familiar with the area so after driving through the dark towns of Bird City and McDonald we was startin' to worry we'd been on the road too long. Word was surely out what we'd done. The lead car took a right four miles east of McDonald. The Beaver Creek was that direction and there'd be trees. There weren't none along the main road we'd been traveling.

The whole way, Rich Read was sobbin' and keenin' and singin' in an unhuman way. He talked to hisself some, too. Like he was havin' a argument in his head. Finally he just settled into a steady hum.

About three miles south we dropped down into the valley. A farmhouse was off to our right, but no lights were on. We cross't a rough board bridge and started a little ways uphill, but turned off to the west, going through an open gate, before the tree line ran out. Our headlights cast stripes of shadow in the trees. The moon were just coming full and shone down upon us clear as if God were helping our task. Huge cottonwoods with trunks that would'a took three men to span, trees that had survived buffalo, fires and droughts, who had long tapped into the deep waters of the drainage, stood stark against the black sky. White plum blossom glowed and sweetened the air. When the cars all shut down and the doors had stopped clos'n, I heard a big ol' hoot owl call off in the distance. Fit the night just perfect, somehow.

Several of the men had ropes. More than we would ever need. A loop were formed from one, no fancy knots or nothin', just a lasso loop. We just wanted the man dead. Richard kept on at his burrin', hummin' sounds, never seeming to stop. He made his sounds on breathing in an' out both, like my mouth harp. I'd never heard a thing like it.

"We are here tonight to end a life of a monster what took an innocent child into his keeping, brutally treated her and left her like a cast off carcass." The voice was a man from Selden. I'd heard it before and knew him but we were all careful not to look at each other. All eyes were on the man before us, his shoulders hunched around the rope, hands tied behind his back. We listened to the quavering sounds that was comin' from him.

The end of the rope were thrown over a limb about 8' off the ground. The tree were close to a bob wire fence and there was posts in an orderly row followin' the tree line. Three men took a holt of the rope and give it a little tug, testing the limb and the resistance of the man on t'other end.

He didn't fight. He didn't plea. He sang his in and out song, tears seemin' to run without end, like the rivers of the earth was behind his eyes.

"Anythin' you got to say, say it now."

The man, his posture one of complete acceptance, said, "There's... some... neighbors.... that owe... me... money... for work... I... done. That... should... go... to my... mother. Give... my... watch... to my... father. If... it... hadn't... been... for liquor... I... wouldn't... have done... it..., and I... would... not do... it again." His words were oddly spaced with long pauses between as if his lips and tongue had no feelin' left in em'. I 'membered how little he spoke in the harvest field and now I know'd why. It must of been a terrible handicap to speak so.

"You won't have a chance," one of the men said loudly and raised his arm. "Is that all?"

"Thank… you… " With that his crying song started up but now there was a tune to it, a sad and mournful tune that seemed familiar.

The leader dropped his arm and the three men pulled the rope taut, raising Richard about three feet off the ground while one other man tied the end to a post with a knot that weren't going to slip or be untied.

As his body thrashed and jerked, his keening cries was stopped by a choking gurgling sound. Urine dripped from the bottom of his pants and stained his front. A strong outhouse odor passed by my face. I felt ill, my face hot and cold all of a time. More cars began to pull in behind ours. I guess the word were out. None was a sheriffs' though. There was women and children coming to see the spectacle and I knew I were done with the whole mess. This job were done.

I drove home alone, scrubbed long and hard at the wash basin and climbed into bed with Tater Pie. Her softness and moist heat wrapped around me, drivin' back the cold in my bones. She didn't ask a thing of me, then or later. Though she checked the papers for weeks and weeks to see what were reported, to see if me and the others was in any danger of being arrested, we never spoke of it. Never ever.

CHAPTER 45

Newsmen tracked me to my office at the Colorado State Industrial Commission where I work as an investigator. A reporter for The Denver Post was first in line, but when he finished telling me the horrid story from Kansas I was so distraught I gave instructions to my secretary that I'd not be interviewed further and fled for home. Considering I've not missed a day's work in ten years I believe that says something of my distress.

The monster struck again. I knew he would. I'm surprised something of the kind didn't happen sooner, though we will never know if he had committed other atrocities that were not attributed to him. A man like that, well, I can't imagine he could control himself for very long.

So much hurt, so much pain! Unwillingly I find myself thinking back to the battered child in 1916. Such viciousness! Such unmerciful damage done to a young girl! I am horrified and sickened once again.

Now I am told he took an even younger child, an eight year-old, by God! Ravaged her and crushed her skull with some type of farm tool. Oh Lord, maybe it was a mercy she didn't live, knowing like I do what happened to Pauline, a girl nearly twice that age.

The quote placed in The Denver Post doesn't begin to express what I wish I could have said. Words come into my head that I am ashamed to admit to. Words I don't even want to acknowledge knowing. I was recorded as saying,

"I am convinced he was mentally unbalanced." Well, as the phrase goes, 'that is an understatement'.

I was also quoted thusly: "But one thing is certain. He was a chronic menace to society. His huge bulk and steel muscles, his stunted intelligence, his ugliness when drunk, all combined to make him irretrievably dangerous."

Take note that I used the word chronic even though the 1916 event was the first time he'd been incarcerated. I truly believe there were likely other events before Pauline's and again following his premature release from prison.

For days the Post fanned the flames of their readers' passion for horror and though I wished not to, my eyes sought the columns for further revelations. A California investigator questioned crimes committed in his state. With Read's family connections on the west coast, I have my suspicions. Though I abhor mob action, I commend those who ended the life of this fiend with sure and swift justice. I grieve for those involved as I know their lives will forever be tainted and indelibly changed.

I will always question the night when a choice of outcome was in my power. At the completion of each pondering, of each sounding of my heart, I believe I took the lawful and upright action for Richard Read, that spring night in 1916, rather than to allow his hanging from a barn rafter. I pray to the Almighty Father that I did.

Tomorrow I have the satisfaction of seeing Mr. Lester Smith, Mr. Frank Baldauf and Mr. Frank Penley held accountable for greed and thievery through their practice of billing Douglas County for labor at a rate of $4.00 per day while paying out $2.00 or less to their workers, something which they have been doing for nearly a decade, but which had gone unnoticed. I am pleased to say my case is clear with adequate documentation to assure a fair judgement on behalf of the laborers. It remains to be seen if any money will find its way back to those who earned it. I've done all I can to pursue justice.

It pleases me to think I might be remembered as one who fought for the victim, who stood against the tyrant and through diligent work gave satisfaction. I pray to the Almighty Father I might stand with a clear conscience at the end of my days.

CHAPTER 46

April 19, 1932: SARAH LOU READ WARNER

Prairie Dog Creek

"Oh dear brother! Oh my sad, sick brother! What happened to you? How could you have done this unbelievable thing?" Word came to Burlington by telegram that we had to come home, Art and me and the little ones. Come back to Rexford for Richard's funeral. We took the train and Joe met us at the depot. His expression was carved from marble.

No one said much on the ride to the ranch, not wanting the children to hear. When they asked, as children will who sense silent adults mean something is being kept from them, they were told 'it's a sad time, honey, and mama doesn't want to talk just now'. Art wouldn't even answer them. I believe he wanted to say what he thought about Richard, but held back for my sake.

I know they will hear whispers. They will get the looks. It is bound to happen. We'll get it here and back home at the store. The German families will have heard. They will be glad to know of Richard's end. News travels so much faster now than it once did. I suppose our business will fail over this.

"Oh dear brother! Oh my sad, sick brother!"

Mother looks near death. She has no color to her lips. Her hair is thin, wispy as dried grass and just as pale as winter milk. She can't even smile for the grandchildren she's not seen in months. When I hug her, her bones crack audibly. She can't last much longer after this blow.

"Oh dear brother! Oh my sad, sick brother! How could you do this to your family? How could you do this to your sweet mother, the one who loved you no matter what you did?"

Father still has some fire, but he is very confused. His once sharp mind is failing. He announced at supper, when we had all gathered the night before the funeral, that he wanted Richard to have a Lodge burial.

Tim said, his voice biting in bitter irritation, "Father, do you remember how Richard died? Do you remember why?" With all the children at table he was careful not to go further.

Father said, "Now, now, Tim. There's no reason for you to get hot!" But his eyes turned inward and he didn't bring up a Lodge burial again.

The next day, April 21st, folks started arriving early, bringing covered dishes and cold tea in glass jugs. I hate to say, but I saw some other jugs being passed around by the men who kept finding reasons to step over to the barn.

My focus went to those true friends of the family, like the Geisenheners. Their eyes and faces tell me how heart sick they feel, on all accounts. They pat and fuss and help smooth the way for the service.

Musicians Wilbert Thayer, Mrs. McIntyre, Mrs. Jud Keefer and her brother-in-law Walt Keefer provide somber hymns, and they, too, are here out of sincerity. But there are many here who are only curiosity seekers, thrill seekers, the ones who want to gawk at the family that raised a fiend. Well, let them look. There's nothing to see but sorrow upon sorrow!

I pray there will be no rude outbursts or worse.

Reverend Harry C. Elema of Colby's First Baptist was willing to conduct the service. It took some doing to find a religious man open hearted enough to do so. That made Mother cry and cry, to think that her son might not have a minister to pray over him. It was a fine Christian act of love and his words were powerful.

He spoke, "Today we mourn together for the family of Pleasant Richardson Read who was the first born of Jacob and Mary Ellen Read. He came to Kansas as a child and worked his life in honest labor." Here, Pastor Elema paused, scanned the faces and took a preparatory breath.

"We are all aware he found difficulty relating to others and others to him. This impaired his inclusion in the community, but he continued to do his part through productive work. His strong physical form was useful, but because of his slowness or his impaired speech or for whatever other reasons he didn't mesh well. He was not welcomed when the work was done.

"I ask you, each of you, if he had carried a wound or infirmity upon his physical body wouldn't you have given understanding and allowance? Cruelly for Richard, with an infirmity of the mind, there was no understanding, no allowance. Instead there was mockery, there was abuse. At the very least he found himself outcast and isolated. That is an unnatural place for a child of God.

"I grieve that we, each of us whose lives touched that of Richard Read, may have played a part in his sorrowful actions. Whether through intention or through a lack of Christian love each of us may carry some measure of responsibility for the damage and sorrow this man, whose soul cried out for comfort and found none except in devil drink, inflicted on two known occasions.

"Let us recall the love of our savior Jesus who welcomes all to his embrace. Let us never ever again turn our backs on another human being. Untold misery may be averted if we reach out in understanding, not judgement. Love your neighbor as yourself. Such simple words, yet so difficult to practice."

Reverent Elema gathered the silence of the room, waited for shifting feet to quiet further before he spoke again.

"Especially difficult if the neighbor doesn't fit our definition of normal.

"Today we mourn together, not just for the Read family, but also for the family of Dorothy Eileen Hunter and the families of everyone involved in this tragic event. As you say your prayers tonight and each night, ask yourselves: have I lived as Jesus would have me do? Have I? With prayer and action, let us never find ourselves so grieved again!"

I felt peace come over the room. It was spirit, I had no doubt, nor had I ever felt anything like it. I could never have imagined the profound sensation gathered like a down filled comforter around the shoulders of those listening. In the silent room Mother started Richard's music box, the one she'd given him all those many years ago, the one he'd cherished and protected as the one solace in his life, and in the silence of the room, the music played.

Pleasant Richardson Read, my big brother, was buried in the Hawkeye Cemetery. No one traveled with his body to the graveyard. The instructions given to the caretaker were, "put him in a corner away from everyone".

CHAPTER 47

April 20, 1932: PAULINE WEISSHAAR
SCHLICHENMAYER
The Settlement Bethune, Colorado

Lena came to visit, to tell me about a little girl's death and a lynching in Rawlins County, Kansas a few days ago. The news smashes into me with the force of a sledge hammer.

I am shattered! The earth drops from beneath me. My heart hammers so strongly I believe it can be seen beneath the cover of my dress. Illness as sudden and real as bad food brings me to my knees and I heave, cold sweat beading across my forehead. My lips turn to ice. I hear a whistling, see glittering stars and drop into blackness.

I wake to the sound of Shirley, not quite six months, demanding her feeding. My breasts leak milk in response. Edna whimpers at my side. I've been put to bed, though I have no memory of how this has happened. Lena is rocking Shirley, shushing her with a knuckle to her mouth. It has been too long since her last child or she would have suckled the babe. Sisters do that for each other. Mothers offer what they can to the little ones.

"Lena, bring her to me. I'll get up in a moment, but I can feed her first. How long have I been like this?" I prop myself against the headboard and unbutton my bodice, reaching for a shawl to cover myself.

"Oh Pauline, dear sister! I am so sorry! My God, I had no idea you'd take the news so hard! I thought you'd be happy."

Shirl has been swaddled tight like Lena does with her children. I loosen the wrappings, hating the thought of anyone being restrained against their will. "I don't know, Lena...I never expected to hear...I always thought...Oh God in Heaven, he killed a child? And he's dead? Truly? He's truly dead? Hung? Oh my God!"

"We don't have to talk about this anymore, Pauline. You know, maybe I shouldn't have said anything, but I was afraid you'd hear from others. I'm sure you would have. I know how they will talk again. I know how you will hate it all coming back up. I wanted to spare you, but I didn't expect you to collapse! It's been such a long time!"

"Not so long, Lena. Not so long, really. I can never forget. I will never forget, but perhaps I won't have to be afraid anymore. Perhaps."

"It's true, we all feared when we knew he'd been let go early from the prison. We all wondered if he might return, having family here and all. You never let on, though, Pauline. You never said you were afraid."

"How could I say it? How could I open my throat and say his name or put my mind onto him?" I felt bile rising again and heat come to my cheeks. Turning down to look at sweet, innocent Shirley, stroking her velvet cheek, helped me settle. "Come up here beside us, Edna. Snuggle with your Momma and baby sis." Edna's round head burrows under my arm that is supporting the baby. I feel her hot breath and quivering shoulders.

"Lena, after... well, you know, afterwards... when I left for a time, no one wanted to ask me, no one wanted to hear about it from me. They didn't speak about it to me, but I knew the talk. I was blamed, Lena! It was my fault! And I shudder to think that anyone who was as mistreated as I was should also be punished. It made me furious! I was a victim, Lena! Being blamed, well that was nearly as bad as what that beast did to me! Maybe worse, because it went on so long and it was my community. I was shut out, Lena! I was judged and found guilty!" I gasped, unable to catch my breath. Edna whimpered and I tried to calm my voice. "Oh Lord, my God! To think another child, a baby child – she was how old?"

"Eight, Pauline. Only eight. And he a man old enough to be her father, grandfather even. I am so, so sorry! For you and for her and for her family!" Lena's face, splotchy with crying, was bound into the shape of a tight fist. "And I am sorry for the ones who were forced to do what they did. The men in Kansas that hung him. But I'm proud of them, too. You might not remember, but the men here were set to do the same. If they had then this little girl would be alive. Maybe he hurt others. We'll never know."

"Lena?" I asked. "Will you talk to me now and then we'll not speak of it again? I have so many questions. I have so many blank places in my mind over that time. Will you tell me?"

"I will try, Pauline. I will try." Lena drew a deep breath and settled back into the rocking chair, patting the wooden arms rhythmically with her palms. "There was much that only the men knew. What do you need?"

"After... after I was found... when the others came upon me... how did they know who had done it? How did they find him?"

"Well, when the others came back from Bauders it was getting on toward chore time. The cows were home, but they couldn't find you. They called and called. Then Father and Mother returned from my place, you remember they came to play with little Pete. Father sent Jake to ring the church bell while the others started searching. When they came past the Barnesberger farm, they saw something white, caught on a bush like a flag. They might have walked right past you without that cloth. It was part of your dress."

I remembered the printed fabric then. With a flash of pain I remembered the sound of tearing and his vicious teeth. Gasping, I pulled Shirley away from my breast, but then moved her gently to the other side so she would complete her feeding.

"They weren't even sure what you were at first! Bill thought coyotes had taken a calf when he saw the blood, but then it all came clear. Still, they had no way of knowing what had happened. You were so hurt, Pauline. Bill carried you home. You were just torn apart, you were. Mother was so upset she couldn't even care for you, but she refused to let the ladies in. John rode for me and I came right away. You slept for more than a day. I washed you and dressed your wounds. We didn't know how bad you were hurt inside, Pauline. We didn't know if you'd ever have babies. When you woke and could travel, Mother and Father thought it best you stayed with the Idalia cousins for a time."

"Where did they find him? How long after?"

"Right away, Pauline. Once you were in the house and they saw where," Lena paused with eyes turned inward remembering, "how, you were hurt, they knew it had to be a man. They knew it had to be the Kansas Read man. By then the bell had called all the men and they were gathered at our place. They spread out from where you'd been found, taking ropes and shovels. He was hiding like a jack rabbit behind a big sagebrush. I don't think they were too kind to him. They planned to hang him in the Bauder's barn.

"But Reverend Adolf thought it best to get outside help, since this man was from the outside, you know, so he rode to Burlington for the Sheriff. Mr. Ruberson it was then.

"He was sick, Pauline, that man. He was sick from liquor and from what he'd done. But we all knew, even then, that he was sick inside his head. I guess that has been proved true once again."

"I don't understand what happened to me Lena. I know that there are men who are rough and don't feel tenderness for a woman, who take what they feel is theirs to take, but I was not a woman, I was a child and I remember... I don't want to and I've fought it for 16 years... it was spring, April

and the moon was so big... Oh God! Lena! I just realized...
this little girl, this little eight year old girl was taken on
the very same day he hurt me! It was April 14, the VERY
SAME DAY but 16 years later! What can that mean, Lena?
What can that mean?"

I was crying hard, without reservation and my babies
were crying with me. Lena, too. We sobbed for things we
would never understand.

CONCLUDING STORIES

READ FAMILY:

Art and Sarah Lou Warner had twin daughters who did not survive. They lost their son Warden Wayne the year following the lynching at the age of 29 while he was working in Norton.

Art died just before Thanksgiving in 1934, less than a year after burying Warden. Sarah Lou and her daughter Leila (Lela B.) continued to run the store in the German Settlement.

Mary Ellen (Kell) Cardwell Read was gone by January 1936. Jacob Hoffman Read passed in 1938. They are both buried in the Hawkeye Cemetery in Decatur County, KS.

Leila married Ray Plummer and moved to Burlington. Ray became a sheriff!

Sarah Lou managed the Warner store until 1946 when a neighbor, Mr. Ed Knodel, expressed an interest in buying it. She moved into the town of Burlington and died there at the age of 88. She was buried in Burlington rather than her hometown of Rexford.

Attie Read Leach died in Stanislaus, California in 1960.

John Jacob Read, his wife Ollie Geisnehener and two children Maxine and Harold (a twin Gerald died at the age of 6) moved onto the home place and farmed until returning to Iowa. 'Little Jake' died in Iowa in 1970.

Tim Johnson Read married Millie Stradley. They also had two children, Robert and Fawn. He died in California one month after his brother John.

Villa Read married Claude Brantley and they moved to Oklahoma to farm. They had three daughters and one son and in 1920 were living in the Siebert, CO area. Her husband passed away in 1964 and all of her children are deceased at the time of this writing.

Joe Glenn Read moved onto the homestead after John returned to Iowa. He and his wife Hannah had one son, Lifus. Joe ended life in Buena Vista, CO in 1977.

Edmee Ellen Read Gardner resided with her husband Will in Republic County, KS through most of her life. They had only one son. She died in Hoxie in 1972 and is buried in Belleville, KS.

The last son of Jacob and Mary Ellen Cardwell Read, George Wayne Read and wife Lora operated a cream and egg station in Rexford. Baseball was his passion. In later years he lived in north central KS, ending in Hays as a custodian at the Fort Hays University. His three children are deceased. At his death in 1986 he was 89.

Pleasant Richard Read is buried in the Hawkeye Cemetery. He has a headstone beside his mother's with this engraving:

BROTHER PLEASANT R. READ
JAN 30, 1879 APR 18, 1932

McGINLEY FAMILY:

Edward Henry McGinley controlled the office of Thomas County Sheriff from the election in 1930 to 1939, alternating between acting Sheriff and Under-sheriff with his son Don. From all appearances, the father was in charge regardless.

He was included in the "Illustriana Kansas" as a notable Kansan in the early 1930's. His demeanor was said to have influenced James Cagney's acting career as a detective.

There were several sensationalized stories written and published in detective magazines about the cases Ed

McGinley handled during his years as Thomas County Sheriff. One such magazine, the Dynamic Detective, September 1938 issue, included an adaptation of the 1932 event with the title: KANSAS MISSING SCHOOLGIRL AND THE PRAIRIE MONSTER by Richard Enright.

Don married Vada Miller in 1935 and a son was born that same year. He was named after his grandfather, Edward.

Despite Sheriff McGinley's renown his wife Stella Emilie (Bess) found herself in financial difficulty when he died from stomach cancer the day after Christmas 1939. She moved to Colorado with their son Bill to run a café. Following a failure in this business she relocated to Denver and worked as a house-keeper, having lodging at the home of her employer.

In 1941 Bill married Wanda Horner, the best friend of Dorothy Hunter who had waited vainly for her to return from school. The couple had five sons.

Later, Bess moved into an old Victorian home in Denver owned by her mother Frannie and worked in a clothing factory as a seamstress. For a time in the early 1950's Don joined his mother and grandmother, living in the basement

Following his father's death, alcohol and mental illness destroyed Don McGinley. His unharnessed brutality had lost the restraint of his father's control. He spent his last years in an institution in Pueblo, Colorado.

He and Vada's son Ed had mental and behavioral problems as well and at an early age was also institutionalized in a Kansas mental hospital. Around 1975 during the national de-institutionalization movement Ed, at age 40, was placed in the community based program in Atwood called Prairie Development Center (PDC), a branch of Developmental Services of Northwest Kansas (DSNWK).

JOHN RICE (J.R.) RUBERSON:

In 1932 J. R. Ruberson was married and living in Denver, CO. He and his wife, Grace Gladys Cox, had a daughter 2 ½ years old, Betty Lou. His employment as an investigator for the Colorado State Industrial Commission proved well suited to his sense of protecting the 'little man'.

The Governor of Colorado at this time was Edwin (Big Ed) Johnson whose birth in Scandia, KS in 1884 made him a contemporary and fellow Kansan with J.R. Ruberson. Big Ed is remembered for his work in developing Colorado highways, a project which opened up many opportunities for graft. J.R. Ruberson had a keen eye for graft.

Mr. Ruberson lived in Colorado during an era of intense persecution of the Mexican labor class, due mostly to the Depression and resulting unemployment of so many. He is recorded as delivering information directly to Governor Johnson regarding relief and deportation issues. While Governor Johnson was a mighty force for the eradication of Mexican families, federal laws prevented many of his efforts.

I believe that J.R. Ruberson was, by character, a fair and honest man who would have used his position to uphold decent treatment of those unfairly impacted by these times. As all men of honor do amongst those without, he did what he could.

John Rice Ruberson died in 1960 at the age of 72. From painter, insurance man, real estate broker and prairie town sheriff to advising the Governor of Colorado, J.R. Ruberson stood for integrity.

ADDISON ALANSON (A.A.) BACON:

The notoriety of having been the sheriff to lose a prisoner, one who was then killed by mob action, could not have been to the benefit of Addison Alanson Bacon. In a small community there would have been no escape from the ongoing 'peanut gallery' comments.

In 1940, at age 50, he was the proprietor of the St. Francis grocery. That same year he lost his brother Ezra Martin, the third brother to have died. Both of his parents were also gone.

Two years later another brother, George Willis, passed away with his dear sister Chloe soon to follow. Chloe had married in Colorado and had eight daughters, but no more sons.

I was told a story by a family member regarding her little boy Rollo, the one who was taken from her as a child. Tragedy followed tragedy. When Rollo was grown, he and his mother were finally able to reconnect. They had only a short time together before he was killed in a lime pit accident.

Mr. Bacon's first marriage ended and he was remarried in 1957 to Bertha Talmon. She had been married twice before. He was 68, she was 57.

His two sisters, Ethel and Maude were the next to pass. He and Bertha remained married until his death.

He is buried in the St. Francis Cemetery.

PAULINE WEISSHAAR SCHLICHENMAYER:

The crime of rape against a girl or woman is often doubly damaging when a sense of culpability is placed upon the victim by themselves and/or others. This was especially true in a closed group such as the Settlement. Pauline had no outside resources to turn to, no therapists or counselors and the additional pressure of a judgmental religion that has the power to support or strangle. It must have been crippling for this young woman, not quite 16 years old.

Tragically Pauline's father died the following December at the age of 53. Perhaps the shame and guilt of letting a daughter be so ill-treated turned inward. A father would naturally hold himself to blame for his failure to protect a child. Especially from a man living in such close proximity. Her mother, a woman who bore 13 children in 25 years, lived on to the age of 80. Her endurance was not uncommon, but it was remarkable in every aspect.

On February 11, 1923, Pauline married Jake Schlichenmayer, the nephew of her sister Lena's husband. One has to wonder about their courtship, shadowed by what had happened seven years earlier. During a phone interview with a person who was raised in the Settlement and knew the family intimately, I was told he remembered how Pauline was treated as a 'black sheep'. She had become a topic for the after Sunday dinner sewing circle where women met to 'measure and find wanting' those who did not strictly abide by the old ways.

What a strong woman Pauline was! Just like her mother, just like the tough prairie grasses, she endured. She let judgement and gossip blow over her like the prairie wind. I imagine she lent a sensitive ear to any young woman in need.

She and her husband continued in the faith, remained in the Settlement and raised seven children. Becoming a widow in 1971, she moved to Longmont, Colorado in 1985. In 1993 she died at the age of 92 and was buried in the Fairview Cemetery in Burlington, Colorado.

DOROTHY EILEEN HUNTER FAMILY:

The magnitude of having a child taken under such horrid circumstances would be overwhelming. Jennie Lucille was so traumatized that she was unable to attend Dorothy's funeral. Her pregnancy made the collapse even more worrisome.

There is no knowing how the lynching of Richard Read added to the family's burdens, but Mr. Hunter was reported as saying, "I only wish I could have been there."

By 1935 the family had relocated to Sharon Springs, Wallace County, KS. Four years later they had moved to San Bernardino, California where there were other family members including Jennie's parents.

Another tragedy occurred in 1940 with the drowning death of Fred Weaver, Jennie's father, while on a fishing trip in Lake Elsinore, California. Her mother, Alice, died from cancer six years later.

Floyd died in 1970 in San Bernardino and was buried in Hoxie. Jennie remained in California until her death at age 88.

When she passed away in 1994, her remains returned to the Hoxie Cemetery to be buried near her husband and daughter.

Alice, Dorothy's older sister, was married in California and remained in that state until her mother's death. At the time of her husband's death they were living in Colorado Springs. That same year, 1996, she moved to Virginia at age 74. At the age of 92 she passed away in Oregon.

Doyle and Dale Dean also spent much of their lives in California. There is record of Dale's death in 2007.

At the time of this writing the author believes Dorothy's youngest brother is living.

In communicating with one of the living family members I received this note written by Brenda Barnum-Rasmussen dated 6/29/2016:

"I do have a story. Alice told me that she blamed herself for her sister dying. They were walking home from school and about halfway home Dorothy realized she didn't have her lunch pail. Alice didn't want to walk back with her so she told Dorothy to walk back and get it by herself. If Alice had walked with her she may not have been kidnapped...."

Jennie would not allow anyone to talk about Dorothy after she died. I can only imagine the pain she went through surviving her daughter. Alice said that she had forgotten about Dorothy till I started talking about her.

Alice had her and Dorothy's trinket boxes as well as the two little crocheted dresses that she and Dorothy wore in their picture with Doyle as a baby. Uncle Dale had Dorothy's baby doll. There is only one picture with all four older kids in it, a snapshot from far away.

That's all I know. I'm really interested in your research."

—Brenda

WILLIAM L. THOMAS:

The story of William Thomas was based upon an interview done with him by Robert Lewis Sr. and Marvel Lewis in Delta, CO in preparation for a talk given to the Atwood Rotary in 1987. From the typed pages recorded by Mr. Lewis came the re-creation of a life impacted by the lynching.

Mr. William L. Thomas had written a letter to the Atwood Historical Society to say that "the stories you read about the hanging of Read are all wrong – I know for I was there," That letter is what sent Mr. Lewis to Colorado.

William was 86 years old at the time of the interview. His wife had passed away just a couple of years prior. He had been without sight for over a decade.

A few of the details he gives are incorrect, but most importantly, his first-hand account clears away much of the sensationalized newspaper reports. His memories show that the lynching was done with no intent to cause difficulty for the lawmen tasked with protecting Richard Read. He states when asked if there were guns used, "Oh, no, oh, no, I don't think there was a dozen in the crowd, it was just as quiet as it could be, I don't think there was a horn blew. Now, that's what I know of it. It ain't nothing like what that paper said." Mr. Thomas felt the event was one that needed done, was done and then was best forgotten. He said, "My daughter never even knew it. We never did tell my daughter at all." William and Ellen's only child was not born until they'd been married 13 years as a result of a mule accident shortly after their wedding.

William L. Thomas died not too long after this interview with Mr. Lewis. It is my belief, from reading his condensed life story as recorded by Mr. Lewis, that William Thomas was a very gentle natured man, who could never have imagined being part of a mob action that ended the life of a near neighbor. His willingness to be involved demonstrates he believed there was justice in the act and that a man must take action to protect, but does not find pleasure in violence.

ED McGINLEY 1953-2009: A FINAL CONNECTION

Long before this manuscript was conceived, Ed McGinley, grandson of Sheriff Ed McGinley and great-grandson of pioneer John James McGinley, was one of eight men with dual diagnoses of developmental disability and mental illness who shared a group home with our family. As employees for Developmental Services of Northwest Kansas (DSNWK) in the Atwood branch of Prairie Developmental Center (PDC) we cared for these men in a family teaching home through their residential program.

We knew him intimately. In the town of Colby, where he was born, he'd earned the nick-name of 'Hoppy' which came from a jerking movement when he walked. It was not a name we used.

Ed McGinley was tall with a thin build like his grandfather. From his father Don he had inherited a frighteningly explosive temper. His time in an institution had not given him any tools for self-control. Punishment and removal would have been typical responses in that setting.

Often, during the years we shared in his life, if another of the men we cared for acted out Ed would say "put him in the hole!" which we assumed was a type of solitary confinement he'd experienced himself. However, with consistency, reward- based programs and caring, we saw a real change in his ability to interact with others.

Our daughters, (the youngest was just starting pre-school when we became Family Teachers), were privileged to grow up seeing the disabled population as 'people first'. We ate family meals, took house vacations, went to the circus, and traveled to Ed's home town of Colby to swim at the college pool. For the first time in his life Ed was part of a functioning family. He was treated with respect and given a sense of value.

This early exposure to the feelings and needs of the men and women who were cared for through DSNWK gave our daughters empathy for those who 'stand apart'. Their career choices have reflected this sensitivity with positive impact for many.

Ed McGinley – another connection between the author and the last lynching in Kansas – died in Russell, Kansas.

SUPPLEMENTAL READING

FIRST CONNECTIONS: Chapters 1-2

The route from Iowa to Kansas in the time of the Read family's journey likely brought them through Council Bluffs where they crossed the Missouri River into Nebraska near Omaha and then followed the Platte westward to Republic City at the junction of the Republican River and the Platte. There they entered Kansas and began a west-southwest course towards the town of Rexford. Many of the major highways and interstates of today follow closely those original trails. What now takes a traveler 10 hours in a comfortable car was a brutal, grueling battle lasting nearly two months.

Families joined together for support and safety. Folks relied on each other for information on what was ahead and the best watering places for their livestock. They shared their misery in terse terms with no boast. They shared a dream. Bonds formed that lasted generations.

The Reads became acquainted with the Gardner family while in Republic City. Many years later these families joined with the marriage of the youngest Read daughter, Edmee to Will Gardner. The two families made many trips back and forth and Richard was noted to have been in Republic City to learn the cement trade just weeks before his first punishable offense.

Though the Reads must have felt they were trail breakers, they were not the first to imagine Kansas as a welcoming home. In 1862, roughly 20 years before, the Homestead Act sent the initial wave of pioneer farmers into the central states followed by those displaced by the Civil War. When the Reads made their way to Kansas, many of these original homesteads had been forfeited or given over to tenants. The great grasshopper plague of 1874 had starved-out many as crops and grass were devoured by hordes of insatiable insects so dense the clouds of their migration blocked the sun.

A flow of families into and out of the plains occurred on a regular basis. Abandoned dugouts, remnants of sod walls, headstones and plowed soil reverting to grass were the only footprints left from these first attempts at taming the prairie. The Read family was part of a final movement spurred by railroad magnates who used their political power to 'create towns'.

Their destination was in Thomas County along the Prairie Dog Creek in Wendell Township 4 ½ miles northeast of Rexford. The Chicago, Kansas and Nebraska Railroad (later the Rock Island Railroad), completed in 1888, became a vital draw to homesteaders of the time. With its arrival commerce was possible and isolation lessened.

The Read homestead along Prairie Dog Creek, within traveling distance of the Rexford depot, gave them grass, tillable ground, tree cover, timber and water in addition to a market for their crops. Despite the extremes of heat, cold, drought, violent storms and insect pressure, this family held on with grit and determination. A new child was born every 15-20 months creating a labor force and opportunities for land acquirement.

Amazingly the nine Read children escaped the high death rate common of most prairie families and they prospered, becoming notable names in the local newspaper. Their ties with the earlier pioneer families who had succeeded were a strong and important part of a limited social support system.

The Union Pacific Railroad, among other railroad companies, published and distributed pamphlets promoting the so-named Golden Belt Lands of the central states. Using beguiling phrases they gave promise of fail proof success, riches and prosperity. Many statements were complete fabrication in denial of a harsh reality. Slogans such as 'rain follows the plow' and 'champagne air' drew interest from the east. If these brochures had held truth, Kansas was a welcoming Eden.

Railroad magnates with government given land to sell also needed agricultural products for shipment on their newly built and proposed lines. They sought out and found willing souls in limitless numbers: men dreaming of land ownership in an empty, treeless environ; men who wished to 'better their selves'.

These men willingly 'proved up' with the lives of wives and children and their own desperate efforts. Those who 'made it' grew a sense of pride based on tenacity and endurance rather than success. These were the 'stickers' who, embedded in the high plains, defied the odds. Nearly a third of the first pioneers failed, leaving behind dugouts and graves scrubbed by wind and blowing dirt. Wave after wave of families followed similar paths.

Intermittent spells of pure delight sandwiched by brutal, life-threatening conditions are trademark of the high plains. Those who claim more than one generation defend vigorously their right to continue the battle.

Though it might be imagined a farm would always have an abundance of food, many settlers arrived in mid to late summer, much too far into the growing season to raise a garden or plant crops. Shelter became first priority. In many cases, if it wasn't in the wagon when they arrived they were forced to do without. Precious seed had to be stored carefully for planting and not ground into flour or meal, though the family might starve while waiting on their next crop. At least one full growing season, hard labor and luck were needed to reach any semblance of sustainability. In Zone 5 of Northwest Kansas frost-free weather doesn't come until mid-May; first frost can take out tender crops by October 10. In between those dates are hail storms, high winds, parching triple digit heat, grasshopper and rabbit plagues as well as rains that either don't come or arrive in a deluge.

Cattle and sheep could graze the prairie grasses, but heavy snows might cover their feed for weeks. If drought was prolonged, as frequently happened, grass was in short supply. Lightning strike prairie fires might eat a year's growth of dry fodder in minutes and burn out a household. A herd of beeves being trailed from Texas to Montana often trampled gardens and fouled springs.

Chickens and pigs, limited in their foraging abilities, needed grains to thrive and grain required the sod to be broken and harrowed into plant-able condition. Buffalo grass sod does not easily lend itself to a plow. Protection from predators was vital. Wolves, mountain lions, bobcats, coyotes, raccoons and opossums viewed the homesteaders' livestock as easy pickings.

Women gave birth nearly every other year, frequently less than 24 months between babies, with no true medical assistance; many without even the support of another woman. With cramped living spaces, questionable water and minimal hygiene illness fell upon the young and elderly. Scarlet fever claimed a high mortality rate. Diphtheria took whole families. It wasn't uncommon for parents to bury 50% of their children or a husband to bury both his wife and newborn, leaving a brood of motherless children in stair-step ages. Horrendous injuries from livestock, equipment, kitchen fires and snakebite or while performing tasks such as well digging, home building and harvests killed or maimed the unlucky.

In the high plains very few native foods are available. Tart chokecherries and wild plums, ripening in summer and fall, could be stewed or made into a fine jelly if there was enough sugar to preserve them. Grapes were small and sour but might be dried. These fruits are only found along the creeks. Currants were a prized find. Birds, raccoons, opossums and coyotes feasted on them too, taking a large share. Prickly pear cactus made a base for jelly. Cottontails and jackrabbits could be shot, but there were no apples, no nuts, no roots. The tri-state area of Northwest Kansas, Eastern Colorado and Southwest Nebraska is a grass desert with little relief.

Historically, wildlife had been abundant, but as early as 1878 the buffalo were gone and the deer much diminished. Antelope had been hunted heavily. Geese and ducks might be shot during their bi-annual migration but with no large lakes nearby few summered or wintered locally. Pheasant weren't introduced to the area until after 1900. Wild turkey did not exist on the shortgrass prairie though a few might be found along the creeks where cottonwoods offered roost. Prairie chickens were a welcome source of protein but didn't go far in feeding a large family. Competing with hungry humans were the buffalo wolves that still hunted, taking down deer, antelope and livestock, once their prime source of food was gone. Bobcats and far ranging cougars sought meat for their kittens. Coyotes scavenged and ate everything from mice to frogs to the eggs and chicks of ground nesting birds.

A traveling pioneer family ate beans with flour or cornmeal gravy. When an old hen who no longer laid eggs was sacrificed to the plate, the meal was not finished until the bones were broken for marrow and sucked clean. Coarse bread spread with lard and a sprinkle of precious sugar made lunch. Photographs show children of that era with heads too large for their shrunken bodies; their expressions pinched and hard. It was said a woman lost a tooth for every child she bore. Fathers dried into sinew and bone. Hunger prowled close.

Yet the pioneers dug in and held. First families to arrive have 7th generation descendants still calling the area home. Year after year hope rises with spring rain and a softening south wind. The land has never been tamed but it has been subdued by mechanical inventions, seed improvements, infrastructures of roads and highways – though the original railroad spurs that brought these families forth have recently been abandoned.

Perhaps propaganda becomes reality over time.

REXFORD, KANSAS: Chapters 7-10

The town of Rexford, named for a family of early settlers who had died when their home burned, is one bead along a chain of tiny communities linked by the Chicago, Kansas and Nebraska railroad, part of the Rock Island line. The vital tracks came through Rexford on their way to join the Union Pacific at Colby's hub in 1888.

Its plat reveals north-south and east-west streets with the tracks running at a diagonal through its center. An 1898 photo of the depot, a two story wooden structure, shows crated bicycles, a plow and men standing on the platform sporting official vests and hats.

Businesses formed to meet the needs as needs became apparent. Farm related equipment and myriad supplies arrived in boxcars to be hauled to the outlying farms by wagon. Goods raised in the area were used locally or went east on the return run.

When Jacob Read drove his wagon into town, the population boom had begun. Census records show that in the year of 1885 Thomas County grew from 161 citizens to nearly 2000. Early arriving families wrote home and drew more and more relatives and friends to this empty land of promise. Europeans, fleeing overcrowding and war in their home countries and unable to speak any English, came by the thousands, created settlements, married neighbors, tried to raise crops and buried babies at a steady rate. Everyone soon learned that the prairie was without mercy and months of intense labor could be lost overnight.

The town fathers did their best to mitigate the hardships and provide the services farm families depended upon. 'Going to town' were words imbued with pleasurable anticipation.

SCHOOLS: Chapter 15

The first schools on the plains of Kansas were funded by subscription. A family paid .50 to $1.00 a month for each child attending to support this vital necessity. Initially the school year was in session only two months to minimize impacting farm activities and to avoid sending children out during the worst winter weather. Most young people rode 'shanks mare', a phrase to describe walking to school. A few, with longer distances to travel, did ride a farm horse. Sometimes three or four children were tucked tight together on a wide backed plow horse.

Typically starting life in a dug out or housed in a centrally located home (perhaps that of the family with the most children) it was some time before the communities organized buildings specifically for education. Frequently when a structure was built it served as a multipurpose space, filling the needs of religious meetings and town hall. Furnishings were minimal, textbooks limited and discipline tight.

In Thomas County, typical of other western Kansas communities, the need for schools rapidly expanded as the population increased. From 1886 to 1887 the districts rose from three to forty, with more soon to be organized. One room schools provided social opportunities as well as exposure to the three R's. Extremely important for foreign speaking families, this mixing of children provided a path for them to assimilate into their American communities. Sadly this social soup could be a painful experience for anyone who stood outside the accepted norms. Bullies and cliques and divisions based on any number of criteria made the 'outsider' miserable, indeed.

1888 CHILDREN'S BLIZZARD: Chapter 13

Despite modern technology and much effort by those dedicated to the subject we are still mostly powerless against catastrophic natural events. Blizzards, droughts, wild fires, dust storms, floods, hail, high winds, tornados, plagues of insects and outbreaks of disease are intimate bedfellows for the determined citizens of the central states. In 1888, without warning systems and with very limited protection from the elements, there were no strategies to prepare for the brutal winter storm that hammered the plains. No agencies were available to provide relief. Neighbors helped bury the dead and shared in mourning. Frozen animals were butchered before spoiling. The pioneer families took their hits.

Much has been written about the 'children's blizzard' of January 1888 which cut farming communities deeply. Many young lives were lost as the children tried to return home from school when the storm roared in at midday. An estimated loss of upwards of 500 human lives with one fifth being children has been documented.

Coming only two years after the devastating blizzard of 1886, the Read family now faced a brutally cold existence until late spring finally ended their bitter existence. Jacob and Mary Ellen Read endured, assessed the damage and began repairs. They were fortunate to have kept all their babies alive. Indeed, it appears likely their next child, Villa Belle, born the following September, got her start as the family occupied themselves within the protective walls of their home.

EDWIN LYMAN (1872-1953) McDONALD, KANSAS Chapter 17 & 44

Select men make a greater impact in their lives than others. It is common to find they come from a lineage that boasts a pattern of productivity and success. Setbacks occur, as circumstances beyond control shove a man off course, but these men do not falter long. They view the changed world and adjust. They sense with anticipation that the stars will continue to shine on their endeavors.

Edwin Lyman was just this type of man. Coming from Table Rock, NE he and his father W.G. Lyman brought a threshing machine to Rawlins County. This was a marvel of mechanical ingenuity developed in 1786 by Scottish engineer Andrew Meikle which revolutionized grain harvests around the world. By the time Edwin and his machine arrived in McDonald the equipment had been modified and perfected. Ultimately the thresher would become a 'combine' which cut and separated the grain from the straw in one operation.

Edwin was so impressed with the bounteous area that he returned to purchase land. On Christmas Eve 1899 with his wife (Anna Cleaveland) of five years and newly born son, Roy, they located on a prime section of the Beaver Creek south of McDonald.

He did not limit his efforts to farming and ranching but utilized his inborn attributes to bring prospective settlers to the area, providing real estate services and encouragement.

Seeing many needs in the new town of McDonald and surrounding communities while quickly becoming acquainted with others of natural vision he established lumber yards, grain elevators and the 1905 McDonald State Bank. His father, W.G. Lyman was supportive in these endeavors, coming to live in Kansas in 1913.

The 1919 A Standard History of Kansas and Kansans gives the following information regarding Edwin Lyman: "Owing to the increased valuations set upon productive activities as a result of the great war, popular attention is fixed upon and fired by the statement that one man's supervision and enterprise has raised in a single season 35,000 bushels of wheat. Such an achievement was the performance of Edwin Lyman of McDonald for the season of 1916. With wheat worth at the price of a dollar a bushel, his yield signified a modest fortune to its owner and was a generous contribution to the big undertaking of feeding the world from American farms. ...he owns thirteen sections of land, totaling 8,320 acres..."

Shortly before this, in 1915, Edwin Lyman lists in the Topeka Daily the following ad:

"Closing-Out Sale of the McDonald Ranch This ranch consists of about ten thousand acres adjoining the town of McDonald In the western part of Rawlins county, and is one of the best ranches in northwestern Kansas, consisting of level wheat lands, rolling pasture lands, alfalfa creek lands, with five miles of running water, plenty of shade for stock, a large acreage all ready set to alfalfa. This ranch can be cut up and sold in small tracts. Terms are one-third down, balance on or before five years. Price from fifteen to thirty dollars per acre. For further information please call on or write to EDWIN LYMAN McDonald, Kansas Cheyenne County Abstract Company. Having just completed my second term as treasurer in the county, I am again engaging in the Real Estate and Abstract business. Crops in this section this year will pay for the lands upon which they were grown. I have lived in northwestern Kansas for thirty years and have witnessed but one crop failure...."

Five months after Edwin's first wife passed away from a short illness he remarried to Margaret Cochran, the sister of this author's great-grandfather.

IT WAS ON THE LYMAN RANCH SOUTH OF MCDONALD THAT THE LAST LYNCHING IN KANSAS OCCURRED IN THE SPRING OF 1932.

SHIRLEY'S OPERA HOUSE, ATWOOD, KANSAS
CULTURE on the PLAINS: Chapter 41-42

Opera Houses followed the rail lines. As towns prospered and were filled by transplants from the East, a hunger for culture, preceded only by the construction of churches and schools, resulted in private citizens with the wherewithal to construct multi-purpose entertainment halls. The design was frequently two stories. The main floor housed at least one and sometimes multiple business enterprises while the upstairs offered a large public space for a variety of activities.

These buildings represented civic pride and a sense of 'having made it' to contrast with the wildness so recently experienced. Style and décor matched the area's level of wealth from simple to highly ornate.

Theatrical companies formed to meet the demand. Reduced costs of rail transportation and increasingly abundant connecting lines allowed even the smallest communities to access live entertainment. Spacious boxcars provided a means for theatrical companies to 'bring the stage to the town' and an entertainment circuit was born.

Coming from Chicago and other points east, a troupe would set up for two or three, offering several opportunities for citizens to be enthralled. Music, magic, political debates, wrestling matches and three-act dramas could all be enjoyed. As the term 'Opera House' lent respectability women and children were able to attend and attend they did.

Thus was born the 1907 Shirley Opera House in Atwood, KS.

The January 10, 1907 edition of The Republican Citizen stated, "The Shirley Opera House, which he (Judge Shirley) is now building in Atwood, will be a lasting monument to his memory in Rawlins County." When completed, the main floor first housed The Cash Grocery, run by owner and entrepreneur William Riley Shirley. His motto was to 'sell a dollar's worth of candy' then close the doors and go fishing. Knowing how little extra cash was available in Rawlins County and the worth of a dollar, it would seem he didn't fish much.

Mr. Shirley became a citizen of Rawlins County in 1879 and was another of those men who were not satisfied with a single role. He was a census collector and elected as a township trustee. He served as the county clerk, sheriff and probate judge. In 1905 his enterprises expanded to include a brick yard, helping to provide local builders with "good brick at a minimum price". That same brick continues to support the Opera House.

As a venue for performances and community gatherings, the upstairs was reached via shallow concrete steps on the exterior's east side. While originally having no plumbing or electricity and using wood heat for warmth this 'Queen of the Prairie' proved adequate for the times.

The first public event held in the attractive two story brick building was on May 10, 1907 featuring "A Prince of Liars" produced by home talent, directed by Miss Beulah Monroe. The Atwood Orchestra played for dances and the Woodmen held their First Annual Grand Ball there.

Traveling performances were soon on the agenda. Newspaper ads announced: "FOUR NIGHTS in ATWOOD" with the Ruth Craven Company bringing drama to the upstairs stage. Lyda Munger is quoted in Ruth Kelly Hayden's book The Time That Was as saying "We were even glad to go to a funeral and when Shirley's Opera House opened, I remember we walked through snow up to our knees three nights in a row to watch a stock company that was traveling through."

The Ted North Players and the Hillman Stock Company were other well-publicized performance groups whose shows were eagerly anticipated. Roller skates became a popular sport and today the undulating floor bears the marks of much use.

The 1907 Shirley Opera House holds many stories. It nearly burned down before it was fully built when a barrel of hot tar ignited and then reignited hours later. One of the upstairs workers fell through the floor, but escaped serious injury. There are lasting energies within its walls.

ON APRIL 15, 1932 PLEASANT RICHARD READ BOUGHT BREAKFAST FOR DOROTHY EILEEN HUNTER AT THE OWL CAFÉ IN SHIRLEY'S OPERA HOUSE. THAT WAS THE LAST TIME SHE WAS SEEN ALIVE.

1910 – 1930s: Chapters 26-47

In 1910 drought returned to Thomas County and the surrounding area. Crops failed in '11 and in that year a horrid plague appeared, killing horses with a ferociousness unseen by any of the old settlers. No cause was ever found, though theories were many. It did not end until winter. The horses who survived were of little use. Valuable animals, now in short supply, were dear to replace. 1912 continued abnormally dry, adding more strain to those barely holding on.

With the winter of 1912/1913 the drought broke. Many say it takes snow to break a drought and this time the adage proved true. The blizzards cut families off for days and shut down the trains with 15 foot drifts. Jack rabbits, well-known as survivors and just the past year considered a plague of such magnitude that three railcars were filled with their carcasses to be shipped east, froze to death in the bitter cold. Spring thaw with heavy rains caused flooding of the Prairie Dog and nearby Solomon River with huge cakes of ice piling up, exacerbating the floods.

Changes came to the land. Mechanical devices not reliant on horseflesh are arriving. One patent led to another. Crews of men are no longer needed. The upcoming war machine fuels an exploding need for grains and record acres will be put into crops. With these changes another promise of prosperity circulates the farming communities but will soon collapse from its own greed.

In 1916, Congress passed the Federal Farm Loan Act, allowing for long-term low interest loans through twelve federal land banks for expansion. Many with an eye for opportunity took this way and mortgaged land they owned free and clear.

It is very interesting to note that during these years the United States government took control of the grain trade. In 1918 farmers were told their 1916 and 1917 wheat stores would be seized if not taken to market by May 1, 1918. Grains, in short supply worldwide were needed for the Allied troops. Control of farm commodities via the United States Department of Agriculture (USDA) was in its seminal stage.

During and after the war years of 1917-1920 more than 40 million acres of uncultivated land in the US went under the plow, including 30 million acres in the wheat and corn producing states of the Midwest. Land values nearly doubled, allowing greater borrowing leverage.

European relief efforts resulted in continued demand for US agricultural products. Exports of grain and livestock products reached phenomenal levels. It was a formula for economic disaster that could only be summed up by the phrase 'Boom and Bust'. Production continued to climb with the expectation that demand and prices would hold. Supply and demand in relation to grains is tricky business due to the length of time from seed to harvest, weather patterns and the independent nature of farming.

Catastrophically, as recovery overseas stabilized, the US farm economy began its collapse and reached a crisis during the Great Depression. The very environment had been changed as a result of the millions of acres of grass lost to the plow. It is believed this destruction of native prairie was directly related to the climactic events leading to the Dust Bowl.

When prices fell to pennies a bushel for grain crops, farmers, burdened heavily with debt they'd been encouraged to take on, felt the only solution was to plant more and more acres. Too little, too late the federal government attempted to undo the damage and began to promote a decrease in production and programs to stabilize prices. This self-created cycle of boom and bust was well established. The bust years often last decades.

SELDEN, KANSAS: Chapter 27

To the northeast of Rexford, about 15 miles up the track, is the town of Selden. Secured in 1888 with bonds of $12,000.00 it now exists as one of only two towns remaining in Sheridan County.

Absorbing families and buildings previously loyal to the towns of old Sheridan, Shibboleth and Jackson its strength lay in the railroad's proximity. Among the first stout hearted families was Caleb Geisenhener who would later become tied to the Read family through the marriage of a daughter to a son.

Following a total crop failure in 1890 and acting with the authority as county commissioner Mr. Geisenhener was given a pass by the Rock Island Railroad to travel to eastern Kansas and Missouri to bring supplies of clothing, seed and food back to his starving citizens. At that time the Read family had at six children under the age of ten.

From 1880, when the census recorded 1500 citizens county-wide, to 1930 when Sheridan County's population had grown to 6000, nature had battered the families who came and went. As reported by the 2016 census these numbers have nearly returned to that of its beginning, standing at 2500, most residing in the county seat of Hoxie. Economics of farming coupled with years of drought and limited opportunities for non-ag income result in an area little changed from the past. Today the town of Selden holds just over 200 citizens. Many carry direct ties to those who were the first to settle.

As any native will tell you, the cycles of weather, crop prices and the vagaries of USDA programs strain the greatest die-hards. Chemical farming has become the norm. Mega-feedlots and dairies have absorbed the small family producer. Not many eat their own food, but rely like city folks on the nearest Walmart or Dillons. Cancer and diabetes rates have skyrocketed.

Young folks graduate from high school and rarely return. Drugs, most recently the national meth epidemic, hammer the resources which protect the integrity and sense of safety a small town deserves.

It is difficult to know what the future holds for Selden, just past its 130th year of survival. There continues much potential, but it will take people such as Caleb Geisenhener, people with vision, to take it forward.

COLORADO STATE PENITENTIARY:
Chapter 31, 35 & 45

The legal system was remarkably efficient. Just three days after his act of brutality, Pleasant Richardson Read is convicted of rape on April 18, 1916 following trial. Four days later he is received into the Colorado State Penitentiary with a sentence of 15 to 20 years. It is notable that a man admitted four days prior to Richard Read, also for the crime of rape, was given a sentence of three to five years. This is likely an indicator of the viciousness of Mr. Read and the age of his victim.

His Prison Record gives his number as 9951, age 38, his height at 5' 11 ¼", his weight at 187, with a ruddy complexion, hazel eyes and brown hair. His occupation is listed as cement worker.

Under 'Marks, Scars and Remarks' is written: Pit marks on his face, mole on each breast – Scar R. side of nose, Scar L side of back of head, Teeth Fair. He was shown to be literate but not temperate and did use tobacco. He was not married. He had not been in prison prior to this offence. His signature is neat and very legible.

Richard's intake photo shows an almost handsome man wearing a broad striped prison jacket and cotton-ticking buttoned shirt. His deep eyes reflect troubled sorrow. A furrowed brow reveals a serious demeanor. His ears stand away from his head, but not unduly so. A small cleft in his strong chin draws attention to a well formed mouth.

When he entered the Colorado penal system, the Canon City buildings designed to house 444 men held nearly twice that number. Women prisoners were kept in separate areas. In 1907 a hospital had been built to include a ward for the insane. Many famous criminals have been held in this penitentiary. The author has visited the nearby museum and found it impacting.

Prison labor was integral to the institution. Activities included skills incarcerated men might have arrived with including blacksmithing, general maintenance, construction and carpentry as well as training programs such as shoe cobbling. Indeed, a contract between the Colorado Shoe Company and the Colorado State Prison Commission established a cooperative effort of materials, machinery and training to the prison in exchange for payment of .30 per man per day. This income was used to offset prison costs with a stipend going to the prisoner's family or to the convict upon discharge if he had no family.

On site brick work and stone quarries created building materials and marketable products for the prison, while keeping the men occupied with meaningful activity. (The author has visited this prison in the past as it is part of the Wild Horse Inmate Program. The location, buildings and grounds are very attractive with extensive native stone construction.)

Large gardens were cultivated to feed the prisoners as well as to generate income. Over two million pounds of farm produce was raised in one recorded year. Livestock, especially swine, was integral to the self-sufficiency of the system.

In March 1909 Warden Thomas J. Tynan put his belief in redemption through hard work into practice. He took advantage of legislative approval allowing for highway construction to use convict labor. The highway known as Skyline Drive and the road to the Royal Gorge was built with manpower provided by the prison. Warden Tynan stated that "instead of sending broken revengeful men back into the world – in no wise reformed but simply trained to greater cunning – there are being restored mended men eager and willing to be made as such use as society will permit. By removing the continual threat of arms, by eliminating oppression and brutalities, by establishing a system of graded rewards for cheerfulness and industry, the penitentiary has been given a wholesome, helpful atmosphere."

Legislation allowed these workers, some with life sentences, to add "a ten-day reduction of term for every thirty days in a road camp" onto the existing good-behavior allowance. This proved significant.

With Richard's strength, willingness to follow instruction, quiet demeanor and protection from strong drink he was one of those who subtracted sentencing time rapidly. It was noted he was an exemplary prisoner earning status as a trusty.

As a result his sentence in the Colorado Prison system is cut remarkably short. Through the 'automatic parole' system Read was released in six years, two months and eleven days and returned to Rexford, KS (in violation of parole laws which should have kept him in Colorado).

The Denver Post, April 18, 1932 article under the bold headline 'KANSAS CITIZENS LYNCH APEMAN SLAYER OF GIRL' and the follow up article 'CODDLING OF COLORADO CONVICTS COST CHILD'S LIFE' describe in detail the system of "Automatic Parole" which released Richard Read less than halfway through his sentence. The article writer seems perplexed at the math allowing such early release.

Included in these articles are quotes made by J. R. Ruberson. He points out that during the trial it became evident that Richard Read was a man of "stunted intelligence" and possible mental illness. He is quoted as follows: "During the trial there was considerable argument as to whether Read was insane. Many persons maintained he should be sent to an asylum… When news of his automatic parole from prison after serving six years of his fifteen to twenty-year sentence reached Burlington, the citizens of that town weer(sic) actually frightened by the knowledge that he was at large."

Regardless, Pleasant Richardson Read returned to Kansas in July 1922, stepping off the train (noted in the Rexford News) to surprise his parents. Despite an exhaustive reading of Thomas County newspapers to discover details of this event the author found no reference at all to the 1916 crime, Richard's incarceration or the fact that they now had a convicted rapist in residence with no official oversight. Whether this was an intentional kindness to the Reads by the community papers or the family had been vigilant in preventing the spread of information is not known at present.

THE AFTERMATH: Chapter 43-45

In a strange coincidence, the 12th Annual District Convention had drawn Democratic Governor Harry Hines Woodring to Atwood on Sunday, April 17th. This was the same day of Dorothy's funeral and, since the governor remained in town overnight, he was likely intimately aware of Richard Read's lynching.

The District Convention had been planned for months with many prominent guests feted. It was reported in circumspect phrasing that spectators from this group had attended the 'cutting down' of Richard Read's body by Dr. Henneberger in the pre-dawn hours of April 18th.

Governor Woodring was an opponent of capital punishment and had recently vetoed bills pertaining to the death penalty. On March 14, 1931 his statement regarding this veto seemed prognosticating, "There is certainly no crisis in Kansas which would necessitate the retrogression toward the dark ages in our criminal laws."

Later, the Governor was reported as saying, "While the offense committed by Richard Read was a most dastardly crime, mob lynching cannot be countenanced and every effort will be made to discover and prosecute the members of the mob.

"For a mob to take the punishment of crimes out of the hands of the constituted authorities results in a breakdown of government, and it cannot and will not be permitted to go unpunished in Kansas."

Despite his strong words and investigation, no one was held accountable for the death of Richard Read. Sheriff A. A. Bacon claimed 'darkness prevented a close scrutiny of the mob leaders'. Public sentiment generally favored the actions taken by the people.

This is evident in the words of an Atwood woman whose previously secure life was disrupted by these events, "But you know the attitude of everybody in those days if you went out and stole a horse, they found that man and they hung him up and he didn't steal any more horses. So I think that would be the same reaction this man did not deserve to live because he had committed this terrible thing and my belief today is I think we're a little bit too lenient on our criminals. And to me it's not right." Hattie Toth Bliss – Atwood, KS - interview June 2016.

The 1923 Kansas statute was clear. An unlawful assembly, defined as at least three individuals having intent to act with violent force against a person or property, was illegal. If death resulted as a result of this action all parties should be, upon conviction, placed in the state penitentiary for a period determined by the jury.

The law also specified that the sheriff who allowed this to occur, in this case Sheriff A. A. Bacon, was required to vacate his office. The Governor had the discretion of reinstatement if the officer of the law petitioned for such within ten days and was found to have done all in his power to protect a prisoner.

Sheriff Bacon was indeed 'out of a job' for a brief period following this event in 1932. However, his reinstatement came quickly after an investigation was completed by

Roland Boynton, state's attorney general, who traveled to the northwest corner of the state. By telegraph messages the county attorneys for Rawlins and Cheyenne had been instructed to begin the process. It is interesting that Sheriff Ed McGinley escaped being named during this scrutiny.

After hearing evidence presented by the sheriffs and county attorneys of the four involved counties, charges against Sheriff Bacon were dismissed by April 20, 1932. No vigilante was identified.

Thus the LAST LYNCHING IN KANSAS was culminated.

An interesting detail noted in the April 21, 1932 Citizen Patriot, Atwood, KS is that the convention headquarters were in the Hill Garage owned by the author's husband's grandfather, W.H. Hill.

EPILOGUE

Great effort was made to be guided by verifiable sources while writing UNDER A FULL MOON. I frequently found errors of fact or conflicting details regarding the 1932 event during my research. Rather than base this record on those sensationalized versions I chose to reflect the more likely common sense actions of Kansas citizens. On occasion I had to readjust my own preconceptions. Accounts recorded by families who lived the times support historical accuracy.

Pleasant Richardson Read was viewed as deviant.

In consequence he suffered ostracism. He was 'cut from the herd', most painfully by his own family. It is notable that during the last years of his life he was no longer listed among his siblings during family gatherings, even while living at home.

UNDER A FULL MOON alludes to explanations for Richard's abnormal nature. Possible oxygen deprivation at birth, a traumatic head injury and the likelihood of nutritional deficits during his infancy and childhood could combine to explain his perceived retardation. His mental status would have been impacted further by the psycho-emotional complexities of driven men with their first born sons. It is known that Richard was able to function normally as evidenced by the jobs he held, but that he was also seen as menacing.

Pauline Weisshaar and Dorothy Hunter were obviously innocent victims of violence. Less obvious was the damaging abuse suffered by Richard throughout his lifetime. His aggressive and psychotic behavior may have been directly related to social isolation to the extent that his only recourse for human contact was through violent acts

Ingestion of 'moonshine' alcohol, (a product which frequently included madness inducing ingredients), during both known events compounded these physiological and mental aberrations. Most inhuman acts involve mind altering substances.

Great tragedies are often triggered by actions or inactions of others not directly involved in the culminating behavior. If there had been proper action at appropriate times Pleasant Richardson Read might have been protected from becoming the 'Prairie Monster', Pauline Weisshaar could have been spared untold pain and fear, Dorothy Hunter's life would have been preserved and her family freed from unbearable grief while those that were forced to react with primitive justice could have been spared deep psychological scars.

"To be made to feel invisible, unloved, or non-existent is perhaps the cruelest act we can inflict on another. Few events in life are more painful than feeling that others, especially those whom we admire and care about, want nothing to do with us.

"Whereas there is a consensus among social and biological scientists that ostracism has a strong negative impact on its targets... Some biologists and physiologists claim ostracism causes "general deregulation": interferes with our immunological functioning and hypothalamic reactions that are related to aggression and depression (Kling,1986; Raleigh & McGuire, 1986). Psychotic behaviors are more likely to occur in prisoners who are subjected to solitary confinement." (Raleigh & McGuire, 1986) Ostracism: The Power of Silence by Kipling D. Williams, 2001

If you are impacted by this story do not turn away if you suspect a child is in danger of physical or emotional abuse. Opportunities that might have altered the events leading to the last lynching in Kansas were presented but allowed to slip past for all the typical excuses. These opportunities are before us as well.

Do not be party to ridicule and estrangement from society those we deem 'odd'. Your kindness may be their only 'soft' hand. Your acknowledgement of their existence may save lives.

Do warn your small people that danger is present and protect them from harm. Let this message from history protect the safety of all vulnerable children. If this is done, perhaps Dorothy's young spirit and Richard's broken soul had purpose.

In memory of Pleasant Richardson Read and in the memory of Dorothy Eileen Hunter: Be kind. Do no harm.

RESOURCES

These resources are not listed in any particular order or in order of importance.

PUBLICATIONS:

1. History of Rawlins County, Kansas Volumes 1-4
2. Sheridan County, Kansas – A History of Faith and Labor Volumes 1-2
3. The Time That Was Ruth Kelley Hayden
4. The Time That Was – The Second Forty Years, 1915-1955 - Ruth Kelley Hayden
5. Golden Heritage of Thomas County, Kansas
6. Old West Lawmen – Legends of America
7. The Golden Jubilee Anniversary of Thomas County and its Neighbors
8. Lynchings, Hangings & Vigilante Groups – Legends of America
9. Great Plains – Ian Frazier
10. Lynchings in Kansas, 1850-1932 - Harriet C. Frazier
11. Family Remembrances - Ann McGinley-Bok
12. Come Spring - Charlotte Hinger
13. Land of the Windmills Thomas County, Kansas A Photographic Perspective
14. Dynamic Detective September, 1938 "Kansas' Missing Schoolgirl and the Prairie Monster" Richard Enright

15. Next Year Country – Dust to Dust in Western Kansas 1890-1940 - Craig Miner

16. Pioneer Women The Lives of Women on the Frontier Linda Peavy & Ursula Smith

17. The Legacy of the Homesteaders Albert L. Hardon

18. Deadly Days in Kansas Wayne C. Lee

19. Tales of Western Kansas Amy Lathrop

20. From the Files of the Decatur County Museum Compiled by Sharleen Wurm, Museum Director

NEWSPAPERS OF THE TIME:

The Colby Free Press – Colby, KS

The Citizen Patriot – Atwood, KS

The Rexford News – Rexford, KS

The Hoxie Sentinel – Hoxie, KS

The Denver Post – Denver, CO

The Chicago Daily Tribune – Chicago, IL

The Selden Independent – Selden, KS

Republic City News – Republic City, KS

The Grinnell Record – Grinnell, KS

The Colby Tribune – Colby, KS

The Belleville Telescope – Belleville, KS

Greeley Daily Tribune – Greeley, CO

The Square Deal – Atwood, KS

INTERNET SITES:

http://www.nathankramer.com/settle/

www.newspapers.com

www.ancestry.com

https://www.coloradoci.com/serviceproviders/whip

https://www.kansasmemory.org/

https://www.kshs.org/

http://genealogytrails.com/kan/

SPECIAL THANKS TO:

Dr. Kipling Williams, PhD., Department of Psychological Sciences Purdue University

https://williams.socialpsychology.org/

MUSEUMS:

Rawlins County Museum – Atwood, KS

Prairie Museum of Art & History – Colby, KS

Museum of Cheyenne County – St. Francis, KS

Mickey's Museum – Hoxie, KS

Old Town Museum – Burlington, CO

Coffey County Library - Burlington Branch – Burlington, CO

Denver Central Library – Denver, CO

Colorado State Archive & Public Records – Denver , CO

Museum of Colorado Prisons – Canon City, CO

To see original articles and photographs from this book,
please visit **http://wbp.bz/underafullmoonphotos**

For More News About Alice Kay Hill,
Signup For Our Newsletter:

http://wbp.bz/newsletter

Word-of-mouth is critical to an author's long-term success. If you appreciated this book please leave a review on the Amazon sales page:

http://wbp.bz/underafullmoona

AVAILABLE FROM PATRICK GALLAGHER AND WILDBLUE PRESS!

'Til Death Do Us...' by Patrick Gallagher

http://wbp.bz/tildeathdousa

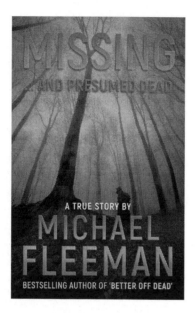

See even more at:
http://wbp.bz/tc

More True Crime You'll Love From WildBlue Press

A MURDER IN MY HOMETOWN by Rebecca Morris
Nearly 50 years after the murder of seventeen year old Dick Kitchel, Rebecca Morris returned to her hometown to write about how the murder changed a town, a school, and the lives of his friends.

wbp.bz/hometowna

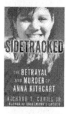

BETRAYAL IN BLUE by Burl Barer & Frank C. Girardot Jr.
Adapted from Ken Eurell's shocking personal memoir, plus hundreds of hours of exclusive interviews with the major players, including former international drug lord, Adam Diaz, and Dori Eurell, revealing the truth behind what you won't see in the hit documentary THE SEVEN FIVE.

wbp.bz/biba

SIDETRACKED by Richard Cahill
A murder investigation is complicated by the entrance of the Reverend Al Sharpton who insists that a racist killer is responsible. Amid a growing media circus, investigators must overcome the outside forces that repeatedly sidetrack their best efforts.

wbp.bz/sidetrackeda

BETTER OFF DEAD by Michael Fleeman
A frustrated, unhappy wife. Her much younger, attentive lover. A husband who degrades and ignores her. The stage is set for a love-triangle murder that shatters family illusions and lays bare a quiet family community's secret world of sex, sin and swinging.

wbp.bz/boda